Angel City
&
Other Plays

Sam Shepard

Angel City
&
Other Plays

Sam Shepard

Introduction by Jack Gelber

APPLAUSE
THEATRE BOOK PUBLISHERS
100West 67 St.•New York,N.Y.10023•(212)496-7511
ISBN 0-87910-200-4 $ 9.95

Fifth printing, 1981

Library of Congress Cataloging in Publication Data

Shepard, Sam, 1943-
  Angel City, curse of the starving class & other plays.

    I. Title.
PS3569.H394A8   812'.5'4   76-21289
ISBN 0-916354-18-0
ISBN 0-916354-19-9 pbk.

All inquiries concerning performing rights should be addressed to the author's agent, Ms. Toby Cole, 234 West 44th Street, Suite 402, New York, N.Y. 10036.

Rock Garden © 1968 by Sam Shepard
Cowboys #2 © 1968 by Sam Shepard
Killer's Head © 1972 by Sam Shepard
Mad Dog Blues © 1972 by Sam Shepard
Action © 1976 by Sam Shepard
Angel City © 1976 by Sam Shepard
Cowboy Mouth © 1976 by Sam Shepard and Patti Smith
Curse of the Starving Class © 1976 by Sam Shepard

The Playwright as Shaman © 1976 by Jack Gelber

Printed in the United States of America

Contents

SAM SHEPARD:
The Playwright as Shaman

By *Jack Gelber*

I've been told more than once tna. plays, modern plays in particular, are difficult to read. Faced with the spare printed page with its scanty stage directions and ellipitical dialogue, the reader must summon an intense and vivifying concentration if he is to get anything out of the experience. Often in our best plays there is as much happening below the lines of dialogue as there is action implied in them. Dialogue is the air in the bubbles breaking sea surface from the very deep, highly condensed, poetically charged experience intended by the author. Asked to read and project an ideal performance of a new play without benefit of the weeks of rehearsal where actors, director, and playwright confront and clarify the text, many readers abandon the effort and read a novel or get out of the house and see a movie.

No wonder then that introductions are commissioned to guide the reader. Unfortunately, I am all too aware of the tendency in our society to substitute the guide for the thing itself: the critic as star. The following is not meant to be a substitute for Sam Shepard's work, nor is it meant to assign a number showing where he stands on someone's hit parade. It is an all too fallible approach intended to aid the reader in getting into the plays. And "getting into" or immersing oneself within the depths of the text is what it's all about.

Since plays are meant to be complete, I try to get a sense of the whole before I attempt to decipher any specific bit of dialogue. I skim. I flip through the pages of the play searching for hints of the playwright's design. I try to get a sense of the characters, of the story and of the place, but I do not stop the forward momentum in the face of the stumbling blocks of inexact appreciation or less than satisfactory understanding. I push on to the end, for as Kenneth Burke has said, whether we consider life a dream, a pilgrimage, a labyrinth, or a carnival makes all the difference in the world.

What's going on? And is it happening on one set or many? Twentieth-century playwrights have been obsessed with the livingroom, so it should come as no surprise to meet one of the many variations of this theatrical metaphor in *Cowboy Mouth* or *Action*. All but one of Shepard's plays in this collection call for one set, a condition to which I will return. Whether we are in a Hollywood office in *Angel City* or the stage itself in *Mad Dog Blues* I am interested in any event which binds together the characters: a daily ritual, a meal, a particular kind of language. Does the playwright stress the interpersonal relationships as in *Cowboy Mouth?* Or pageantry as in *Mad Dog Blues?* These are the kinds of questions which are held open in order to sniff out a working hypothesis as to what constitutes the moving spirit of the whole.

Are playwrights conscious of this "moving spirit?" The answer is: only dimly while at the writing desk.

Applying this method to Sam Shepard's plays, it takes a glance to recognize that they are trips. Not only are the characters in them on trips, for they tell us as much, but also the shapes of the plays themselves are in the form of trips, quests, adventures. Many of the characters are high on drugs, some are high on music, still others are flying on their own words. These characters speak directly to us or to each other or to their visions, the likes of Mae West, Paul Bunyon, Jesse James, or Lobsterman. These visionary beings are in search of gold, fame, or love, as indeed are the principals. Along the way we see cures, clairvoyance, the finding of lost objects, and the foretelling of the future. And all of this action takes place in play after play on a bare or nearly bare stage accompanied by spell-binding music and trance-inducing monologues.

Anthropologists define the shaman as an expert in a primitive society who, in a trance state induced by drugs or music or other techniques, directly confronts the supernatural for the purposes of cures, clairvoyance, the finding of lost objects, and the foretelling of the future. Sam Shepard, my working hypothesis runs, is a shaman—a New World shaman. There are no witches on broomsticks within these pages. That's the Old World. Sam is as American as peyote, magic mushrooms, Rock and Roll, and medicine bundles.

North and South American Indian shamans regularly use drugs to induce trancelike states which carry them on their trips to the spirit world. The primitivist in Shepard parallels this experience *(Mad Dog Blues, Cowboy Mouth)* with certain characters in his plays who actually take drugs, go on trips, and live out what they hear and see. The emphasis is on the trip, the personal visions, the shamanistic goals fulfilled along the way—in short, the metaphysical. It is not important for Shepard to examine the social, economic, or political implications of drug taking. One must not ask him to answer questions he hasn't asked. Drugs are one technique in altering the conception of space-time between audience and actor. This alteration is essential if anything remotely resembling the metaphysical is to occur. Shepard's design is to promote a theatrical condition between audience and actor similar to an ecstatic state which will allow him to fulfill his shaman's role within the play and between audience and actor.

Even when a particular play does not have a character altering his consciousness with a chemical substance the trance strategy remains. The sound of the cricket in *Cowboys # 2* and the saxophone in *Angel City* would be mesmerizing in production. The reader ought to make an effort to keep them alive in the background of his mind, for Shepard's obsessively minute instructions regarding music and off-stage dialogue are the expert's choices to invoke another world.

One effect of the volcanic monologue, which is one of Shepard's favorite forms of address, is the near hypnotic state it promotes. These riffs, these poetic ejaculations are incantatory. They reaffirm the contiguous time between audience and actor without which the playwright as shaman could not function.

Still another element in the preparation of the audience in accepting the metaphysical nature of the evening is the matter of the bare or open stage. The open stage theatrically forces the audience to concentrate on a few suggestible props and use its imagination to provide the rest. The playwright need not depend on expensive stage machinery to move his characters from place to place because the audience makes the necessary mental adjustments. In Shepard's plays the abstract quality of the open stage lends credibility to the mythical figures in *Mad Dog Blues* and *Cowboy Mouth*. Having everything happen in one set with the audience doing the mental traveling also reinforces the continuity with the actors. Combined with the time element, which is usually left unbroken, the use of one set, the open stage, solidifies the sense of immediacy.

This sense of "nowness" celebrates in a personal way the human scale of the theatrical experience. Of course, if Shepard is to make the world of the spirit palpable he must have the cooperation of the audience. How else is he to effect a cure or find a lost love?

One exception to the shaman theory is the earliest play included here, *The Rock Garden*. The presentation of the man and woman as endlessly mouthing boring American claptrap goes beyond boring into irritation, and as irritation reaches its apex the young man in the play erupts in a monologue designed to shock a puritanical old man with its sexual explosiveness. It literally knocks him over and kills him.

Despite the hilarious table dance and bear imitation, *Action* resonates a European sensibility which appears to be set off by visions of a holocaust. Although the four young people in the play have their counterparts in his other work, here they are isolated, trying to survive apart from society.

There is a definite movement in Shepard's work to center shamanism in one character rather than spreading it around. That character is the artist, the poet-visionary. In the latest Shepard play, *Angel City*, the character "Rabbit" has been called for to help doctor a disaster movie which is in great danger of becoming a disaster itself. Rabbit shows up with his medicine bundles and does his stuff. It is when I begin to describe this play that I begin to sense how inadequate this introduction is. It is here that the content of Shepard's work blinks on and off like a neon sign at Hollywood and Vine, and my text touches content hardly at all, which means that it must be time for me to stop and for you to get the message yourself.

Angel City

Angel City was first produced at the Magic Theatre, San Francisco, on July 2, 1976. It was directed by the author, with the following cast:

Lanx: *Jack Thiebeau*
Wheeler: *John Nesci*
Miss Scoons: *O-Lan Shepard*
Rabbit: *Ebie Roe Smith*
Tympani: *James Dean*
Sax: *Bob Feldman*

Original music composed and performed by Bob Feldman.

NOTE ON THE MUSIC:

The dominant theme for the saxophone is the kind of lyrical loneliness of Lester Young's playing, occasionally exploding into Charlie Parker and Ornette Coleman. The musician should be free to explore his own sound within that general jazz structure and may find other places in the script, not indicated in the stage directions, to heighten or color the action. The saxophonist should remain cut off from the other characters in the play, even when he appears on stage. His presence is felt as a shadow to the other actors. His playing remains aloof and above the chaos for the most part. At moments when it does become chaotic it tends to explode right through the action and out the other side.

The actor who plays Tympani should either know how to play drums or at least be able to carry out some basic rhythm patterns without falling apart. Ideally his musicianship should be on the same level as the saxophonist's.

It might be useful for the musicians to listen to some of the recordings of Japanese theater to hear how the actor's voice is used in conjunction with the instruments—especially in the Act 2 contest between the generals.

NOTE TO THE ACTORS:

The term "character" could be thought of in a different way when working on this play. Instead of the idea of a "whole character" with logical motives behind his behavior which the actor submerges himself into, he should consider instead a fractured whole with bits and pieces of character flying off the central theme. In other words, more in terms of collage construction or jazz improvisation. This is not the same thing as one actor playing many different roles, each one distinct from the other (or "doubling up" as they call it), but more that he's mixing many different underlying elements and connecting them through his intuition and senses to make a kind of music or painting in space without having to feel the need to completely answer intellectually for the character's behavior. If there needs to be a "motivation" for some of the abrupt changes which occur in the play they can be taken as full-blown manifestations of a passing thought or fantasy, having as much significance or "meaning" as they do in our ordinary lives. The only difference is that here the actor makes note of it and brings it to life in three dimensions.

ACT 1

SCENE:

Basically bare stage. Upstage center is a large suspended blue neon rectangle with empty space in the middle. The rectangle is lit from time to time. Behind the rectangle the upstage wall is covered by a scrim which can be back-lit in different colors. Upstage, directly behind the rectangle is a narrow platform, raised about two feet above the stage floor and running horizontally the width of the stage. When the actors enter on this platform they become framed by the rectangle. Directly center, in front of the rectangle, is a large black swivel chair with the back of it facing the audience. The back is high enough to conceal whoever is sitting in it. There is a hand-held microphone attached to one arm of the chair which is used to amplify the narration sequences. There are two copper tympani drums placed at the very edge of the stage in the down-left corner. As the audience enters, the stage is set like this with the rectangle unlit and no color in the scrim. Lights go to black. LANX *and* TYMPANI *enter in blackout.* LANX *seats himself in the swivel chair with the back still facing audience so he's unseen.* TYMPANI *stands facing audience behind the two drums and begins to play a slowly rising drum roll in the dark. The drumming rises in volume. The blue rectangle is lit with the rest of the stage dark. The drumming rises slowly, and with it the scrim slowly turns a pale yellow with the stage lighting still dark.* TYMPANI's *form begins to be made out in the light. He is dressed in an English working-class cap, white T-shirt, suspenders, baggy pants and heavy construction boots. He is playing the drums with mallet type sticks. His expression is very serious as he watches the audience as he plays. Slowly yellow light begins to fill the stage area as* TYMPANI *begins to reach a thundering pitch on the drums. The drumming and light reach their full intensity. Suddenly* TYMPANI *stops playing, and makes a short bow to the audience and exits left.* LANX *begins to speak immediately from the chair over the microphone. Still unseen.*

LANX: *(as though reading from a script)* "It's a great office. A great window. A great life. All hell passes before me, and I can watch it like a junkie. With no pain." *(flatly, as though contained in the speech)* Yes, come in.

RABBIT BROWN *enters from right.* LANX *goes on talking, still unseen.* RABBIT *is dressed in a tattered detective's type suit and overcoat, hat, and tennis shoes. He seems fatigued. He has bundles of various sizes attached to him by long leather thongs and dragging on the floor behind him. He makes his way to center stage and stops. He scans the space for the source of* LANX'*s voice.*

LANX: "From the blackest black to the lightest light. It's all happening. The amazing thing to me is that despite its desolate appearance, the city teems with living things. Things crawl across upholstered seats. Deals are made in remote glove compartments. And we exist, here, walled in. A booming industry. Self sufficient. Grossing fifty million in just two weeks. Our own private police. Our own private food. Lawyers, doctors, technical staff, a laboratory of the highest caliber." Help yourself to anything. I'll be with you when the time comes.

RABBIT *looks around the space for something to help himself to but finds nothing. He tries to locate the voice as* LANX *rambles on, getting more intense. Sax could be used underneath some of this.*

LANX: "Outside, the smog strikes clean to the heart. Babies' eyes bleed from it. Paint blisters from it. Grown men keel over. Dogs go paralyzed. Used-car lots melt away into the black macadam. The Tar Pits squirm with animal life. And all along through the terrifying shopping centers the doom merchants whisper our fate. They hide behind the grape counters twisting their boney faces at us. Pointing their narrow hands and marking our death as though they themselves stood somehow out of time and judged us from eternity. Even so, it would seem that, after all these years, after all these plagues and holocausts, the city is finally being re-built."

The voice stops. LANX *whirls the chair around facing front. He is short and powerfully built with his hair greased straight back, dark glasses, black suit and shoes, starched white shirt with a high collar, gold cuff links which he's constantly snapping and adjusting, a ball point pen which he clicks continuously. In his lap he holds a few sheets of paper. He puffs and chews violently on a huge cigar and cracks his knuckles.* RABBIT *looks at him nervously.* LANX *just stares at him for a while.*

LANX: So, as pure narration, what do you think of it?

RABBIT: *(looking around)* You're asking me?

LANX: You're the Rabbit aren't ya?

RABBIT *nods.*

LANX: So, it's you I'm askin'. What do ya' think?

RABBIT: Terrible. Old time.

LANX: Exactly!

LANX *rips the papers into shreds and then sits on them.*

RABBIT: Worse than Jack Webb I'd say.

LANX: Very good, very smart. That's enough now. Shut up.

RABBIT: Did you write it?

LANX: No, I didn't write it! What do you think I am! What kind of a question is that!

RABBIT: Sorry.

LANX: Don't apologize. And wet your lips.

RABBIT: What?

LANX: Your lips! Wet them! Run your tongue around the outside.

RABBIT *does it.*

LANX: That's better. What've you been, out in the elements or something?

RABBIT: It's the smog.

LANX: Right. We don't get smog in here. You'll notice that.

RABBIT: Yeah.

LANX: We don't tolerate it in here. Out there, yes. *(indicating toward rectangle)* It's necessary. But in here, no.

RABBIT: Right. It's very nice the way you've got it controlled.

LANX: Well, it's either we control it or it controls us. You know what I mean? *(short tense laugh)*

RABBIT: Yeah.

LANX: *(suddenly serious)* So, you don't fly, huh?

RABBIT: No, I rode the buckboard down. I got a team a' horses. Stopped off at all the missions.

LANX: The missions? What for? Missions are stupid.

RABBIT: To pray.

LANX: You stopped and prayed on the way down?

RABBIT: Yeah.

LANX: You stopped at all the missions?

RABBIT: Right.

LANX: Terrific. Well, it woulda' been faster a' course if you'd a' flown down. That's gonna' be a problem. I mean time-wise and money-wise.

RABBIT: Well, I don't fly.

LANX: That's what I understand. You don't have to repeat what I already understand. Would you like a drink or something?

RABBIT: No.

LANX: A chair? Would you like a chair? It's my job to offer things. To make offers.

RABBIT: Yeah, I wouldn't mind a chair.

LANX: *(bellowing off left)* MISS SCOONS! COULD WE HAVE A CHAIR IN HERE RIGHT AWAY! *(to* RABBIT, *confidentially)* What are these items you have tied to yourself?

MISS SCOONS *enters from left. Very sexy. Short dress, high heels, typical secretary type. She carries a chair on her back, sets it downstage left and exits left again.*

RABBIT: *(to* LANX *but watching* MISS SCOONS*)* Oh, these are different bundles. Some of them are medicine bundles and some are just practical bundles.

LANX: Well, which is which? I'm not a mind reader.

RABBIT: *(picking up one of the bundles which looks like a weasel carcass)* Well you see this one? This one's particularly magical. It's a power bundle. Extremely dangerous. It was stolen from a museum.

RABBIT *sits in the chair which* MISS SCOONS *brought.* LANX *moves down right, puffing clouds of smoke, clicking his pen, snapping his cuffs, etc.*

LANX: I see. Well, let's get down to brass tacks shall we? I mean, in my book a bundle's a bundle. To cut it short, my partner, Wheeler, and I are in kind of a jam. A little bit of a fix. We've got ourselves in over our heads in this one particular project and uh—we're looking for an ace in the hole.

RABBIT: *(dropping the weasel bundle to the floor)* How far in have you got yourselves?

LANX: Well, in round figures let's call it eight million. But that's neither here nor there. The point is we need a slight miracle to boost us out, and we heard through the grapevine that you were the doctor.

RABBIT: That's right.

LANX: Of course, I myself, personally, have never even heard of you, but your reputation seems to be widespread in the areas where we're dependent. If you catch my drift?

RABBIT: I do.

LANX: Very sharp. Now try to stick close to my next line of reasoning.

RABBIT: Uh—I think I would like something to drink.

LANX: *(pausing, staring hard at* RABBIT *then yelling for* MISS SCOONS)
MISS SCOONS! A GLASS OF WATER PLEASE!

RABBIT: Thanks.

LANX: That's quite all right. Basically, you'll find that it's better to be direct around here. If you want something you say so. If you don't want something you don't say so. Simple as that.

RABBIT: Right.

MISS SCOONS *enters again slowly from left balancing a glass of water on the back of her hand. She gives it to* RABBIT, *who takes it off her hand, then she exits.* LANX *continues talking through this.*

LANX: Now, essentially, what's missing at the heart of the material is a meaningful character.

RABBIT: That's pretty basic isn't it?

LANX: Well, yes. But that's why we're considering this a state of emergency. I mean, after all we woulnd't have called someone in of your particular ilk if all we needed was a script writer.

RABBIT: Oh.

LANX: I mean you're not just that are you? You're not just another ordinary hack. You're supposed to be an artist, right?

RABBIT: Right.

LANX: A kind of magician or something.

RABBIT: Something like that.

LANX: You dream things up.

RABBIT: Right.

LANX: Right. So what we need in this case is a three-dimensional invention. Something altogether unheard of before. We have the story, the plot, the stars, the situation, but what's missing is this uh—this development. Something awesome and totally new.

RABBIT: I see.

LANX: It has to somehow transcend the very idea of "character" as we know it today.

RABBIT: Well, that's a big order.

LANX: Exactly! We're prepared to pay through the teeth, of course. I mean we're already over the budget, so what the hell. *(short laugh)*

RABBIT: Have you tried holographs or whatever they're called?

LANX: No, no! You don't get the picture. We're looking for an actual miracle. Nothing technological. The real thing.

RABBIT: A miracle.

LANX: That's right! Right here in Culver City.

RABBIT: Well, I've never exactly worked on a case like this before. I mean you want some "thing" to make an actual appearance in the middle of your movie?

LANX: SHHHH! Not so goddamn loud! The air has ears around here. There's spies all over the place.

RABBIT: *(whispering)* But that's the general idea, right?

LANX: *(whispering)* Exactly.

RABBIT: *(whisper)* A kind of an apparition?

LANX: Well, I don't want to explain your business to you. I mean you could call it whatever you want. All I know is that in order to pull this budget out of the hole we've got to have something happen that's never ever happened before. Something unearthly.

RABBIT: Well, I don't know. I mean I'll have to have a lot more information before I can take something like this on. I mean I'll have to know the story, who the other characters are, the plot. All that kinda' stuff.

LANX: Sure, sure. I'll get Wheeler in here right away. He's the backbone of the whole project. You just take it easy for a second. I'll be right back. He'll fill you in on all the details.

LANX exits quickly off right leaving RABBIT alone. Slow lurking music from the saxophone is heard from off stage. Stage lights dim slightly. Scrim turns pale green. Rectangle lights up blue. RABBIT stands and gathers the bundles around him. He starts arranging them in a large circle around him as he talks directly to the audience. Sax continues underneath.

RABBIT: *(to audience)* I make an adjustment. I'm basically geared in the old forms. Pre-bop, Lester Young, Roscoe Holcombe. I could run a list of hip references to make your tail swim. I've connived in the deepest cracks of the underground. Rubbed knuckles with the nastiest poets. Done the "Rocky Mountain Back Step" in places where they've outlawed bubble gum. But that's neither here nor there.

The SAXOPHONE PLAYER enters from up left on the platform playing his horn. He crosses slowly into the space behind the rectangle so that he's framed in the blue neon light with the green scrim behind him. The stage lighting continues to dim. Sax plays slow and mournful.

RABBIT: *(continuing)* The point is I've smelled something down here. Something sending its sweet claws way up North. Interrupting my campfires. Making me daydream at night. Causing me wonder at the life of a recluse. The vision of a celluloid tape with a series of moving images telling a story to millions. Millions anywhere. Millions seen and unseen. Millions seeing the same story without ever knowing each other. Without even having to be together. Effecting their dreams and actions. Replacing their books. Replacing their families. Replacing religion, politics, art, conversation. Replacing their minds. And I ask myself, how can I stay immune? How can I keep my distance from a machine like that? So I wind up here, in the city of the South. Not knowing a thing but convincing them through mysterious gestures that I'm their main man. (HE *hears* LANX *coming; secretly to audience*) I'm ravenous for power but I have to conceal it.

LANX *enters fast from right with* WHEELER. *The lights go out behind scrim and rectangle goes out. Stage lights back up.* LANX *chases the* SAXOPHONE PLAYER *who exits at a run off left.* LANX *is yelling at him as* WHEELER *stands sheepishly to stage right.* WHEELER *wears a bow tie, glasses, short-sleeved shirt, white and brown brogans, and holds a golf club which he's constantly turning in his hand. His whole manner is shy and intimidated.*

LANX: *(to* SAXOPHONE*)* GET OUTA' HERE YOU CREEP! GET AWAY FROM THE WINDOW! I'VE TOLD YOU A HUNDRED TIMES I CAN'T STAND THAT SOUND! YOU'RE GONNA' CRACK MY WINDOW! *(turning back to* RABBIT *after* SAX *exits)* Continuously trying to reverberate us into the past with that solo crap. When will these guys wake up? Oh, uh—this is Wheeler, my partner. Rabbit Brown.

WHEELER: *(stepping toward* RABBIT *shyly, offering his hand)* How do you do.

RABBIT *just stares at his hand but doesn't shake.*

WHEELER: I'm afraid this is all my fault in a way. I'm very sorry for having to bring you down all this way.

LANX: *(to* WHEELER*)* Now don't start apologizing right off the bat. We haven't even made a deal yet. *(laughs nervously to* RABBIT*)*

WHEELER: *(to* LANX*)* I'm sorry.

LANX: *(to* RABBIT*)* He's new to the business even though he is a genius. Wishy-washy. Spineless. Came up through the cutting rooms. We gotta just work around him. Take it as a necessary handicap.

RABBIT: I'm a little confused.

LANX: You look confused. But don't worry. Looks are deceiving. That's one a' the first things you learn around here. Nothing is the way it appears to be. In fact, very often, it's the opposite.

RABBIT: I see.

LANX: No you don't. But don't worry.

RABBIT: What is it exactly that you're looking for?

WHEELER: Well, we don't know exactly. We have a hunch. We have a feeling. But we don't know for sure.

LANX: Exactly. I thought I made that clear before. We have an idea that this town is ripe for another disaster.

RABBIT: *(pause)* Disaster?

WHEELER: Cinematically speaking. *(nervous laugh)*

LANX: In the profit sense of the word of course. A disaster on the screen, not in the box office. *(laughs)*

WHEELER: Yes. You see, all of the really major box office smashes have dealt with disaster to one degree or another. Either a disaster is about to happen, it's already happened, or it's actually taking place right now.

RABBIT: Right now?

WHEELER: In the movie. Right now in the movie.

RABBIT: Oh.

WHEELER: We have come to believe that it's only through a major disaster being interjected into this picture that we'll be able to save ourselves from total annihilation.

RABBIT: You mean financial?

WHEELER: *(suddenly serious)* And otherwise. Have you taken a look out the window? *(gestures toward rectangle)*

RABBIT *looks toward the rectangle then back to* WHEELER *without understanding his point.*

RABBIT: I don't get ya'.

WHEELER: *(to* LANX, *amazed)* Hasn't he looked out the window yet?

LANX: Well, he's just traveled the full length of California by buckboard, stopping off at all the missions on the way down. I assumed that he knows.

RABBIT: What's going on anyway? There's nothing but a city out there.

WHEELER: The city is eating us alive. Can't you see my skin? Look at my skin.

WHEELER *steps close to* RABBIT, *holding out his arm.* RABBIT *inspects the skin on* WHEELER'S *arm.* LANX *stands by, puffing and clicking his pen.*

WHEELER: It's turning us into snakes or lizards or something. Can't you feel that? We need protection.

RABBIT: Oh. *(steps back away from* WHEELER)

LANX: What we're getting at here, Brown, is that we're desperate for a device. We need something which is the next step forward. A step beyond the usual, if you get my meaning.

WHEELER: *(sudden intense secrecy)* That's right. Not simply an act of terror but something which will in fact drive people right off the deep end. Leave them blithering in the aisles. Create mass hypnosis. Suicide. Auto-destruction. Something which will open entirely new fads in sado-masochism. Penetrating every layer of their dark subconscious and leaving them totally unrecognizable to themselves. Something which not only mirrors their own sense of doom but actually creates the possibility of it right there in front of them. That's what the people are crying out for and that's what we must give them. It's our duty. We owe it to the public. For without the public we are nothing but a part of that public. We must stand apart, on another plane. We must rise to the challenge. We must help them devour themselves or be devoured by them. The time is ripe for this obliteration. We must rise to the occasion or be lost forever in a tidal wave of oblivion!

RABBIT: Now hold on a second, man. This sounds like something totally out of my ball park. I mean, I'm a stunt man. I fall off horses. I've done some sleight of hand. I've conjured a little bit. I collect a few myths, but this sounds like you need a chemical expert or something.

LANX: Exactly! A chemical expert. Very well put. Now we've prepared this room especially for your needs. You'll have two assistants and, of course, Miss Scoons will be at your complete disposal.

RABBIT: Wait a second!

WHEELER: We'll be checking in from time to time to see how you're coming along. Of course we don't want to interfere with the creative process but we do need to protect our investment.

RABBIT: What investment! I haven't cost you a thing yet!

LANX: There is, of course, a time element involved.

WHEELER: Yes. *(coldly)* If, by the end of the week you haven't come up with anything useful your entire motor functioning will cease to be a private concern. You can see what it's like outside, Brown. You can see what it's doing to us. You can help stop it. It's up to all of us to stop it before it's too late.
They both exit left, leaving RABBIT *alone. He stares around the space numbly. Lights dim slightly.* TYMPANI *enters abruptly from left with his drum sticks and stands behind the drums. He looks at* RABBIT. *They are silent for a while.*

RABBIT: *(to* TYMPANI*)* Are you in on this?

TYMPANI: *(facing front)* "It's a great office. A great window. A great life."

RABBIT: Aw, knock it off!

TYMPANI: *(blankly)* "The city thunders with the hollow moan of despair."

RABBIT: Have they got you working on something too? *(no answer from TYMPANI)* What's your position, if you don't mind my asking?

TYMPANI: I play drums.

RABBIT: I get it. I thought it might be more complicated than that.

TYMPANI: They have a theory about rhythm.

RABBIT: I was right.

TYMPANI: I'm experimenting with various rhythm structures in the hope of discovering one which will be guaranteed to produce certain trance states in masses of people.

RABBIT: Have you found it?

TYMPANI: Not yet. I've been here several months now. They take care of me though. I get everything I need here. It's not a bad life.

RABBIT: So we're in the same boat.

TYMPANI: *(matter of factly)* No. I'm above you. You're below me.

RABBIT *studies* TYMPANI *for a second.*

RABBIT: Who else have they got here?

TYMPANI: All kinds. I'm not allowed to talk about it. They all like it here though. We're well paid. Nobody complains.

RABBIT: What about the saxophone player?

TYMPANI: Lanx hates him. The guy wants in on the action, but Lanx can't stand him. Says he belongs in the wax museum.

RABBIT: Have you tried to escape?

TYMPANI: What for? You know what it's like out there. In here we're well protected. Nothing can touch us. Besides, I love the movies. I'm proud to be a part of the industry.

RABBIT: You're a sap.

TYMPANI: *(coldly)* Don't talk nasty or I'll break your back. Nobody talks nasty in here. We all get along. We eat Louis B. Mayer's chicken soup every day. It's a tradition. Louis is dead but his soup lives on.

RABBIT: I'm gettin' outa' here! *(starts to leave, then stops)*

TYMPANI: You won't go far. They've already busted up your buckboard and sold your horses. On foot you're as good as dead in this town. They'll swallow you whole and spit you out as a tax deduction.

RABBIT: Listen, I didn't ask for this! They called me in for consultation! That's all! That's as far as it went!

TYMPANI: Well things happen fast down here. You gotta be prepared. One day you're raising chickens, the next day you're buying up half of Mexico. *(He clucks like a chicken)*

RABBIT: I don't want half of Mexico!

TYMPANI: Then you'll want something else. Sooner or later you'll want something, and they'll find out what it is.

RABBIT: What do you mean?

TYMPANI: Some little fantasy. Some dream. Some tiny little delusion that you've got tucked away. They'll pry it out of you.

RABBIT: What do they care?

TYMPANI: Because then they've got you. They'll feed off your hunger. They'll keep you jumping at carrots. And you'll keep jumping. And you'll keep thinking you're not jumping all the time you're jumping.

RABBIT: Is that what's happened to you?

TYMPANI: What does it look like?

RABBIT: Well, how can you know it and still keep doing it?

TYMPANI: What else is there to do?

RABBIT: Are you crazy? They've got you kidnapped in here and you like it.

TYMPANI: So will you. You'd be surprised how fast it happens.

RABBIT: Listen, Mack, no matter how many greasy skinbags think the city's turning them into snakes it's still better out there than it is in here!

TYMPANI: Then why don't you leave? You can walk out easy enough.

RABBIT *considers a second. Suddenly stage lights dim sharply. Rectangle lights. Scrim turns deep blue. Saxophone comes in slow, heard off stage.* MISS SCOONS *appears from up left on the platform reading from a notepaper and crosses slowly behind the rectangle so that she's framed by it.* TYMPANI *fills in on the drums as* RABBIT *watches her.*

MISS SCOONS: *(overly dramatic)* "No more pain, she cried, as they lowered half the bleeding city into a deep dark hole and covered it over with smoking rubber tires. She slowly became aware of the truth behind the power of money. The very thing she had desperately tried to avoid all these long months as she shuffled aimlessly up and down the length and breadth of the City of Angels with a toothpick in her hand. Now it stood before her. Glaring down like some awesome demented saint. Its teeth chattering through rusted-out alleyways. Its breath blowing lasciviously at her gingham skirt. All innocence was now behind her. All dreams of the life of man free and unfettered as she once knew it was on the plains of Nebraska. Here was the hard core cement. The concrete reality of the dreaming-machine. The terrifying destruction which faced her head-on was now met by her own indivisible courage which she felt welling up from some deep primeval source which she knew not of. Suddenly the solution was clear. In her mind's eye was a simple equation. It appeared like a flashlight in a hooker's nightmare. 'Money equals power, equals protection, equals eternal life.' And with that she collapsed at the foot of La Cienaga.''

Sax stops, drums stop, stage lights back up. Special lights out. MISS SCOONS stands on the platform smiling down at RABBIT who stares at her in disbelief.

RABBIT: What was that?

MISS SCOONS: *(jumping down from platform)* Something I cooked up at the commissary during my lunch break. What do ya' think?

RABBIT: Great stuff. Really great.

MISS SCOONS: Really? You think it'll sell?

RABBIT: Positive.

MISS SCOONS: What did you think of it, Tympani?

TYMPANI: It's all right. A little wordy maybe.

MISS SCOONS: That's what I was thinking. Sort of too much showing off. Too many big words maybe.

RABBIT: No, I don't think so. In fact, on the whole I think it showed a remarkable economy of language.

MISS SCOONS: Gee, thanks.

TYMPANI: You mean like, ''. . . some deep primeval source which she knew not of''?

RABBIT: Well, that was a little sticky in that area, but otherwise I thought it was surprisingly original.

MISS SCOONS: Well, it is based on my own experience.

RABBIT: I could tell. It had that kind of a ring.

MISS SCOONS: Do you think I oughta' present it at the next tribunal?

RABBIT: Sure, why not.

TYMPANI: Are you kidding?

MISS SCOONS: No, I'm not kidding as a matter of fact. I wanna' advance my position. I can't remain a secretary forever.

TYMPANI: You show up with that kinda' crap they're gonna cut you right back to part-time lab duty. That stuff is strictly third rate.

MISS SCOONS: What do you know, beef sticks! You can't even come up with a simple thing like an original rhythm.

TYMPANI: All I know is that you'll never get to third base with that kinda' drivel. That went out with Raymond Chandler.

RABBIT: Yeah, he's right. Ayn Rand sorta' did it to death too.

MISS SCOONS: That's the trouble, ya' know.

RABBIT: What?

MISS SCOONS: Nobody knows what's good. Everybody's too easily swayed. One minute it's great, the next minute it's garbage. You have to just go on your own intuition. *(suddenly noticing* RABBIT's *bundles)* What are these things you have tied to yourself anyway? Nobody's ever showed up here with things tied to them like that before.

RABBIT: I'm working on something for the big fellas. Special project.

RABBIT *and* TYMPANI *exchange looks.*

MISS SCOONS: Really? You need any help?

RABBIT: Well, yeah. Sure. I mean I don't know exactly what it is I'm doing yet, but I sure could use some help.

TYMPANI: Nobody helped me when I was in a jam

MISS SCOONS: When were you in a jam?

TYMPANI: The day I arrived. I was just like him when I first got here, and nobody helped me.

RABBIT: Well, I'll help ya'. We can all help each other.

TYMPANI: Too late.

MISS SCOONS: That's for sure in your case.

TYMPANI: *(to* MISS SCOONS) At least I have a firm position. A title.

MISS SCOONS: Yeah, "Frozen in the Act of Creation."

RABBIT: Listen, I'm not sure if I can accurately assess the danger that we're in here, but I have a feeling we oughta' come up with something fast. I mean these guys are desperate. One of 'em's skin is crawling.

TYMPANI *smiles at* RABBIT, *satisfied that he's swallowed the bait.*

MISS SCOONS: Yeah, that's what I been saying all along. We should try to put our heads together and work as a team.

RABBIT: I mean they even threatened me. Did they ever threaten you?

MISS SCOONS: Oh yeah, every once in a while. It's sort of part of their whole approach.

RABBIT: I mean, didn't you uh—get scared or anything?

MISS SCOONS: Scared? What for? They're just crazy, that's all. Nothin' to worry about.

RABBIT: But aren't you being held here against your will?

MISS SCOONS *looks to* TYMPANI *for an explanation.* TYMPANI *shrugs.*

MISS SCOONS: What's got into this guy? *(back to* RABBIT*)* Do I look like a prisoner to you?

RABBIT: No, I guess not. Well, look, maybe we can fool them.

TYMPANI: Hah! You must have a screw loose or something. Lanx and Wheeler have been through every trick in the book.

RABBIT: Yeah, but what if we could come up with a character that nobody's ever seen before. Something in flesh and blood. Not just an idea but something so incredible that as soon as they came in contact with it they'd pass out or go into convulsions or something. That's what they're looking for.

TYMPANI: How could you do that?

RABBIT: We'd have to invent it. Right here. Between the three of us.

MISS SCOONS: That's fantastic! What an idea! A real live experiment!

TYMPANI: It'll never work.

RABBIT: How come?

MISS SCOONS: Like a monster or something!

TYMPANI: First of all, because they're looking for something beyond the imagination. Something impossible.

RABBIT: Well, if they can imagine the possibility of it maybe we can imagine the thing itself.

MISS SCOONS: Yeah, it'd be a great challenge, Tympani. You could get that diner that you're always talking about.

RABBIT: What diner?

MISS SCOONS: *(to* RABBIT*)* He's always wanted a diner, ever since he was a little boy.

TYMPANI: SHUT UP!

MISS SCOONS: Well, it's true isn't it? You're always talking about it.

TYMPANI: I'm not always talking about it! I mentioned it once!

RABBIT: Take it easy. It's nothing to be ashamed of.

TYMPANI: I'M NOT ASHAMED!!

RABBIT: All right, all right. Jesus, I could care less if you've always wanted to have a diner. I happen to like diners.

TYMPANI: I HAVEN'T ALWAYS WANTED TO HAVE A DINER!

RABBIT: Oh, brother.

MISS SCOONS: He'll be okay in a minute. Shall I get us all some coffee?

RABBIT: Sure.

MISS SCOONS *turns toward the rectangle as though to leave but stops suddenly. She seems to go into a hypnotic state and just stares at the rectangle.*

RABBIT: What's the matter, Miss Scoons?

She speaks in a kind of flattened monotone, almost as if another voice is speaking through her.

MISS SCOONS: I look at the screen and I am the screen. I'm not me. I don't know who I am. I look at the movie and I am the movie. I am the star. I am the star in the movie. For days I am the star and I'm not me. I'm me being the star. I look at my life when I come down. I look and I hate my life when I come down. I hate my life not being a movie. I hate my life not being a star. I hate being myself in my life which isn't a movie and never will be. I hate having to eat. Having to work. Having to sleep. Having to go to the bathroom. Having to get from one place to another with no potential. Having to live in this body which isn't a star's body and all the time knowing that stars exist. That there are people doing nothing all their life except being in movies. Doing nothing but swimming and drinking and laughing and being driven to places full of potential. People never having to feel hot pavement or having to look at weeds growing through cracks in the city. People never having to look the city square in the eyes. People living in dreams which are the same dreams I'm dreaming but never living.

She suddenly snaps out of it and exits left. RABBIT *watches her go. He looks at* TYMPANI.

RABBIT: Is she all right?

TYMPANI: I don't know.

RABBIT: What's going on around here anyway? Doesn't anybody know each other?

TYMPANI: What's to know?

RABBIT: Well, I mean, you see each other every day don't you?

TYMPANI: Look, don't go gettin' humanitarian on me, mister. The environment can't take it.

RABBIT: What environment?

TYMPANI: This is a city.

RABBIT: So what?

TYMPANI: We're the brain of the city. The brain's demented. It's a demented brain. You understand? If we disturb that demented condition, the city will collapse around us. Now you don't want that to happen, do you?

RABBIT: Is that what Wheeler's afraid of?

TYMPANI: *(menacing)* Don't poke too deep, you're still on the guest list.

RABBIT *stops short. Pause.*

RABBIT: Don't you ever sit down?

TYMPANI: No.

RABBIT: You won't mind if I sit down?

TYMPANI: No.

RABBIT *sits upstage in the black swivel chair, facing front.* TYMPANI *stays behind the drums facing front.*

RABBIT: You're always standing?

TYMPANI: Always. Waiting for it to happen.

RABBIT: What "it"?

TYMPANI: "It."

RABBIT: Oh. "It."

TYMPANI: The rhythm. The one, special, never-before-heard-before rhythm which will drive men crazy.

RABBIT: That's a tough one.

TYMPANI: It's possible.

RABBIT: Sure. I guess.

TYMPANI: *(facing front)* One time I could almost taste it. I was standing here just like this. I was playing a standard four-four cross pattern. I'd been into it for maybe half an hour when I began to feel something taking over my left wrist. I was curious at first because I'd never had quite that kind of a feeling enter into a simple four-four pattern before. It was like I could hear a whole other shape and sound to the basic structure. Something behind what I was playing. Then I looked straight down at my hands and I saw somebody else playing the pattern. It wasn't me. It was a different body. Then I got scared. I panicked when I saw that, and right away I lost it. It just vanished like that, and I never have come across it again.

RABBIT: It'll come back.

TYMPANI: What do you know? Your optimism isn't reassuring; it's stupid. You can't make me feel better about it, because I already know what it is. I know it's lost and I'll never find my way back to it. It was the chance of a lifetime.

RABBIT: So now you're just taking up space?

TYMPANI: I'm facing my death.

Loud screech from the saxophone off stage. RABBIT *suddenly whirls the swivel chair around so it's facing upstage. At the same time the lights go black and the rectangle is lit. The scrim turns dark red.*

TYMPANI *pulls the other chair downstage center, facing front and sits in it like a little boy, eating popcorn and watching the movies.* RABBIT's *voice is heard but he is unseen.*

RABBIT: *(little kid voice)* I love the newsreels! I could watch the newsreels forever!

TYMPANI: *(little kid voice)* Not me. News is stupid. It has a stupid voice. Sounds like a grown-up. Grown-ups sounding important and not knowing they're stupid.

RABBIT: *(adult newscaster voice)* A two-headed St. Bernard was born to normal parents in Grand Rapids, Michigan. The pup was the only one in the litter, which is unusual for St. Bernards.

LANX *enters on the platform up left in boxer shorts, black boxing shoes, towel around his neck and swollen eyes, his nose bleeding profusely. He is raising his arms to a distant cheering audience, in victory. He crosses into the rectangle and keeps acknowledging his audience silently.*

TYMPANI: I wanna' see the one where they find the guy's face in the vacant lot full of shotgun holes.

RABBIT: *(newscaster voice)* The mother died in birth and the baby died shortly thereafter. Medical experts are still uncertain as to the exact causes of death; however, they believe the unusual size of the double-headed baby may be at the root of it.

TYMPANI: That could never happen in this town. Too many cops.

RABBIT: *(newscaster)* Tom Mix got caught stealing towels from the Beverly Wilshire and refused to make a comment.

TYMPANI: I wish it would happen in this town. Wouldn't that be neat? A real murder right here. Where they can't find who did it and everybody's scared to go to bed at night!

RABBIT: The "Howdy Doody Show" will not be seen on television this season due to a contractual disagreement between the producers. The "Sheriff John Show" will fill in the missing slot.

Sax backup. Suddenly LANX *starts talking from the rectangle as though he were being interviewed. Sax builds through this.*

LANX: Yeah, I love fightin' in this town. There's somethin' about the atmosphere here. The people. The people love me here. They go bananas. This town is crazy. That's why I love it. I go back to Jersey City and I'm just another mug, ya' know what I mean? But out here in the West they can appreciate a real boxer, ya' know? I mean I give the people what they want. They like to see some action when they come to the fights. They don't wanna' see a couple of GIs up there doin' the fox trot all over the canvas. They wanna' see some boxin'. And that's what I'm here for. And the fans know that. They know when they come to a Jimmy Muldoon fight that they're gonna see the real stuff. They're gonna' see some leather thumpin'!

Sax fades to low backup. LANX *continues talking to his audience in mime as* RABBIT *and* TYMPANI *go on.* LANX *shadowboxes in the rectangle.*

RABBIT: *(newscaster)* The kidnapping has stirred the emotions of millions. Everywhere the voice of outrage is on the people's lips.

TYMPANI: *(like an old lady)* Such a sweet little boy too. All alone in the bedroom with the wind blowing the curtains. Only a monster could have dreamed of such a thing.

LANX *cuts back in with his voice.*

LANX: Well, I figure I got maybe two or three good years left. You know how it is in this profession. Here today, gone tomorrow. *(laughs)* Anyway, I figure there's a future for me right here in Hollywood. I mean, I still got my looks and my muscle to get me through. I've already been talkin' to a major studio about doin' my life story. Soon's a good offer comes along I just might take it. Who knows? Anyhow, I just wanna' wish all my fans in L.A. the best of luck and thanks for supportin' me and helpin' me to become a challenger for the title. Thanks a million.

LANX *raises his arms in victory and waves to the fans. Suddenly* TYMPANI *stands on the chair facing front and shouts like a little kid to his mother upstairs.*

TYMPANI: I just wanna' go to the movies, Ma! I don't care about anything else! Just the movies! I don't care about school or homework or college or jobs or marriage or kids or insurance or front lawns or mortgage or even the light of day! I don't care if I never see the sun again, Ma! Just send me to the dark, dark movies!

Rising sax. Sound of mass applause. LANX *exits right, shadowboxing as he goes. Rectangle goes unlit. Scrim out. Stage lights back up.* RABBIT *whirls the chair around facing front again.* RABBIT *and* TYMPANI *freeze a second. Sudden silence as* MISS SCOONS *enters slowly trying not to spill two Dixie cups full of coffee. She crosses to center stage and sets the cups down extremely slowly on the floor, so as not to spill them. This sequence should be almost in slow motion. Once she has the cups safely on the floor she breaks back into her normal tempo.*

MISS SCOONS: All I could find was Dixie cups. Wheeler smashed all the real cups the other day. Went totally crazy. Better drink these fast before the wax melts. Makes the coffee taste really weird.

TYMPANI: *(leaving chair and crossing back to drums)* I don't want any coffee. Makes my teeth itch. Bad enough with smog choking you, making your eyes run, cops giving you walking tickets. Everything's bad enough without coffee to make things worse.

MISS SCOONS: Well, that's just perfect because I only brought two cups anyway!

TYMPANI: What is coffee anyway! Some goddamn bean they invented to make you stay up late.

RABBIT *gets up from the chair and picks up a cup of coffee.* MISS SCOONS *sits in the other chair.*

RABBIT: I've got an idea.

MISS SCOONS: Great.

RABBIT: What if we start with ourselves. One of us.

TYMPANI: What do you mean, one of us?

RABBIT: One of us volunteers to be worked on by the other two. To be transformed into this character they're looking for.

TYMPANI: Back to that again. It's not just a character. Why can't you get that straight? If they were just looking for a character they'd be going through the casting agencies. They want a phenomenon.

RABBIT: Why're you in such a bad mood all of a sudden?

TYMPANI: I have no good moods! Every mood I have is a variation on a bad mood. Good moods don't fit into the scheme of things. Good moods are stupid! GOOD MOODS ARE WORSE THAN DIXIE CUPS!

MISS SCOONS: *(to RABBIT)* I'll volunteer.

RABBIT: Great, Miss Scoons will be the guinea pig.

TYMPANI: *(to audience)* And suddenly they were all transported to the world of magic.

RABBIT: This coffee tastes really weird.

MISS SCOONS: It's the wax melting.

RABBIT: Oh.

MISS SCOONS: Come on Tymp, you can sit in the director's chair. It'll be fun.

TYMPANI: Fun? What is this supposed to be? Mickey Rooney and Judy Garland get their big break and move to Philadelphia with the Dorsey brothers? What is this? We're in the middle of a dung heap here. Where do you think we are anyway? You don't work your way up from the bottom anymore. You rip flesh! You tear your eyeballs out and watch them get kicked down the street.

MISS SCOONS: *(to RABBIT)* He's had some bad breaks.

TYMPANI: It doesn't work that way anymore! Nobody gets breaks! You get broken in half!

MISS SCOONS: Just relax for a while. Let's just try this idea he has. You got nothing to lose. Just pretend everything's all right. Pretend you've had so many successes that now you're retired and living in the East. Boston or Maine or someplace cozy. You can afford to relax. You have a Golden Retriever at your feet, the *New York Times Review of Books* in your lap, an after-dinner mint in your mouth. You've created more disasters in your time than the whole of Hollywood put together. You're known as "The Master of Disaster."

TYMPANI's mood begins to change as RABBIT *crosses to him and escorts him upstage to the black swivel chair and sits him down in it. He coaxes him along with his voice.*

RABBIT: That's right. Pretend you've been called from a far-away place by the head chiefs of the whole city. You're the only one who can solve the mystery. Millions and millions are riding solely on your powers of imagination. There's nobody quite like you on the entire planet. You've been called in on similar cases and solved every one of them. But this is something special. This is the case to end all cases. Even you, with all your powers, with all your stature and reputation, are left somewhat puzzled and dumbfounded. Even you, the High Prophet of Disaster. The Master himself.

TYMPANI begins to take on the characteristics which RABBIT *attributes to him. He seats himself in the swivel chair with his hands folded in his lap. He speaks with an air of authority.*

TYMPANI: *(to* RABBIT*)* So tell me—this particular entity, I assume it's evil?

RABBIT: *(deep voice)* Can any fear be construed as good?

TYMPANI: That is not my question! I'm not here to dilly-dally in quasi-philosophical meanderings! I'm here to solve a problem.

RABBIT: But you see, the consistent product of this being is paralyzing fear. Even in its dormant state it can produce severe nausea and depression.

TYMPANI: Would we be safe in assuming then, at the outset at least, that this "thing" is more a kind of force than anything resembling a character?

RABBIT: We could assume, yes.

TYMPANI: Good. Then let's begin.

Low lurking sax music bleeds in from off stage. Lights shift. MISS SCOONS *becomes very still in her chair as* RABBIT *moves steadily around the space.* TYMPANI *remains in the swivel chair with hands folded. Green light on his face. The scrim turns orange.*

RABBIT: We find it, somehow, at the present, inhabiting the body of a woman.

TYMPANI: What is her age?

RABBIT: The age of the body or the "thing"?

TYMPANI: THE BODY, OF COURSE!

RABBIT: In its twenties, roughly.

TYMPANI: Roughly? How roughly?

RABBIT: Mid-twenties.

TYMPANI: Thank you.

RABBIT: Can you picture it now?

TYMPANI: DON'T RUSH ME!

RABBIT: Sorry.

TYMPANI: I'm having difficulty with the form.

RABBIT: We could change it to a man.

TYMPANI: DON'T BE STUPID! That's not the form I mean. I can't go from drums to this just like a duck to water.

RABBIT: Oh.

TYMPANI: I need some time to work into it.

RABBIT: Well, take your time then.

TYMPANI: Could you stand her up for me?

RABBIT: Yeah, sure.

RABBIT goes to MISS SCOONS *and stands her up. She stands very still, staring straight ahead as though hypnotized.* TYMPANI *faces out and doesn't look at her directly.*

TYMPANI: She doesn't seem grotesque at all.

RABBIT: Well, she's not. Not now.

TYMPANI: She seems abnormally normal in fact. What's the matter with her?

RABBIT: Nothing's the matter with her! We have to cook up something that's the matter with her! That's the whole point. We have to transform her.

TYMPANI: But maybe that's where the terror lies.

RABBIT: Where?

TYMPANI: In her very normalness. She's terrifyingly normal.

RABBIT: Are you kidding! That won't sell.

TYMPANI: No. She passes herself off as one of us, but then these weird events take place. She demolishes entire populations with her normalness. She enters an advanced civilization where deranged citizens rule the planets. Her normalness destroys them utterly.

RABBIT: That won't scare anybody!

TYMPANI: So, the only alternative is to make her grotesque then. It's either one or the other.

RABBIT: We have to go beyond that! This is a challenge!

TYMPANI: It's either an Angel or a Devil. Which one's it going to be?

RABBIT: There must be something in between.

TYMPANI: But that's totally boring.

RABBIT: How do you know?

TYMPANI: *(getting up from chair, quits the game)* Because that's where we are right now! IN BETWEEN!

Lights come up again. Sax stops. MISS SCOONS *keeps swaying hypnotically back and forth.*

RABBIT: *(to* TYMPANI*)* What's the matter?

TYMPANI: The matter is that you're trying to approach this whole thing in an ordinary way. Like an amateur seance or something. I mean we're just fishing around in the dark for some kind of vague creepiness. This is an eight million dollar project your talking about!

RABBIT: Well, what's your idea then?

TYMPANI: I DON'T HAVE AN IDEA! I already told you. It's impossible. I don't want any part of this thing.

RABBIT: Great.

TYMPANI: *(returning to drums)* It's your predicament, not mine. I'm already sidetracked enough as it is.

TYMPANI *picks up the drum sticks and begins to play softly on the drums.* MISS SCOONS *starts to sway more intensely. Pause. She slowly starts moving around the stage in a trance. Sax comes in underneath.*

RABBIT: *(to* TYMPANI *who continues drumming softly)* I don't see it that way.

TYMPANI: What way?

RABBIT: Yours or mine. If one of us escapes, we all escape.

TYMPANI: I'm not looking to escape! This is my job! I like it here. Stop trying to squeeze me out of a good thing.

MISS SCOONS: *(to herself, still moving; drum continues)* In those days God had no need to create anything apart from himself. He was self-contained.

RABBIT: *(to* MISS SCOONS*)* God?

MISS SCOONS: *(dancing slowly, speaking in trance)* There was such an overflow of divine love that the angels came bursting forth of their own accord. Circle upon circle of spirit lights radiantly dashing the heavens, whirling about the sun in clouds of crystal fragments.

RABBIT: *(to* SCOONS*)* We have to go the other direction! Fear! Devils! Serpents, not angels! What's the matter with you people! You should know what's commercial by now.

MISS SCOONS: They were blasted out of eternal sleep by the blinding light of a direct vision of Glory. So devastating was this light that only their flaming wings could offer protection from this fire that also gave them their birth.

RABBIT: *(to* SCOONS*)* We have to work on fear, not glory! Terror! Devastation! That's where the money is! Devastation!

MISS SCOONS: And all at once they began to sing. All nine choirs in descending rank.

> RABBIT *turns to* TYMPANI. MISS SCOONS *whirls around the stage in ecstasy.* TYMPANI's *rhythm on the drums builds. Sax fills in behind.*

RABBIT: What is the most frightening thing in the world?

TYMPANI: *(blankly)* A space. *(He continues drums)*

RABBIT: What is the most frightening thing in the whole world?

TYMPANI: A life cut off from all life.

RABBIT: What is the most scary thing in the world!

TYMPANI: Death.

RABBIT: *(pacing)* WHAT IS THE MOST FRIGHTENING THING IN THE WHOLE WIDE WORLD!

TYMPANI: Dying.

RABBIT: WHAT IS MORE FRIGHTENING THAN ANYTHING ELSE?

TYMPANI: Dying alone.

RABBIT: WHAT IS IT THAT EVERYBODY IS SCARED OF!

TYMPANI: The expectation of a death unknown.

RABBIT: What is fear!

TYMPANI: THE IMAGINATION OF DYING!

RABBIT: Now we're getting somewhere!

TYMPANI: Now we're cooking!

RABBIT: THE IMAGINATION OF DYING IS MORE SCARY THAN ACTUALLY DYING!

TYMPANI: How do you know?

RABBIT: I assume.

TYMPANI: You assume, but you don't know.

RABBIT: Having never died my death, I assume that imagining it is more scary than doing it.

TYMPANI: You don't do it. It does it by itself.

RABBIT: Yes. That's true. That must be true.

TYMPANI: But you don't know.

RABBIT: I don't know.

Through this the rhythm from TYMPANI'*s drumming is getting more frenetic.* MISS SCOONS *dances with more and more abandon.* RABBIT *paces.*

TYMPANI: He doesn't know.

RABBIT: NOT KNOWING IS MORE SCARY THAN KNOWING.

TYMPANI: But since you don't know you can only assume.

RABBIT: NOT KNOWING WHEN OR HOW OR WHY OR WHERE!

TYMPANI: But only that you will.

RABBIT: I will. I WILL DIE!

TYMPANI: HE WILL!

RABBIT: We all will.

TYMPANI: You will.

RABBIT: So will you.

TYMPANI: WE ALL WILL DIE AND NOT KNOW HOW OR WHY OR WHERE!

RABBIT: AND THAT IS WHAT'S FRIGHTENING BEYOND ALL REASON!

TYMPANI: AND THAT'S WHAT MAKES A BOX OFFICE SMASH!

RABBIT: AND THAT'S WHAT MAKES AN INDUSTRY!

TYMPANI: AND THAT'S WHAT MAKES A MILLION BUCKS!

RABBIT: WE'VE GOT IT! WE'VE GOT IT! MISS SCOONS! WE'VE GOT IT! Miss Scoons?

Sax stops. Drums stop. MISS SCOONS *is frozen in place, center stage. She speaks as though in a trance.*

MISS SCOONS: You haven't got a thing. None of us has got a thing. We're only going in circles. We're only going around and around. We're only getting nowhere. We're going nowhere fast.

RABBIT: No, we've really hit on something! Tympani and me. We both discovered something while you were dancing.

MISS SCOONS: It's nothing. You only got excited by the sound of your own voice. There's nothing in here. The city's dead. The living are replacements for the dead. Nothing moves in this town.

TYMPANI: She'll be all right.

RABBIT: I thought we had something there. *(to* TYMPANI*)* Didn't you feel like we were on to something?

TYMPANI: I don't know.

RABBIT: Boy, you people are really weird.

TYMPANI: You don't know what weirdness is, chump.

LANX *enters fast from right, dressed in his suit again, puffing on his cigar. He stops center stage next to* MISS SCOONS *and glares at all of them.*

LANX: What's going on! I'm not paying you to stand around salivating! Do you realize what's happening! Wheeler's condition is getting worse! He's turning completely green and his top layer is beginning to peel!

RABBIT: We've been trying our damndest to come up with something.

LANX: THAT'S NOT GOOD ENOUGH! THIS IS CULVER CITY, NOT THE BORSCHT CIRCUIT! WE DEAL IN HARD CORE PRODUCTS! CASH ON THE LINE!

RABBIT: It's not my fault! I can't work with these people! They don't have any gumption! All the fire's gone out of them.

MISS SCOONS: *(still in trance)* The Cherubim. The Seraphim. The Thrones. The Dominions.

LANX: THEN DO IT ON YOUR OWN!

RABBIT: Where? In this nut house? I want a suite of my own with room service. I deserve better than this. I'M AN ARTIST GODDAMN-IT! I CAME ALL THIS WAY BY BUCKBOARD!

MISS SCOONS: The messengers of God.

LANX: *(to* RABBIT*)* That's very quaint, but that's not the point. The point is that you came. Something drew you down here to us. Isn't that so? Something indescribable?

TYMPANI: I can describe it. Money.

RABBIT: That's right. So what?

LANX: So don't go pulling rank on me with that "Artist" crap! You're no better than any of us.

RABBIT: That's not what I meant.

LANX: You thought you'd come down and whip off a few quick lines, collect a little traveling expenses and a fat contract, and then sashay on outa' here. Right?

MISS SCOONS: *(trance)* The urge to create works of art is essentially one of ambition. The ambition behind the urge to create is no different from any other ambition. To kill. To win. To get on top.

LANX: What's got into her?

RABBIT: Part of our experiment.

MISS SCOONS: Greed is greed.

LANX: Why is she talking like that! She's never talked like that before. I can't even follow it.

TYMPANI: You know what I think? I think it was the rhythm I was playing. THAT MUST BE IT! I MUST'VE FOUND IT ACCIDENTALLY!

RABBIT: I told you we were on to something!

TYMPANI: THAT'S IT, LANX! THAT'S IT! LOOK, SHE'S COMPLETELY ZONKED OUT!

MISS SCOONS: The Angel is against all evil. He appears in the midst of destruction.

LANX: What's going on! Miss Scoons, snap out of it!

TYMPANI: No, you don't understand. I was playing a rhythm on the drums and she was moving to it. I must've hit on the one that I was looking for and didn't even know it.

LANX: So what! If you didn't know it then, you still don't know it.

TYMPANI: But I could find it again! I could trace it down!

LANX: What I want to know is what are we going to do about Wheeler! If he goes under, all of us go with him!

MISS SCOONS *travels around the space and speaks with a different voice.* TYMPANI *watches her closely.*

MISS SCOONS: The ambition to transform valleys into cities. To transform the unknown into the known without really knowing. To make things safe. To beat death. To be victorious in the face of absolute desolation.

LANX: Whose script is that? Where did she memorize that?

TYMPANI: It's coming from her!

LANX: Don't give me that! I recognize the style. Sounds like Fritz Lang or early Howard Hawkes.

RABBIT: She's going to need some help. Is there a doctor around?

LANX: There are no doctors in this town. They've all been sued to death. What's the matter with you! We're all on the verge of disaster, and you talk about it like it was a simple medical problem. Wheeler's condition can only be solved by you!

RABBIT: But what about Miss Scoons?

LANX: She doesn't count! Only Wheeler counts! His condition is precarious!

RABBIT: But I don't care about Wheeler one way or the other.

LANX: Then you have no business in this business!

RABBIT: Then let me go!

LANX: NO!

RABBIT: This is insane.

MISS SCOONS: The Authorities. The Powers. The principalities. The Arch-angels. The Angels.

TYMPANI: *(watching* MISS SCOONS*)* I think she's going deeper. She's definitely contacting other entities. Listen to her breathing.

LANX: GET HER OUT OF HERE! SHE'S UPSETTING THE WHOLE PROJECT!

MISS SCOONS: El Pueblo de Nuestra Senora la Reina de los Angeles de Porciuncuta. En la ciudad. En todo el mundo. La muerta esta es el rey supremo. Viva la muerta!

LANX: PLEASE! I NEED SOME KIND OF ORDER! SOME KIND OF ARRANGEMENT! WHEELER'S SKIN IS TURNING GREEN! WE'LL ALL BE EATEN ALIVE!

From this point on everyone is in their own world. They speak to themselves.

TYMPANI: I have a diner in my dream. One diner.

RABBIT: What's keeping me from leaving? I could leave. Nobody's holding a gun to my head.

LANX: It's not the same for me. My power lies in manipulation. If no one is manipulated, then I'm sunk. I have no purpose!

TYMPANI: One diner. Basically green. Pale green walls. Chrome stools with black leatherette seats. Everyone's face is reflected in those stools.

MISS SCOONS: The Spanish took over. The Spanish Hunger. Spanish stomachs made a sound that rumbled through these canyons. You can still hear it in some parts. The Spanish had no idea they'd ever be in the movies.

LANX: There has to be some form! Even chaos has a form!

TYMPANI: The main dish is chicken gumbo. Served on Saint's Day. The Chef's Special. People go a hundred miles out of their way just to taste it.

RABBIT: It's me! It's me who wants to stay! I could leave but I'm staying.

MISS SCOONS: Absolute greed devoured them whole. Their viciousness was beyond belief. Tearing the gold teeth from half-dead victims. Crushing jade jaguars into green dust. They set the stage with Catholic blood.

LANX: *(looking out through rectangle)* Once there was an industry! A magnificent industry! The studios dominated the scenery. The villages sprang up around them like serfs spawning at the feet of their master. Then there was order! Everyone knew their place!

TYMPANI: In one corner is a chrome juke box with nothing but Hank Snow records.

RABBIT: *(to audience)* I'm staying and I don't regret it.

MISS SCOONS: Their voraciousness knew no bounds. They were a bottomless pit.

WHEELER rushes on from stage right. Everyone stops. WHEELER's skin has turned green, big open sores on his face and arms. He is panting for breath. He screams in desperation.

WHEELER: WHERE'S MY DISASTER!!!!!!!!!!!!!!!!

Lights black out. Sax rushes into high wailing riff and continues into black out.

ACT 2

SCENE:

Same basic set as Act 1. LANX can be heard shadowboxing in the dark. He makes the sharp exhaling sound of a boxer when he throws a punch. The stage lights rise slowly on TYMPANI, dressed up in a chef's hat, long white apron, and a spatula in his hand. He is using the two tympani drums as a make-believe griddle. WHEELER is seated in the swivel chair, upstage, facing the audience. His skin is a slimey green. He now has two fangs and extra-long fingernails. His posture is slumped over and painful. He seems to be having trouble breathing, and in general his health has depleted considerably. Downstage right, on the floor on hands and knees, MISS SCOONS is scrubbing the floor with a big brush and a bucket full of soapy water. She is dressed as a nun and speaks with a light Irish accent. Center stage, RABBIT is laying out the bundles to form a large circle on the floor. WHEELER watches his every move very closely, as though his life depended on it. LANX is dressed in a suit, but his hands are bandaged and bloody. His nose has a wide bandage across it, and his eyes are black and blue. He shadowboxes around the loose space. MISS SCOONS sings softly to herself as she scrubs the floor. Lights rise slowly. LANX keeps boxing the air. TYMPANI cooks and WHEELER watches RABBIT.

MISS SCOONS: (*singing*)

I could've married a thistledown
Or Jesus Christ his self
Or climbed a holy mountain top
Or built a ship meself

But, no, I cast meself to sea
And sailed for foreign turf
Whereupon I climbed the highest tree
And searched for my sweet home
And searched for my sweet home

Lights up full. They are all silent for a while but continue with their actions. The dominant sound is WHEELER's *heavy, rasping breathing and* LANX's *punches.*

WHEELER: *(to* RABBIT, *having difficulty speaking)* I can't understand the necessity for getting so elaborate with the design.

RABBIT: *(as* HE *works, arranging bundles)* Well, under ordinary circumstances I'd plunge right in and just see what I'd come up with by chance. But this situation seems to call for a more traditional approach.

TYMPANI: *(to* LANX, *cooking imaginary eggs)* Did you say you wanted those over-easy or straight up?

LANX: *(still boxing air)* I want the whites firm. That's the most important. If the whites aren't firm you don't get the full nutrition from the egg. Might as well eat it raw. An athlete has to watch his eggs.

TYMPANI: Right. Don't worry. I'm used to this kind of cooking. Sugar Ray used to stop in here on his way to the Garden. Now there was a finicky eater.

WHEELER: *(to* RABBIT) What do you mean by traditional?

RABBIT: There's a long history to the Medicine Wheel. I'm just learning it myself.

WHEELER: That's what you call this? A Medicine Wheel?

RABBIT: That's what the Indians called it.

WHEELER: Don't get cute. I'm not interested in ethnic origins.

RABBIT: Well, we're taking a risk any way you look at it.

WHEELER: Why's that?

RABBIT: This was always used for prayer, not destruction.

WHEELER: Well this isn't for destruction. It's for entertainment.

MISS SCOONS: Oh, Mister Wheeler, would you have me clean the entire floor then, or just the alcoves?

WHEELER: Is she talking to me?

MISS SCOONS: Aye, it's you, Mister Wheeler, that I'm addressin'.

WHEELER: *(standing suddenly)* What's happened in here! Something's happened in here since I was last here! I want to know what it is! The air smells different.

The rest continue, ignoring WHEELER. LANX *tries to comfort him.*

LANX: Don't worry, buddy. It's just the smog. The smog and the Spanish. We're doing something about both problems. We've got our man on it right now. They can't get away with it for long.

WHEELER: I don't understand what's going on. Have I changed as much as you?

LANX: We're exactly the same, old buddy. Everything's exactly the same. I'm in top condition. Look at me pivot!

LANX *pivots for* WHEELER.

WHEELER: Show me the window! I WANT TO SEE THE WINDOW!

LANX: Sure thing. Right this way.

TYMPANI: *(to himself)* Cripples and lames. Cripples and lames. All the same as far as I'm concerned. I see all kinds in here. They come and go. All I do is cook and watch.

LANX: *(at window with* WHEELER*)* There now. Just take a gander out there! Isn't that something. The "City of Angels"! Magnificent! Just like it always was. Palm trees. Duck ponds. Sculptured hedges.

WHEELER: WHAT'S HAPPENED TO THE LEMON ORCHARDS!

LANX: Now take it easy. Those were plowed under to make room for the new lots.

WHEELER: *(backing away from window as if about to faint;* LANX *supports him)* Oh, my God, I feel I'm going to die right here. What's happening to me. The entire scenery's changed!

LANX: It'll be okay. Just sit back down and take a load off. Would ya' like something to eat?

LANX *escorts him back to the swivel chair.* WHEELER *collapses into it.*

WHEELER: I couldn't keep it down. Everything's shrunken inside me. I can feel it. All my organs are tiny.

LANX: How 'bout some nice chicken broth?

WHEELER: NO! LEAVE ME ALONE, YOU IDIOT!

LANX: *(backing off)* Yessir.

WHEELER: Are you taking care of me? Is that it? Am I an invalid now?

LANX: Well, someone's got to look after you.

WHEELER: What about these others? What are they doing here?

LANX: Working on the project, sir.

WHEELER: Project? What project!

LANX: The disaster.

WHEELER: Oh, that. Do you still think it's worth it? Aren't we beyond that now?

LANX: Hard to say. Seems like our only choice now.

WHEELER: *(suddenly switching)* YES IT IS! OF COURSE IT IS! You don't have to tell me that. Of course it's our only chance. It always was our only chance. It's our purpose for being here. Right from the start. That's how the town got started isn't it?

LANX: "Choice," I said, not "chance."

WHEELER: AND I SAID "CHANCE"!!

LANX: Yessir.

WHEELER: Go on boxing, will you. You make me nervous when you talk.

LANX: Yessir.

WHEELER: You're not a good talker. You're dumb, in fact. In fact you never should be allowed to open your yap.

LANX: Yessir.

LANX *begins to shadowbox again.*

WHEELER: Box your ass off! It's the only way you'll understand the importance of a dollar.

LANX: You're right, sir.

WHEELER: And wet your lips! Your lips!

LANX: Yessir! *(wets his lips with his tongue as* HE *boxes)*

WHEELER: You're not just another boxer, you're a personality now. You have to look good. Above all else, you have to look good.

LANX*: Yessir.*

WHEELER: *(to himself)* The whole business has gone to pot.

TYMPANI: *(to himself, referring to* WHEELER*)* Bananas.

MISS SCOONS: Could you tell me one thing, Mister Wheeler?

WHEELER: *(looking around for the voice)* Who's that talking!

RABBIT: It's Miss Scoons, I think.

WHEELER: Why is she talking like that?

RABBIT: Tympani and I were conducting an experiment, and in the middle of it Miss Scoons fell into a trauma of some kind.

TYMPANI: *(to* RABBIT*)* Don't explain it. He had his chance already.

LANX: *(still boxing)* "Choice," I said!

WHEELER: I don't understand!

RABBIT: Something to do with rhythm.

TYMPANI: *(to RABBIT)* Don't explain it. I'm cooking now!

WHEELER: Yes, we had a man on that once. A young man. Worked for several months and then died mysteriously. What happened to that young man we had, Lanx?

LANX: He's still with us, sir.

WHEELER: YOU JUST KEEP BOXING!

LANX: Yessir.

WHEELER: You've got a press conference in two hours.

MISS SCOONS: Mister Wheeler?

WHEELER: What is it!

MISS SCOONS: Could you tell me one thing?

WHEELER: Maybe and maybe not.

MISS SCOONS: How come the tide has turned? How come now the people want disasters? I mean what's happened to all those nice stories they used to have where everyone got along? Jeanette McDonald and all that lot?

WHEELER: *(suddenly professorial)* Very simple. No wars. No major war, that is. No big, major world war. No focus. That's what a big, major world war does. It brings a focus to the people. They take sides. Us against them. Simple as that. Now there's no war. No big, major world war. Just gook wars. Jungle wars. Espionage wars. Secret little creepy wars in the swamp. So. No war, no focus. No focus, no structure. No structure spells disaster. And disaster is our business. Simple.

MISS SCOONS: Thank you, sir. *(goes back to scrubbing)*

WHEELER: You're a very intelligent woman, Miss Scoons.

MISS SCOONS: Thank you, sir.

WHEELER: I'd like to talk to you at length some time, but you can see I'm wrapped up at the moment.

MISS SCOONS: Oh, certainly, sir, I was just curious.

WHEELER: No harm in that. Curiosity breeds invention. That's what we're all here for. To invent! It's incredible. We're here to invent and there's no invention. Just a dust bowl. What's going on! We've never spent this much time on a project before! It's been going on for years now.

LANX: We're not sure of our position, sir.

WHEELER: Our position is to coldly calculate the public mind!

MISS SCOONS: Is there such a thing, sir?

WHEELER: Of course there is, Miss Scoons! Don't be silly. We have to find that part of our own mind which corresponds to the masses. We're immune and contaminated at the same time.

MISS SCOONS: A public mind?

WHEELER: Of course! That's what we have to tap into. When you get right down to it, what we are is mind readers. Isn't that right, Mr. Brown?

RABBIT: I don't know.

WHEELER: I don't like your attitude! Lanx, why has Miss Scoons been demoted to scrubbing the floors and this idiot is dancing around making magic circles on the floor?

LANX: *(stops boxing)* Well, she was going off the deep end, Mr. Wheeler. We had to do something.

WHEELER: KEEP BOXING!

LANX starts up again. TYMPANI *begins to speak as though in a world of his own, still cooking, facing audience.*

TYMPANI: "What dya' say we take in a movie?" What a great sound that has. "What dya' say we go out and take in a movie? What dya' say we get the hell outa' here and go take in a movie? *(He pauses, thinks of another way to say it)* How 'bout let's just drop everything and go to the picture show? *(pause, another approach)* What dya' say, just you and me, we leave the kids, get outa' the house, into the old Studebaker, leave our miserable lives behind, and join the great adventure of a motion picture? *(pause; very simply this time)* What dya' say we just lose ourselves forever in the miracle of film? We nestle down, just the two of us, with a big box of buttered popcorn, a big cup of Seven-Up, a big box of Milk Duds, a giant box of 'Black Crows,' and we just chew ourselves straight into oblivion?"

Pause as WHEELER *seems to have dreamed off into* TYMPANI'*s words.* TYMPANI *goes back to cooking.* RABBIT *interrupts the pause.*

RABBIT: I'd like to explain this thing to you if you don't mind, Mr. Wheeler.

WHEELER: *(snapping out of dream)* DON'T EXPLAIN IT! MAKE IT WORK!

RABBIT: Well, it's kind of complicated. I mean I'm just a novice at it myself.

WHEELER: Then what are you doing in such fast company! There's no one I can talk to here! That's the trouble. No one! Everyone's off in their own little world. There's no concern for the industry!

RABBIT: I was trying to resolve the problem from a spiritual angle.

WHEELER: *(standing again)* WHAT PROBLEM! WHAT SPIRIT! FOR GOD'S SAKE, ISN'T ANYONE GOING TO TELL ME WHAT'S HAPPENED HERE? DON'T YOU THINK I'VE NOTICED?

TYMPANI: *(still cooking over drums)* I can tell you exactly.

WHEELER: Who's that talking?

TYMPANI: It's me.

WHEELER: *(sitting back down)* Oh.

TYMPANI: We've been locked out of time, and that's all there is to it.

WHEELER: What kind of a statement is that!

LANX: *(still boxing)* Could I stop for a second, Mr. Wheeler? I can explain this whole thing.

WHEELER: NO! YOU KEEP BOXING! There's nothing worse than a lazy boxer. Good men put their money behind you, and what do you do in return? Sluff off! I'm sick of it!

RABBIT: I just wanted to give you some background on the wheel. That's all.

WHEELER: Well, get on with it then!

RABBIT: Yessir. Now, if you'll notice, there's four main bundles in the wheel. One for each point on the compass. To the North is wisdom, and its medicine animal is the buffalo. The color of the North is white.

WHEELER: I hope this isn't going to take too long. I might die any second you know.

TYMPANI: What's happened is that we're locked into the narrowest part of our dream machine.

WHEELER: WHO'S THAT TALKING OUT LOUD! SHUT HIM UP!

TYMPANI: I was on the verge of discovery. Things were opening up. I could actually see an opening. A rhythm. A whole new pattern.

LANX *boxes his way over to* TYMPANI *and punches him in the stomach.* TYMPANI *doubles over, but continues cooking from this position.* LANX *goes on shadowboxing.* RABBIT *explains the wheel.*

WHEELER: *(to* RABBIT*)* You'll have to excuse me. Go on.

RABBIT: The South is the sign of the mouse, and its medicine color is green. The South is the place of innocence and trust.

WHEELER: Amazing! The Indians dreamed this up?

RABBIT: In the West is the sign of the bear. The West is the "Looks-Within" place, and its color is black—

WHEELER: Hold it! What's that mean? "Looks-Within" place? What does that mean?

RABBIT: Uh—I guess it means the place for looking inside yourself? It's a very dangerous medicine bundle. In fact it's the only authentic bundle I've got. The rest are imitations.

WHEELER: What's so dangerous about it?

RABBIT: There's a warning written on the outside of it saying that if it's ever opened a terrible force will be let loose in the world.

WHEELER: What terrible force? What kind of baloney is that! Go on to the next one. What's the next one?

RABBIT: The East is the sign of the eagle. This is the place of illumination, where we can see things clearly far and wide. Its color is gold.

WHEELER: Very nice. Now, how does it work?

RABBIT: I don't know.

WHEELER: *(standing)* WHAT!

RABBIT: That's what I've been trying to tell you. This is an ancient design. How am I supposed to know. I'm a white man. It took thousands of years to cook this up. I'm just explaining the structure.

TYMPANI: *(still in crouch from* LANX's *blow)* Two over-easy with bacon!

LANX: *(stops boxing and crosses to* TYMPANI) Right.

TYMPANI *serves* LANX *the imaginery food, holding his own stomach in pain.* LANX *sits on the floor and eats it. The rest continue.*

WHEELER: ANCIENT! I'm ancient! We're all ancient! What's ancient got to do with it!

RABBIT: I'm exhausted. I can't keep up with this. I'm just going to look out the window for a while. Maybe something will come to me. Something's got to come sooner or later.

RABBIT *crosses slowly upstage and stares out the rectangle.* WHEELER *watches him for a second.*

WHEELER: There's something deadly going on here! I can smell it. It's the smell of my own skin! You've all given up on me haven't you? That's what it is! That's exactly what it is. Your situation isn't quite so urgent as mine, so you've given up and left me to the dogs. Left me here to rot in my juices! Well, I can tell you one thing! Without leadership you're as good as gone. I know this city inside out! There's nowhere you can go without me! Nowhere!

MISS SCOONS: *(still scrubbing)* I haven't given up on you, sir. I still think you're a smashing gov'nor.

WHEELER: My office used to be swarming with talent, and now it's like a cesspool!

RABBIT: *(looking out rectangle)* You can't see a thing out here. It's all yellow.

WHEELER: It was a gamble right from the start. I gambled on imagination and lost. My dream was to create an industry of imagination! Now look at it! Poisoned! Putrified!

TYMPANI: *(still doubled over)* Would you like some breakfast, sir?

WHEELER: Yes I would. I would like that. That would make things better even though things have never been worse.

TYMPANI: What would you like?

WHEELER: Ham and eggs with the yolks hard. I'll die with the yolk in my chest.

TYMPANI: Right. *(starts cooking)*

RABBIT: You're expecting too much.

WHEELER: I'm expecting to survive! That's all. To live! To be alive! To stay in my skin!

RABBIT: But you haven't even told me who the other characters are, what the story is, or anything. How am I supposed to do anything without information? Even a second-rate hack gets to know what the picture's about!

WHEELER: That's top secret!

RABBIT: Great.

WHEELER: I can see now that I've been abandoned. I should've known.

RABBIT: What is it that's eating you anyway? I mean what is this skin condition that you've developed?

WHEELER: Don't press me, Brown. You're on thin ice.

RABBIT: I mean you've got all of us turning ourselves inside out for you, but nobody really knows what it is you're suffering from.

WHEELER: That's my business!

RABBIT: It's no business! It's a disease!

WHEELER: So what! Something's eating me, and that's all that counts!

RABBIT: You're the disaster, Wheeler. You don't have to look any further. You're it!

WHEELER: You're in no position to be putting the finger on me! I'm the cause for your being here. It turns out you're worthless anyway. All you've brought is a bag of cheap Indian tricks! And only one of those is authentic.

RABBIT: I don't believe there even is a movie. That's it, isn't it? You don't even have a scrap of footage.

WHEELER: Don't be ridiculous!

LANX: I could fix up a cement bathing suit for him real easy, boss.

WHEELER: SHUT UP!

RABBIT: There is no movie! All you've got is a disaster!

WHEELER: I HAVE A MILLION MOVIES! AND DO YOU KNOW WHERE THEY ARE! THEY'RE IN MY BLOOD! THEY'RE CHURNING AROUND IN MY BLOOD! THEY'RE INSIDE THERE WITHOUT ANY FORM OR REASON AND THEY CAN'T GET OUT! EVERY ONE OF THEM IS TEARING ME APART! CHEWING AT THE WALLS! TRYING TO ESCAPE! TRYING TO BECOME SOMETHING! TRYING TO OOZE OUT AND TAKE ON A SHAPE THAT WE ALL CAN SEE! AND EVERY ONE OF THEM IS EATING ME! CHEWING ME APART FROM THE INSIDE OUT! A MILLION DEVILS! MOVIES TO MAKE YOUR HEAD SWIM! DON'T TALK TO ME ABOUT MOVIES!

WHEELER *starts to shake and tremble violently.* MISS SCOONS *gets up and rushes to him. She escorts him to the swivel chair where he collapses.*

MISS SCOONS: Mr. Wheeler, sir! You shouldn't get so wrought up! It's only a movie, for pity sake! You mustn't tax yourself so. You just relax now.

She loosens his collar. WHEELER *gasps for air.*

TYMPANI: Ham and eggs with the yolks hard!

MISS SCOONS: *(to* TYMPANI*)* Not now, you bleeding twit!

TYMPANI: But that's what he ordered.

MISS SCOONS: Can't you see he's about to expire then?

TYMPANI: Well, what am I going to do with this order? He's gotta' pay for it. I can't cook and cook and cook and never get anything in return.

WHEELER: I'll pay for it. I'll pay for everything. All the damages.

MISS SCOONS: Try not to talk, sir.

LANX: *(to* MISS SCOONS*)* Let him die. What do you care?

WHEELER: *(gasping to* LANX*)* We'll have to show him the rushes. That's all there is to it.

LANX: *(pause, standing)* Are you crazy?

WHEELER: There's no other way around it. He's got to know what the material is before it's too late.

LANX: What if he's spying for another studio? It's too big a risk.

WHEELER: We'll have to take the chance.

LANX: Listen, my whole future's wrapped up in this. You may die to-morrow, and I'll be left holding the bag.

WHEELER: Makes no difference. Go and load the projectors!

LANX: You can't order me around! You're half dead.

WHEELER: (WHEELER *leaps at* LANX *like a crazed animal*) GO AND
LOAD THE PROJECTORS!!

LANX runs off stage left. WHEELER *is foaming at the mouth and
snarling at the others.*

WHEELER: ALL OF YOU! GET OUT!

The rest start to run for cover. He stops RABBIT *in his tracks.*

WHEELER: NOT YOU!

Everyone has gone now except for WHEELER *and* RABBIT. *The two
of them stare at each other.* WHEELER *breathing heavily and swaying from side to side.* RABBIT *cringes to one side. Through this next
section the stage lights slowly dim as the rectangle is lit. The scrim
turns pale green. Slowly* WHEELER *stalks* RABBIT *around the stage,
his breathing becomes more and more desperate and seems to control the tempo of the scene.* RABBIT *tries to keep his distance as best
he can.*

WHEELER: *(wheezing in half whisper)* What's that black place called
again?

RABBIT: What?

WHEELER: The black place? That place on your circle? The dangerous
bundle?

RABBIT: Oh, that.

WHEELER: The bear?

RABBIT: The West.

WHEELER: That's right. The West. That's where we are, isn't it? The
West? This is the West? We can't get any further West than this.

RABBIT: This?

WHEELER: What's it called again?

RABBIT: What?

WHEELER: *(suddenly unleashing)* WHAT'S THE WEST CALLED!!
Don't play stupid with me!

RABBIT: Oh. The "Looks-Within" place.

WHEELER: That's right. "Looks-Within."

RABBIT: I didn't understand you at first.

WHEELER: Of course not. That's because you're full of fear.

RABBIT: What?

WHEELER: FEAR!! YOU'RE FULL OF FEAR! YOU'RE FACING ME
AND YOU DON'T KNOW WHAT I AM!

RABBIT: No.

WHEELER: You don't know what's coming next.

RABBIT: No.

WHEELER: That's right. And you're wondering.

RABBIT: Yes.

WHEELER: And your wondering leads you to imagine the worst.

RABBIT: No.

WHEELER: "NO" WON'T HELP!

RABBIT: NO!

WHEELER: Because now, at any moment, what you most fear might actually happen. It might actually crawl out of the walls, and appear.

RABBIT: You don't know what I fear.

WHEELER: There you go again, dreaming you're different. Setting yourself apart.

RABBIT: You can't be inside of me!

WHEELER: WE'RE THE SAME!

RABBIT: NO!

WHEELER: WHAT WE FEAR IS THE SAME! THAT MAKES US EQUAL!

RABBIT: You're crazy, Wheeler! You're a raving maniac!

WHEELER: And you?

RABBIT: What about me?

WHEELER: What are you?

RABBIT: AN ARTIST!

WHEELER *starts laughing maniacally, doubling himself over.*

RABBIT: YOU'RE THE PRODUCER, AND I'M THE ARTIST!

WHEELER *laughs harder.*

RABBIT: YOU CALLED ME DOWN HERE! I'M IN DEMAND! YOU'RE A DIME A DOZEN!

WHEELER *stops himself abruptly.*

WHEELER: That's true. A dime a dozen.

RABBIT: You don't know a thing about creation.

WHEELER: I was created without my knowing. Same as you. Creation's a disease.

RABBIT: What are you talking about?

WHEELER: We're dying here. Right now. In front of each other.

RABBIT: Just stay away from me, Wheeler!

WHEELER: I was turned into this beyond my knowing. I was spawned somehow by a city. I was leaked out. An Angel in disguise.

RABBIT: You're nothing!

WHEELER: I'M SOMETHING AWESOME! I'M FINDING OUT WHAT IT MEANS!

RABBIT: What what means?

WHEELER: The West.

RABBIT: It's just a place.

WHEELER: It's a place of discovery. Things are uncovered here. Gold! Oceans! LOOK INSIDE OF ME!

RABBIT: That's all been discovered.

WHEELER: Only the surface. We're cracking the surface, Brown. We're going into a deep black bear. We're taking the plunge. We're penetrating the flesh and bone.

RABBIT: Get off it, Wheeler. This is a corporation. You're an executive.

WHEELER: We're going straight through all the paraphernalia. All the ponytails, all the jargon, all the Indian lore, all the magic mumbo jumbo. Deeper than California! We're going down, Brown! We're coming face to face with something deadly.

RABBIT: Not me.

WHEELER: You can't get out of it!

RABBIT: I'M NOT IN IT!

WHEELER: What was the sign for the East again?

RABBIT: I'm not playing, Wheeler!

WHEELER: "The place of illumination, where we can see clearly far and wide. The place of the eagle."

RABBIT: So what!

WHEELER: Where's your faith, Rabbit? I thought you prayed regularly? What happened to your missions? Your sense of mission? Your hero?

RABBIT: That's got nothing to do with it. You're twisting things up.

WHEELER: Things are twisted! Monsters are being hatched by the dozens and turned into saints! We can do anything here! Anything is possible here! We can recreate the world and make you swallow it whole! We can make a nightmare out of a mole hill! We can tear you to shreds and make you like it.

RABBIT: You can't mix real life with the movies!

WHEELER *goes into convulsive laughter and starts to have a slight seizure.*

WHEELER: THE MOVIES! THIS IS THE MOVIES!!

RABBIT: *(suddenly covering his head as though afraid to be photographed)* No camera! No camera!

WHEELER *chases him miming a movie camera, trying to photograph him.*

WHEELER: *(talking to* RABBIT *as though* HE *were a primitive child)* You don't understand. It won't hurt you. It's just a machine. All it does is capture light in a certain pattern. It shows you moving.

RABBIT: *(running away)* No! No camera! No capture!

WHEELER: Don't be silly. It's fun. Look. I'll do it on myself. Look! (HE *turns imaginary camera on himself)* See? No pain. It's fun.

RABBIT: It's Devil!

WHEELER: It's not. It's beautiful. It makes us see ourselves. It brings things back to life. It makes us happy.

RABBIT: No happy!

WHEELER: Happy! Everybody loves pictures. It's just like magic. Look, I'll show you.

WHEELER *goes to swivel chair and pulls it down left for* RABBIT. RABBIT *runs.*

RABBIT: No capture! No light!

WHEELER: No. I'll show you the footage. You'll love it. You're the only one outside our crew who's even seen it. It's top-secret footage. Absolutely private.

RABBIT: No secret! Devil!

WHEELER: *(trying to coax* RABBIT *into swivel chair)* But we'd love to get your reactions to it. It's so nerve-racking editing a film. Everyone giving you criticism and opinions, but someone like you would give a raw, gut-level reaction which could prove invaluable to us.

RABBIT: *(settling down a little)* No light.

WHEELER: *(escorting him to chair and sitting him down)* Please. Just as a favor. I promise that no one will photograph you. Just sit down and enjoy yourself. Relax. Everything's beautiful. Everything's going to be just fine. The lights will slowly fade. *(lights follow to dark)* The crowd will grow silent. The screen will light up with beautiful colors. *(scrim turns red slowly)* Your body will go limp and your mind will drift off into a wonderful world of adventure.

RABBIT *is seated downstage in swivel chair facing rectangle upstage, his back to audience.* WHEELER *backs away from him carefully.*

WHEELER: Now just try to relax and watch the movie like a good boy.

Sudden crash of cymbals, bells, and pulsing percussion off stage. SAX PLAYER *enters down-right corner playing low, lurking melody.*

He faces upstage to platform. TYMPANI *enters down left and accompanies on drums. He stands on downstage side of drums facing up to platform. He could bring on another percussion instrument too.* WHEELER *pulls out a long black flashlight and clicks it on in the dark. The only lights now are the neon rectangle, backlighting on scrim, and* WHEELER's *flashlight.* WHEELER *begins to narrate, using the flashlight like a schoolmaster's stick.* RABBIT *stays seated and unseen.*

WHEELER: *(amplified, documentary voice)* Our story opens with the city in a state of siege. A deadlock between two powers so intent upon destroying each other that even the vanishing of their own existence in that struggle means nothing to them. They would sooner die than attempt to co-exist.

LANX and MISS SCOONS *enter from opposite sides of the platform very slowly. They are covered from head to foot in very long, silken robes with oriental designs in bright colors, intricately woven dragons on their chests and backs. The robes cover their heads, which seem to be extended somewhat. Around their waists are wide black sashes with long tassels, and several long black sticks about the size of broom handles are held in by the sashes. They are both barefoot. Their shoulders are huge under the robes. In general they give the impression of menacing Samurai warriors.*

WHEELER: By this time the city has long been in the hands of roving bands of outlaw-warriors. At one time content to work under the shackles of the Lords and Bosses, one after the other they have broken away and taken the law into their own hands, preferring the America of their distant frontier past.

The two warrior figures inch their way slowly forward toward each other, walking on the balls of their feet and releasing low guttural noises from inside the robes. When they reach a certain point, with some distance between them, they slowly move into a crouched position, knees bending slowly, keeping their backs straight and come down so that they're sitting on their heels with their hands resting on their thighs. They face each other in this position for a while. Their sounds continue as WHEELER *shines the flashlight on them and goes on with his narration.*

WHEELER: The siege, however, has become so bloody and so awesome that even the head chieftains of these two deadly powers have agreed to meet in a remote area of the city to see if they can come to some understanding of the future of their predicament. There has never been a summit conference of this kind as long as can be remembered. Every battle in their recorded history was fought to the bitter end out of their strange sense of honor. Even suicides are a thing of the past.

Drums and sax fill slowly as the two chiefs slowly withdraw the sticks from their belts and hold them in front of each other at eye level. This should seem more like an acknowledgment of battle than a threat.

WHEELER: The meeting goes on in silence with the city burning brightly in the distance. There is no talk of peace. Peace would only serve to wipe them out slowly. Their only concern is how to come to a speedy annihilation. They agree to leave their future in the hands of their two generals and to retire themselves to a deep system of caves where they will enact their final duel in solitude.

Slowly the two chieftains rise and take off their long robes, revealing the generals underneath. The robes fall to the ground. Underneath they are dressed in red crash helmets with long black visors covering their faces. They each wear heavy football shoulder pads without shirts, kidney pads tied to their waists, and padded football pants. They have elbow pads and white tape around their wrists. They slowly bend down and pick up a stick from the floor. They square off to each other like Samurai warriors.

WHEELER: The generals see each other eye to eye. There's a meeting in their eyes. They recognize themselves. There's no way out for them. Their roles are well defined. Their armies are in position. There's nothing holding back.

The generals suddenly come crashing down on each other with the sticks. Loud clang of percussion, sax, and high shrieking voices of LANX *and* MISS SCOONS! *They back off and again face each other with the sticks. They charge again. High screams, crash of sticks. Percussion, sax, then back to attack positions. Each return to this position after an attack is marked by stillness and concentration. Music softens.*

WHEELER: The battle lasted days, with the armies agreeing finally to become the audience to their two generals. They watched the sun rise and fall on them with neither one growing any weaker than the other. Gambling grew so rampant between the two armies that soon there grew a bond between them so strong that they were joined together as one vast army. But the generals went on.

Crash of generals again. Percussion, etc. Back to attack positions.

WHEELER: Again and again they crashed into each other with the heavy swords. The cold steel flashed across the City of Angels and cut the stillness of the ruins. No bird sang, no dog barked, no man moved.

LANX *and* MISS SCOONS *continue with their parries and attacks throughout with the musical accompaniment along with their voices.* WHEELER *continues, sweeping the scene with his flashlight.*

WHEELER: The mood of the armies changed from comraderie to one of fear, for they could all sense the impending doom of this last battle. The generals were exactly matched in strength, endurance, and intelligence. In fact they were so exactly the same in every respect that one couldn't be told from the other. The only possible outcome was death to them both. On and on they fought into the night until slowly the armies began to thin out and wander away into the desert. Finally the generals were left all alone. Their sounds were lonely and distant like two wild bucks on an empty prairie. They couldn't remember a city at all. Civilization had come and gone without them knowing. They were battling into another time. They were crossing continents as they fought. They were passing history by.

The clashes between the generals go on with the accompanied sax and percussion. Voices from LANX *and* MISS SCOONS. *They continue to re-position and attack. The stage is very dark still, except for the glowing rectangle. The scrim has faded to a pale red in the background.*

WHEELER: As far as they knew, they were the only living things. The moon raced across the sky. The planets howled in space. Their primitive weapons performed a conversation in empty space.

Battle goes on. Music rises and falls.

WHEELER: Finally, after days of constant combat, one of the generals revealed himself as a woman.

MISS SCOONS *takes off her helmet and visor and sets it on the floor.* LANX *freezes and stares at her, still keeping his helmet on. Music stops.*

WHEELER: In that moment, the opposing general was caught off guard, and the female plunged her weapon home.

MISS SCOONS *lets out a shattering scream and plunges her stick inside the upstage arm of* LANX, *who drops his stick with a groan. He stands there facing her. She keeps hold of the stick without pulling it out of him.*

WHEELER: At last the generals saw their situation. They were one being with two opposing parts. Everything was clear to them. At last they were connected. In that split second they gained and lost their entire lives.

Very slowly LANX *begins to pull himself along the stick toward* MISS SCOONS, *impaling himself more and more with each step. She holds her ground and waits for him. The saxophone and drums enter in here and gather force.* LANX *finally reaches her. They embrace and stand there in each other's arms. Music reaches a peak, then suddenly stops. Stage lights bang up to bright yellow.* MISS SCOONS *and* LANX *release each other and drop right back into their old characters, as they were in Act 1.* LANX *takes off his helmet and they both rest on the platform. (One of them could even go off and get them both some water and then come back on.) This all should be very relaxed and as though they were two athletes just finishing an event.* RABBIT *is still hidden in the swivel chair.* WHEELER *talks to him as he strides nervously around the stage.* TYMPANI *and the* SAX PLAYER *leave the stage.*

WHEELER: *(to* RABBIT) So, what do you think?

RABBIT: *(unseen)* Terrible. Corniest stuff I ever saw.

WHEELER: *(pounding the flashlight with his fist and striding angrily)* What's wrong with it! WHAT THE HELL'S WRONG WITH IT!

RABBIT: *(still unseen)* Everything.

WHEELER: What do you mean! It's got a story, a plot, good meaty characters, tremendous language, colorful locations. It has motion, adventure, conflict, excitement, rhythm, poetry. It's got everything!

Suddenly RABBIT *whips the swivel chair around so it's facing* WHEELER. RABBIT'*s skin has turned slimey green; he has fangs, long black fingernails, and a long, thick mane of black hair. He remains seated.* WHEELER *is the only one who notices the change in* RABBIT'*s appearance.* LANX *and* MISS SCOONS *remain indifferent.* MISS SCOONS *starts massaging* LANX'*s shoulders as they sit on the platform upstage.*

RABBIT: There's no disaster! We're not interested in hankey pankey love stories, romantically depicting the end of the world. We're after hard core disaster. I thought you understood that.

WHEELER: *(moving backwards slightly)* Wait a minute. Wait a minute!

WHEELER *looks for reassurance to* LANX *and* MISS SCOONS *but they only smile back at him.*

RABBIT: *(rising out of chair)* No, you wait a minute, mister.

WHEELER: Don't come any closer! I'm not well! I'm not supposed to have any severe shocks! I might have a heart attack! *(turning to* LANX *who ignores him)* LANX, WHAT ARE YOU DOING! I'M BEING THREATENED!

RABBIT: They can't hear you. They can't even see you.

WHEELER: What do you mean! Of course they can see me! I can see them! They smiled at me before!

RABBIT: You're in trouble, mister.

WHEELER: I'M NOT IN TROUBLE! HOW COULD I BE IN TROUBLE! I'M PROTECTED HERE!

RABBIT: What'd you think, you could come down here in your provincial gear and pull the wool over our eyes? We've had experience, ya' know.

WHEELER: WAIT A MINUTE! I'M NOT YOU GODDAMMIT! I'M ME!

RABBIT: You might as well burn that footage up and go back to making campfires. You're washed up in this town, buddy.

WHEELER: I'M ESTABLISHED! I'M FIRMLY ESTABLISHED! I'm in the business. I'm in pictures. I plant pictures in people's heads. I plant them and they grow. They grow more pictures. And the pictures grow like wildfire. People see them in front of their eyes. While they're shopping. While they're driving. While they're making love. Wherever they go I go with them. I spread their disease. I'm that powerful.

RABBIT: Look, if you don't mind, I've got several appointments, and you're burning my time.

WHEELER: LANX! DO SOMETHING ABOUT THIS!

LANX *and* MISS SCOONS *are now sitting on the edge of the platform, swinging their legs back and forth and eating imaginary popcorn as they watch* RABBIT *and* WHEELER *like two teen-agers watching a movie.* LANX *makes no acknowledgment of* WHEELER's *presence other than that he's an image on a movie screen.*

RABBIT: We've arranged your bus fare back to wherever it is you came from.

WHEELER: LANX! WHAT'S THE MATTER WITH YOU!

RABBIT: You're on the silver screen, buddy. You've been captured in celluloid and you'll never get out. All they're looking at is a moving picture show.

WHEELER: I'M A PERSON! THEY CAN SEE ME! THEY KNOW WHO I AM! MISS SCOONS! MISS SCOONS! IT'S ME! YOUR BOSS! MISS SCOONS! LOOK AT ME! LOOK AT ME! I'M OVER HERE!

WHEELER *starts waving frantically at* MISS SCOONS *and* LANX *but they only smile and chew their popcorn.*

RABBIT: You better get outa' here before you disintegrate right here on the spot.

WHEELER: *(turning on* RABBIT*)* I won't disintegrate! I'M IMMORTAL! I'LL ALWAYS BE REMEMBERED! Right now there's people watching! Right this very minute! There's people all around me! Watching and remembering! As long as they're watching I'll be remembered!

RABBIT: You're dead, Wheeler. You're dead and gone.

WHEELER *stops and stares at* RABBIT. *Pause. He turns and stares at* LANX *and* MISS SCOONS *still eating their popcorn. He turns and looks at the audience. He turns back to* RABBIT.

WHEELER: *(to* RABBIT*)* I'll show you who's dead.

WHEELER *crosses slowly to the medicine bundle depicting the west and picks it up.* RABBIT *watches him, undisturbed.* WHEELER *turns to* RABBIT, *holding the bundle out in front of him.*

RABBIT: Ah, back to your old tricks, huh? What do you think that's going to do?

WHEELER *crosses to* RABBIT *slowly, holding out the bundle.*

WHEELER: *(quietly to himself)* It's going to open up the world. It's going to get me out of here. It's going to reveal something. It's going to change everything from the way it is now to something else.

RABBIT: Can't you stand the way it is?

WHEELER: Can you?

RABBIT: Well, go ahead then. See what happens.

WHEELER: Would you hold my hand while I do it?

RABBIT: Well, how're you going to open it up then?

WHEELER: I never thought of that.

RABBIT: You want me to do it?

WHEELER: No.

RABBIT: You want me to help you?

WHEELER: No.

RABBIT: Well, go ahead then.

WHEELER: *(pauses, staring at bundle)* What if it's worse than we can imagine?

RABBIT: It couldn't be.

WHEELER: No. I guess not.

WHEELER *slowly unties the bundle. As the bundle opens up, a slow, steady stream of green liquid, the color of their faces, oozes from it onto the stage.* RABBIT *and* WHEELER *watch it as they stand there.* LANX *and* MISS SCOONS *are still watching them, as though in the movies. They speak as the lights are slowly dimming.* RABBIT *and* WHEELER *remain still while the liquid drips.*

MISS SCOONS: *(to* LANX*)* I'm not supposed to stay for the second one ya' know, Jimmy.

LANX: Yeah, yeah.

MISS SCOONS: Well, I'm not. I'm supposed to be back before eleven.

LANX: I just wanna' stay for the titles.

MISS SCOONS: Last time you said that we never got back until three in the morning.

LANX: That was last time.

MISS SCOONS: I almost got sent to Juvie. I don't wanna' get sent to Juvie again.

LANX: Relax, will ya'. You're not gonna get sent to Juvie, for Christ's sake. I just wanna' see the titles.

MISS SCOONS: Why, do you know somebody in this movie or somethin'?

LANX: Just shut up will ya'.

Lights slowly fade to black with sax filling in softly over the scene.

CURTAIN

Curse of the Starving Class

CAST

(in order of appearance)

WESLEY	Ebbe Roe Smith
ELLA	Olympia Dukakis
EMMA	Pamela Reed
TAYLOR	Kenneth Welsh
WESTON	James Gammon
ELLIS	Eddie Jones
MALCOLM	John Aquino
EMERSON	Michael J. Pollard
SLATER	Raymond J. Barry

Original New York Production by New York Shakespeare Festival
Presented by Joseph Papp

Directed by Robert Woodruff

ACT 1

SCENE:

Upstage center is a very plain breakfast table with a red oilcloth covering it. Four mismatched metal chairs are set one at each side of the table. Suspended in midair to stage right and stage left are two ruffled, red-checked curtains, slightly faded. In the down left corner of the stage are a working refrigerator and a small gas stove, set right up next to each other. In the down right corner is a pile of wooden debris, torn screen, etc., which are the remains of a broken door. Lights come up on WESLEY, *in sweatshirt, jeans and cowboy boots, who is picking up the pieces of the door and throwing them methodically into an old wheelbarrow. This goes on for a while. Then* WESLEY's *mother,* ELLA, *enters slowly from down left. She is a small woman wearing a bathrobe, pink fuzzy slippers, hair in curlers. She is just waking up and winds an alarm clock in her hand as she watches* WESLEY *sleepily.* WESLEY *keeps cleaning up the debris, ignoring her.*

ELLA: *(after a while)* You shouldn't be doing that.

WESLEY: I'm doing it.

ELLA: Yes, but you shouldn't be. He should be doing it. He's the one who broke it down.

WESLEY: He's not here.

ELLA: He's not back yet?

WESLEY: Nope.

ELLA: Well, just leave it until he gets back.

WESLEY: In the meantime we gotta' live in it.

ELLA: He'll be back. He can clean it up then.

WESLEY *goes on clearing the debris into the wheelbarrow.* ELLA *finishes winding the clock and then sets it on the stove.*

ELLA: *(looking at clock)* I must've got to sleep at five in the morning.

WESLEY: Did you call the cops?

ELLA: Last night?

WESLEY: Yeah.

ELLA: Sure I called the cops. Are you kidding? I was in danger of my life. I was being threatened.

WESLEY: He wasn't threatening you.

ELLA: Are you kidding me? He broke the door down didn't he?

WESLEY: He was just trying to get in.

ELLA: That's no way to get into a house. There's plenty of other ways to get into a house. He could've climbed through a window.

WESLEY: He was drunk.

ELLA: That's not my problem.

WESLEY: You locked the door.

ELLA: Sure I locked the door. I told him I was going to lock the door. I told him the next time that happened I was locking the door and he could sleep in a hotel.

WESLEY: Is that where he is now?

ELLA: How should I know?

WESLEY: He took the Packard I guess.

ELLA: If that's the one that's missing I guess that's the one he took.

WESLEY: How come you called the cops?

ELLA: I was scared.

WESLEY: You thought he was going to kill you?

ELLA: I thought— I thought, "I don't know who this is. I don't know who this is trying to break in here. Who is this? It could be anyone."

WESLEY: I heard you screaming at each other.

ELLA: Yes.

WESLEY: So you must've known who it was.

ELLA: I wasn't sure. That was the frightening part. I could smell him right through the door.

WESLEY: He was drinking that much?

ELLA: Not that. His skin.

WESLEY: Oh.

ELLA: *(suddenly cheerful)* You want some breakfast?

WESLEY: No, thanks.

ELLA: *(going to refrigerator)* Well I'm going to have some.

WESLEY: *(still cleaning)* It's humiliating to have the cops come to your own house. Makes me feel like we're someone else.

ELLA: *(looking in refrigerator)* There's no eggs but there's bacon and bread.

WESLEY: Makes me feel lonely. Like we're in trouble or something.

ELLA: *(still looking in refrigerator)* We're not in trouble. He's in trouble, but we're not.

WESLEY: You didn't have to call the cops.

ELLA: *(slamming refrigerator door and holding bacon and bread)* I told you, he was trying to kill me!

They look at each other for a moment. ELLA *breaks it by putting the bacon and bread down on top of the stove.* WESLEY *goes back to cleaning up the debris. He keeps talking as* ELLA *looks through the lower drawers of the stove and pulls out a frying pan. She lights one of the burners on the stove and starts cooking the bacon.*

WESLEY: *(as he throws wood into wheelbarrow)* I was lying there on my back. I could smell the avocado blossoms. I could hear the coyotes. I could hear stock cars squeeling down the street. I could feel myself in my bed in my room in this house in this town in this state in this country. I could feel this country close like it was part of my bones. I could feel the presence of all the people outside, at night, in the dark. Even sleeping people I could feel. Even all the sleeping animals. Dogs. Peacocks. Bulls. Even tractors sitting in the wetness, waiting for the sun to come up. I was looking straight up at the ceiling at all my model airplanes hanging by all their thin metal wires. Floating. Swaying very quietly like they were being blown by someone's breath. Cobwebs moving with them. Dust laying on their wings. Decals peeling off their wings. My P-39. My Messerschmitt. My Jap Zero. I could feel myself lying far below them on my bed like I was on the ocean and overhead they were on reconnaissance. Scouting me. Floating. Taking pictures of the enemy. Me, the enemy. I could feel the space around me like a big, black world. I listened like an animal. My listening was afraid. Afraid of sound. Tense. Like any second something could invade me. Some foreigner. Something undescribable. Then I heard the Packard coming up the hill. From a mile off I could tell it was the Packard by the sound of the valves. The lifters have a sound like nothing else. Then I could picture my Dad driving it. Shifting unconsciously. Downshifting into second for the last pull up the hill. I could feel the headlights closing in. Cutting through the orchard. I could see the trees being lit one after the other by the lights, then going back to black. My heart was pounding. Just from my Dad coming back. Then I heard him pull the brake. Lights go off. Key's turned off. Then a long silence. Him just sitting in the car. Just sitting. I picture him just sitting. What's he doing? Just sitting. Waiting to get out. Why's he waiting to get out? He's plastered and can't move. He's plastered and doesn't want to move. He's going to sleep there all night. He's slept there before. He's woken up with dew on the hood before. Freezing headache. Teeth covered with peanuts. Then I hear the door of the Packard open. A pop of metal. Dogs barking down the road. Door slams. Feet. Paper bag being tucked under one arm. Paper bag covering "Tiger Rose". Feet coming. Feet walking toward the door. Feet stopping. Heart pounding. Sound of door not opening. Foot kicking door. Man's voice. Dad's voice. Dad calling Mom. No answer. Foot kicking. Foot kicking harder. Wood splitting. Man's voice. In the night. Foot kicking hard through door. One foot right through door. Bottle crashing. Glass breaking. Fist through door. Man cursing. Man going insane. Feet and hands tearing. Head smashing. Man yelling. Shoulder smashing. Whole body crashing. Woman screaming. Mom screaming. Mom screaming for police. Man throwing wood. Man throwing up. Mom calling cops. Dad crashing away. Back down driveway. Car door slamming. Ignition grinding. Wheels screaming. First gear grinding. Wheels screaming off down hill. Packard disappearing. Sound disappearing. No sound. No sight. Planes still hanging. Heart still pounding. No sound. Mom crying soft. Soft crying. Then no sound. Then softly crying. Then moving around through house. Then no moving. Then crying softly. Then stopping. Then, far off the freeway could be heard.

WESLEY *picks up one end of the wheelbarrow. He makes the sound of a car and pushes it off right, leaving* ELLA *alone at the stove watching the bacon. She speaks alone.*

ELLA: Now I know the first thing you'll think is that you've hurt yourself. That's only natural. You'll think that something drastic has gone wrong with your insides and that's why you're bleeding. That's only a natural reaction. But I want you to know the truth. I want you to know all the facts before you go off and pick up a lot of lies. Now, the first thing is that you should never go swimming when that happens. It can cause you to bleed to death. The water draws it out of you.

WESLEY's *sister,* EMMA, *enters from right. She is younger and dressed in a white and green 4-H Club uniform. She carries several hand-painted charts on the correct way to cut up a frying chicken. She sets the charts down on the table upstage and arranges them as* ELLA *talks to her as though she's just continuing the conversation.*

EMMA: But what if I'm invited? The Thompson's have a new heated pool. You should see it, Ma. They even got blue lights around it at night. It's really beautiful. Like a fancy hotel.

ELLA: *(tending to the bacon)* I said no swimming and that's what I meant! This thing is no joke. Your whole life is changing. You don't want to live in ignorance do you?

EMMA: No, Ma.

ELLA: All right then. The next thing is sanitary napkins. You don't want to buy them out of any old machine in any old gas station bathroom. I know they say "sanitized" on the package but they're a far cry from "sanitized." They're filthy in fact. They've been sitting around in those places for months. You don't know whose quarters go into those machines. Those quarters carry germs. Those innocent looking silver quarters with Washington's head staring straight ahead. His handsome jaw jutting out. Spewing germs all over those napkins.

EMMA: *(still arranging charts)* How come they call them napkins?

ELLA: *(stopping for a second)* What?

EMMA: How come they call them napkins?

ELLA: *(back to the bacon)* Well, I don't know. I didn't make it up. Somebody called them napkins a long time ago and it just stuck.

EMMA: "Sanitary napkins."

ELLA: Yes.

EMMA: It's a funny sound. Like a hospital or something.

ELLA: Well that's what they should be like, but unfortunately they're not. They're not hospital clean that's for sure. And you should know that anything you stick up in there should be absolutely hospital clean.

EMMA: Stick up in where?

ELLA *turns upstage toward* EMMA, *then changes the subject.*

ELLA: What are those things?

EMMA: They're for my demonstration.

ELLA: What demonstration?

EMMA: How to cut up a frying chicken.

ELLA: *(back to bacon)* Oh.

EMMA: For 4-H. You know. I'm giving a demonstration at the fair. I told you before. I hope you haven't used up my last chicken.

EMMA *goes to refrigerator and looks inside for a chicken.*

ELLA: I forgot you were doing that. I thought that wasn't for months yet.

EMMA: I told you it was this month. The fair's always this month. Every year it's this month.

ELLA: I forgot.

EMMA: Where's my chicken?

ELLA: *(innocently)* What chicken?

EMMA: I had a fryer in here all ready to go. I killed it and dressed it and everything!

ELLA: It's not in there. All we got is bacon and bread.

EMMA: I just stuck it in here yesterday, Ma! You didn't use it did you?

ELLA: Why would I use it?

EMMA: For soup or something.

ELLA: Why would I use a fryer for soup. Don't be ridiculous.

ELLA: *(slamming refrigerator)* It's not in there!

ELLA: Don't start screaming in here! Go outside and scream if you're going to scream!

EMMA storms off stage right. ELLA takes the bacon off the stove. Slight pause, then EMMA can be heard yelling off stage. ELLA puts some bread in the frying pan and starts frying it.

EMMA'S VOICE: *(off)* That was my chicken and you fucking boiled it! YOU BOILED MY CHICKEN! I RAISED THAT CHICKEN FROM THE INCUBATOR TO THE GRAVE AND YOU BOILED IT LIKE IT WAS ANY OLD FROZEN HUNK OF FLESH! YOU USED IT WITH NO CONSIDERATION FOR THE LABOR IN-VOLVED! I HAD TO FEED THAT CHICKEN CRUSHED CORN EVERY MORNING FOR A YEAR! I HAD TO CHANGE ITS WATER! I HAD TO KILL IT WITH AN AX! I HAD TO SPILL ITS GUTS OUT! I HAD TO PLUCK EVERY FEATHER ON ITS BODY! I HAD TO DO ALL THAT WORK SO THAT YOU COULD TAKE IT AND BOIL IT!

WESLEY enters from left and crosses to center.

WESLEY: What's all the screaming?

ELLA: Somebody stole her chicken.

WESLEY: Stole it?

ELLA: Boiled it.

WESLEY: You boiled it.

ELLA: I didn't know it was hers.

WESLEY: Did it have her name on it?

ELLA: No, of course not.

WESLEY: Then she's got nothing to scream about. *(yelling off stage)* SHUT UP OUT THERE! YOU SHOULD'VE PUT YOUR NAME ON IT IF YOU DIDN'T WANT ANYBODY TO BOIL IT!

EMMA'S VOICE: *(off)* EAT MY SOCKS!

WESLEY: *(crossing up to table)* Great language. *(noticing charts on ta-ble)* What's all this stuff?

ELLA: Her charts. She's giving a demonstration.

WESLEY: *(holding one of the charts up)* A demonstration? On what?

ELLA: How to cut up a chicken. What else.

ELLA takes her bacon and bread on a plate and crosses up to table. She sits at the stage left end.

WESLEY: Anybody knows how to cut up a chicken.

ELLA: Well, there's special bones you have to crack. Special ways of doing it evidently.

WESLEY: *(turning downstage with chart held out in front of him)* What's so special about it.

ELLA: *(eating at table)* The anatomy is what's special. The anatomy of a chicken. If you know the anatomy you're half-way home.

WESLEY: *(facing front, laying chart down on floor)* It's just bones.

EMMA'S VOICE: *(off)* THERE'S NO CONSIDERATION! IF I'D COME ACROSS A CHICKEN IN THE FREEZER I WOULD'VE ASKED SOMEONE FIRST BEFORE I BOILED IT!

ELLA: *(yelling, still eating)* NOT IF YOU WERE STARVING!

WESLEY unzips his fly, takes out his pecker, and starts pissing all over the chart on the floor. ELLA just keeps eating at the table, not noticing.

EMMA'S VOICE: *(off)* NO ONE'S STARVING IN THIS HOUSE! YOU'RE FEEDING YOUR FACE RIGHT NOW!

ELLA: So what!

EMMA'S VOICE: *(off)* SO NO ONE'S STARVING! WE DON'T BE-LONG TO THE STARVING CLASS!

ELLA: Don't speak unless you know what you're speaking about! There's no such thing as a starving class!

EMMA'S VOICE: *(off)* THERE IS SO! THERE'S A STARVING CLASS OF PEOPLE, AND WE'RE NOT PART OF IT!

ELLA: WE'RE HUNGRY, AND THAT'S STARVING ENOUGH FOR ME!

EMMA'S VOICE: *(off)* YOU'RE A SPOILED BRAT!

ELLA: *(to WESLEY)* Did you hear what she called me? *(she notices what he's doing, she yells to Emma)* EMMA!

EMMA'S VOICE: *(off)* WHAT!

ELLA: YOUR BROTHER'S PISSING ALL OVER YOUR CHARTS! *goes back to eating)*

EMMA *enters fast from right and watches* WESLEY *put his joint back in his pants and zip up. They stare at each other as* ELLA *goes on eating at the table.*

EMMA: What kind of a family is this?

ELLA: *(not looking up)* I tried to stop him but he wouldn't listen.

EMMA: *(to* WESLEY*)* Do you know how long I worked on those charts? I had to do research. I went to the library. I took out books. I spent hours.

WESLEY: It's a stupid thing to spend your time on.

EMMA: I'm leaving this house! *(she exits right)*

ELLA: *(calling after her but staying at table)* YOU'RE TOO YOUNG! *(to* WESLEY*)* She's too young to leave. It's ridiculous. I can't say I blame her but she's way too young. She's only just now having her first period.

WESLEY: *(crossing to refrigerator)* Swell.

ELLA: Well, you don't know what it's like. It's very tough. You don't have to make things worse for her.

WESLEY: *(opening refrigerator and staring into it)* I'm not. I'm opening up new possibilities for her. Now she'll have to do something else. It could change her whole direction in life. She'll look back and remember the day her brother pissed all over her charts and see that day as a turning point in her life.

ELLA: How do you figure?

WESLEY: Well, she's already decided to leave home. That's a beginning.

ELLA: *(standing abruptly)* She's too young to leave! And get out of that refrigerator!

She crosses to refrigerator and slams the door shut. WESLEY *crosses up to the table and sits at the stage right end.*

ELLA: You're always in the refrigerator!

WESLEY: I'm hungry.

ELLA: How can you be hungry all the time? We're not poor. We're not rich but we're not poor.

WESLEY: What are we then?

ELLA: *(crossing back to table and sitting opposite* WESLEY*)* We're somewhere in between. *(pause as* ELLA *starts to eat again;* WESLEY *watches her)* We're going to be rich though.

WESLEY: What do you mean?

ELLA: We're going to have some money real soon.

WESLEY: What're you talking about?

ELLA: Never mind. You just wait though. You'll be very surprised.

WESLEY: I thought Dad got fired.

ELLA: He did. This has nothing to do with your father.

WESLEY: Well, you're not working are you?

ELLA: Just never mind. I'll let you know when the time comes. And then we'll get out of this place, once and for all.

WESLEY: Where are we going?

ELLA: Europe maybe. Wouldn't you like to go to Europe?

WESLEY: No.

ELLA: Why not?

WESLEY: What's in Europe?

ELLA: They have everything in Europe. High art. Paintings. Castles. Buildings. Fancy food.

WESLEY: They got all that here.

ELLA: Why aren't you sensitive like your Grandfather was? I always thought you were just like him, but you're not, are you?

WESLEY: No.

ELLA: Why aren't you? You're circumcized just like him. It's almost identical in fact.

WESLEY: How do you know?

ELLA: I looked. I looked at them both and I could see the similarity.

WESLEY: He's dead.

ELLA: When he was alive is when I looked. Don't be ridiculous.

WESLEY: What'd you sneak into his room or something?

ELLA: We lived in a small house.

EMMA'S VOICE: (off) WHERE'S MY JODHPURS!

ELLA: (to WESLEY) What's she yelling about?

WESLEY: Her jodhpurs.

ELLA: (yelling to EMMA) What do you need your jodhpurs for?

EMMA'S VOICE: (off) I'M TAKING THE HORSE!

ELLA: DON'T BE RIDICULOUS! DO YOU KNOW HOW FAR YOU'LL GET ON THAT HORSE? NOT VERY FAR!

EMMA'S VOICE: (off) FAR ENOUGH!

ELLA: YOU'RE NOT TAKING THE HORSE! (to WESLEY) Go down and lock that horse in the stall.

WESLEY: Let her go.

ELLA: On a horse? Are you crazy? She'll get killed on the freeway.

WESLEY: She won't take him on the freeway.

ELLA: That horse spooks at its own shadow. *(yelling off to* EMMA*)* EMMA, YOU'RE NOT TAKING THAT HORSE! *(no answer from* EMMA*)* EMMA! *(to* WESLEY*)* Go see if she went down there. I don't want her taking off on that horse. It's dangerous.

WESLEY: She's a good rider.

ELLA: I don't care!

WESLEY: You go down there then.

    Pause. She looks at him.

ELLA: Well, maybe she'll be all right.

WESLEY: Sure she will. She's been out on overnight trail rides before.

ELLA: What a temper she's got.

WESLEY: She's just spoiled.

ELLA: No, she's not. I never gave her a thing extra. Nothing. Bare minimums. That's all.

WESLEY: The old man spoils her.

ELLA: He's never around. How could he spoil her?

WESLEY: When he's around he spoils her.

ELLA: That horse is a killer. I wish you'd go down there and check.

WESLEY: She can handle him.

ELLA: I've seen that horse get a new set of shoes and he's an idiot! They have to throw him down every time.

WESLEY: Look, where's this money coming from?

ELLA: What money?

WESLEY: This money that's going to make us rich.

ELLA: I'm selling the house.

    Long pause, as WESLEY *stares at her. She turns away from him.*

ELLA: I'm selling the house, the land, the orchard, the tractor, the stock. Everything. It all goes.

WESLEY: It's not yours.

ELLA: It's mine as much as his!

WESLEY: You're not telling him?

ELLA: No! I'm not telling him and I shouldn't have told you. So just keep it under your hat.

WESLEY: How can you sell the house? It's not legal even.

ELLA: I signed the deed, same as him. We both signed it.

WESLEY: Then he has to co-sign the sale. Fifty-fifty.

ELLA: I already checked with a lawyer, and it's legal.

WESLEY: What about the mortgages? It's not even paid off, and you've borrowed money on it.

ELLA: Don't start questioning me! I've gone through all the arrangements already.

WESLEY: With who!

ELLA: I HAVE A LAWYER FRIEND!

WESLEY: A lawyer friend?

ELLA: Yes. He's very successful. He's handling everything for me.

WESLEY: You hired a lawyer?

ELLA: I told you, he's a friend. He's doing it as a favor.

WESLEY: You're not paying him?

ELLA: He's taking a percentage. A small percentage.

WESLEY: And you're just going to split with the money without telling anybody?

ELLA: I told you. That's enough. You could come with me.

WESLEY: This is where I live.

ELLA: Some home. It doesn't even have a front door now. Rain's going to pour right through here.

WESLEY: You won't even make enough to take a trip to San Diego off this house. It's infested with termites.

ELLA: This land is valuable. Everybody wants a good lot these days.

WESLEY: A lot?

ELLA: This is wonderful property for development. Do you know what land is selling for these days? Have you got any idea?

WESLEY: No.

ELLA: A lot. Tons. Thousands and thousands are being spent every day by ordinary people just on this very thing. Banks are loaning money right and left. Small family loans. People are building. Everyone wants a piece of land. It's the only sure investment. It can never depreciate like a car or a washing machine. Land will double its value in ten years. In less than that. Land is going up every day.

WESLEY: You're crazy.

ELLA: Why? For not being a sucker? Who takes care of this place?

WESLEY: Me!

ELLA: Ha! Are you kidding? What do you do? Feed a few sheep. Disc the orchard once in a while. Irrigate. What else?

WESLEY: I take care of it.

ELLA: I'm not talking about maintenance. I'm talking about fixing it up. Making it look like somebody lives here. Do you do that?

WESLEY: Somebody does live here!

ELLA: Who! Not your father!

WESLEY: He works on it. He does the watering.

ELLA: When he can stand up. How often is that? He comes in here and passes out on the floor for three days then disappears for a week. You call that work? I can't run this place by myself.

WESLEY: Nobody's asking you to!

ELLA: Nobody's asking me period! I'm selling it, and that's all there is to it!

Long pause, as they sit there. WESLEY *gets up fast.*

ELLA: Where are you going?

WESLEY: I'm gonna' feed the sheep!

He exits left. ELLA *calls after him.*

ELLA: Check on Emma for me would you, Wesley? I don't like her being down there all alone. That horse is crazy.

WESLEY'S VOICE: *(off)* HE'S GOING TO KILL YOU WHEN HE FINDS OUT!

ELLA: *(standing, shouting off)* HE'S NOT GOING TO FIND OUT! *(pause, as she waits for a reply; nothing; she yells again)* THE ONLY PERSON HE'S GOING TO KILL IS HIMSELF!

Another pause, as she stands there waiting for WESLEY *to reply. Nothing. She turns to the table and stares at the plate. She picks up the plate and carries it to the stove. She sets it on the stove. She stares at the stove. She turns toward refrigerator and looks at it. She crosses to refrigerator and opens it. She looks inside.*

ELLA: Nothing.

She closes refrigerator door. She stares at refrigerator. She talks to herself.

ELLA: He's not going to kill me. I have every right to sell. Every right. He doesn't have a leg to stand on.

She stares at refrigerator, then opens it again and looks inside. EMMA *enters from right, holding a rope halter in one hand, her white uniform covered in mud. She watches* ELLA *staring into refrigerator.*

EMMA: That bastard almost killed me.

ELLA *shuts refrigerator and turns toward* EMMA.

ELLA: What happened to you?

EMMA: He dragged me clear across the corral.

ELLA: I told you not to play around with that fool horse. He's insane, that horse.

EMMA: How am I ever going to get out of here?

ELLA: You're not going to get out of here. You're too young. Now go and change your clothes.

EMMA: I'm not too young to have babies, right?

ELLA: What do you mean?

EMMA: That's what bleeding is, right? That's what bleeding's for.

ELLA: Don't talk silly, and go change your uniform.

EMMA: This is the only one I've got.

ELLA: Well, change into something else then.

EMMA: I can't stay here forever.

ELLA: Nobody's staying here forever. We're all leaving.

EMMA: We are?

ELLA: Yes. We're going to Europe.

EMMA: Who is?

ELLA: All of us.

EMMA: Pop too?

ELLA: No. Probably not.

EMMA: How come? He'd like it in Europe wouldn't he?

ELLA: I don't know.

EMMA: You mean just you, me, and Wes are going to Europe? That sounds awful.

ELLA: Why? What's so awful about that? It could be a vacation.

EMMA: It'd be the same as it is here.

ELLA: No, it wouldn't! We'd be in Europe. A whole new place.

EMMA: But we'd all be the same people.

ELLA: What's the matter with you? Why do you say things like that?

EMMA: Well, we would be.

ELLA: I do my best to try to make things right. To try to change things. To bring a little adventure into our lives and you go and reduce the whole thing to smithereens.

EMMA: We don't have any money to go to Europe anyway.

ELLA: Go change your clothes!

EMMA: No. *(she crosses to table and sits stage right end)*

ELLA: If your father was here you'd go change your clothes.

EMMA: He's not.

ELLA: Why can't you just cooperate?

EMMA: Because it's deadly. It leads to dying.

ELLA: You're not old enough to talk like that.

EMMA: I was down there in the mud being dragged along.

ELLA: It's your own fault. I told you not to go down there.

EMMA: Suddenly everything changed. I wasn't the same person anymore. I was just a hunk of meat tied to a big animal. Being pulled.

ELLA: Maybe you'll understand the danger now.

EMMA: I had the whole trip planned out in my head. I was going to head for Baja California.

ELLA: Mexico?

EMMA: I was going to work on fishing boats. Deep sea fishing. Helping businessmen haul in huge swordfish and barracuda. I was going to work my way along the coast, stopping at all the little towns, speaking Spanish. I was going to learn to be a mechanic and work on four-wheel-drive vehicles that broke down. Transmissions. I could've learned to fix anything. Then I'd learn how to be a short-order cook and write novels on the side. In the kitchen. Kitchen novels. Then I'd get published and disappear into the heart of Mexico. Just like that guy.

ELLA: What guy?

EMMA: That guy who wrote *Treasure of Sierra Madre*.

ELLA: When did you see that?

EMMA: He had initials for a name. And he disappeared. Nobody knew where to send his royalties. He escaped.

ELLA: Snap out of it, Emma. You don't have that kind of a background to do jobs like that. That's not for you, that stuff. You can do beautiful embroidery; why do you want to be a mechanic?

EMMA: I like cars. I like travel. I like the idea of people breaking down and I'm the only one who can help them get on the road again. It would be like being a magician. Just open up the hood and cast your magic spell.

ELLA: What are you dreaming for?

EMMA: I'm not dreaming now. I was dreaming then. Right up to the point when I got the halter on. Then as soon as he took off I stopped. I stopped dreaming and saw myself being dragged through the mud.

ELLA: Go change your clothes.

EMMA: Stop saying that over and over as though by saying it you relieve yourself of responsibility.

ELLA: I can't even follow the way you talk to me anymore.

EMMA: That's good.

ELLA: Why is that good?

EMMA: Because if you could then that would mean that you understood me.

Pause. ELLA *turns and opens the refrigerator again and stares into it.*

EMMA: Hungry?

ELLA: No.

EMMA: Just habit?

ELLA: What?

EMMA: Opening and closing?

ELLA *closes refrigerator and turns toward* EMMA.

ELLA: Christ, Emma, what am I going to do with you?

EMMA: Let me go.

ELLA: *(after pause)* You're too young.

ELLA *exits left.* EMMA *stays sitting at table. She looks around the space, then gets up slowly and crosses to the refrigerator. She pauses in front of it, then opens the door slowly and looks in. She speaks into refrigerator.*

EMMA: Hello? Anything in there? We're not broke you know, so you don't have to hide! I don't know where the money goes to but we're not broke! We're not part of the starving class!

TAYLOR, *the lawyer, enters from down right and watches* EMMA *as she speaks into refrigerator. He is dressed in a smart suit, middle-aged, with a briefcase. He just stands there watching her.*

EMMA: *(into refrigerator)* Any corn muffins in there? Hello! Any produce? Any rutabagas? Any root vegetables? Nothing? It's all right. You don't have to be ashamed. I've had worse. I've had to take my lunch to school wrapped up in a Weber's bread wrapper. That's the worst. Worse than no lunch. So don't feel bad! You'll get some company before you know it! You'll get some little eggs tucked into your sides and some yellow margarine tucked into your little drawers and some frozen chicken tucked into your— *(pauses)* You haven't seen my chicken have you? You motherfucker!

She slams the door to refrigerator and turns around. She sees TAYLOR *standing there. They stare at each other.* TAYLOR *smiles.*

TAYLOR: Your mother home?

EMMA: I don't know.

TAYLOR: I saw her car out there so I thought she might be.

EMMA: That's not her car.

TAYLOR: Oh. I thought it was.

EMMA: It's my Dad's car.

TAYLOR: She drives it, doesn't she?

EMMA: He bought it.

TAYLOR: Oh. I see.

EMMA: It's a Kaiser-Fraser.

TAYLOR: Oh.

EMMA: He goes in for odd-ball cars. He's got a Packard, too.

TAYLOR: I see.

EMMA: Says they're the only ones made out of steel.

TAYLOR: Oh.

EMMA: He totaled that car but you'd never know it.

TAYLOR: The Packard?

EMMA: No, the other one.

TAYLOR: I see.

EMMA: Who are you anyway?

TAYLOR: My name's Taylor. I'm your mother's lawyer.

EMMA: Is she in trouble or something?

TAYLOR: No. Not at all.

EMMA: Then what are you doing here?

TAYLOR: Well, I've got some business with your mother.

EMMA: You're creepy.

TAYLOR: Oh, really?

EMMA: Yeah, really. You give me the creeps. There's something about
  you that's weird.

TAYLOR: Well, I did come to speak to your mother.

EMMA: I know, but you're speaking to me now.

TAYLOR: Yes. *(pause, as he looks around awkwardly)* Did someone
  break your door down?

EMMA: My Dad.

TAYLOR: Accident?

EMMA: No, he did it on purpose. He was pissed off.

TAYLOR: I see. He must have a terrible temper.

EMMA: What do you want?

TAYLOR: I told you—

EMMA: Yeah, but what do you want my mother for?

TAYLOR: We have some business.

EMMA: She's not a business woman. She's terrible at business.

TAYLOR: Why is that?

EMMA: She's a sucker. She'll believe anything.

TAYLOR: She seems level-headed enough to me.

EMMA: Depends on what you're using her for.

Pause, as TAYLOR *looks at her.*

TAYLOR: You don't have to be insulting.

EMMA: I got nothing to lose.

TAYLOR: You *are* her daughter, aren't you?

EMMA: What line of business are you in?

TAYLOR: Do you mind if I sit down?

EMMA: I don't mind. My Dad might mind, though.

TAYLOR: He's not home, is he?

EMMA: He might come home any second now.

TAYLOR: *(crossing to chair at table)* Well, I'll just wait for your mother.

EMMA: He's got a terrible temper. He almost killed one guy he caught her with.

TAYLOR: *(sitting in stage right chair)* You misunderstand me. I'm here on business.

EMMA: A short fuse they call it. Runs in the family. His father was just like him. And his father before him. Wesley is just like Pop, too. Like liquid dynamite.

TAYLOR: *(setting attaché case on table)* Liquid dynamite?

EMMA: Yeah. What's that stuff called?

TAYLOR: I don't know.

EMMA: It's chemical. It's the same thing that makes him drink. Something in the blood. Hereditary. Highly explosive.

TAYLOR: Sounds dangerous.

EMMA: Yeah.

TAYLOR: Don't you get afraid living in an environment like this?

EMMA: No. The fear lies with the ones who carry the stuff in their blood, not the ones who don't. I don't have it in me.

TAYLOR: I see.

EMMA: Nitroglycerine. That's what it's called. Nitroglycerine.

TAYLOR: What do you mean?

EMMA: In the blood. Nitroglycerine.

TAYLOR: Do you think you could call your mother for me?

EMMA: *(yelling but looking straight at* TAYLOR*)* MOM!!!!

TAYLOR: *(after pause)* Thank you.

EMMA: What do you want my mother for?

TAYLOR: *(getting irritated)* I've already told you!

EMMA: Does she bleed?

TAYLOR: What?

EMMA: You know. Does she have blood coming out of her?

TAYLOR: I don't think I want to talk any more.

EMMA: All right.

> EMMA *crosses to table and sits opposite* TAYLOR *at the stage left end. She stares at him. They sit silently for a while.* TAYLOR *squirms nervously, taps on his attaché case.* EMMA *just watches him.*

TAYLOR: Marvelous house this is. *(pause, as she just looks at him)* The location I mean. The land is full of potential. *(pause)* Of course it's a shame to see agriculture being slowly pushed into the background in deference to low-cost housing, but that's simply a product of the times we live in. There's simply more people on the planet these days. That's all there is to it. Simple mathematics. More people demand more shelter. More shelter demands more land. It's an equation. We have to provide for the people some way. The new people. We're lucky to live in a country where that provision is possible. In some countries, like India for instance, it's simply not possible. People live under banana leaves.

> WESLEY *enters from right carrying a small collapsible fence structure. He sets it up center stage to form a small rectangular enclosure. He turns and looks at* TAYLOR, *then turns to* EMMA.

WESLEY: *(to* EMMA*)* Who's he?

EMMA: He's a lawyer.

> TAYLOR *stands, smiling broadly at* WESLEY *and extending his hand.* WESLEY *doesn't shake but just looks at him.*

TAYLOR: Taylor. You must be the son.

WESLEY: Yeah, I'm the son.

> WESLEY *exits right.* TAYLOR *sits down again. He smiles nervously at* EMMA, *who just stares at him.*

TAYLOR: It's a funny sensation.

EMMA: What?

TAYLOR: I feel like I'm on enemy territory.

EMMA: You are.

TAYLOR: I haven't felt this way since the war.

EMMA: What war?

TAYLOR *just looks at her.* WESLEY *enters again from right carrying a small live lamb. He sets the lamb down inside the fenced area. He watches the lamb as it moves around inside the fence.*

EMMA: *(to* WESLEY*)* What's the matter with him?

WESLEY: *(watching lamb)* Maggots.

EMMA: Can't you keep him outside? He'll spread germs in here.

WESLEY: *(watching lamb)* You picked that up from Mom.

EMMA: Picked what up?

WESLEY: Germs. The idea of germs. Invisible germs mysteriously floating around in the air. Anything's a potential carrier.

TAYLOR: *(to* WESLEY*)* Well, it does seem that if the animal has maggots it shouldn't be in the kitchen. Near the food.

WESLEY: We haven't got any food.

TAYLOR: Oh. Well, when you do have food you prepare it in here, don't you?

EMMA: That's nothing. My brother pisses on the floor in here.

TAYLOR: Do you always talk this way to strangers?

EMMA: Look, that's his piss right there on the floor. Right on my chart.

WESLEY: *(turning to* TAYLOR*)* What're you doing here anyway?

TAYLOR: I don't feel I have to keep justifying myself all the time. I'm here to meet your mother.

WESLEY: Are you the one who's trying to sell the house?

TAYLOR: We're negotiating, yes.

EMMA: *(standing)* What? Trying to sell what house? This house?

TAYLOR: *(to* EMMA*)* Didn't she tell you?

WESLEY: She told me.

EMMA: Where are we going to live!

WESLEY: *(to* EMMA*)* You're leaving home anyway. What do you care?

EMMA: *(yelling off stage)* MOM!!!

TAYLOR: *(to* WESLEY*)* I didn't mean to shock her or anything.

WESLEY: *(to* TAYLOR*)* Aren't you going to talk to my old man?

TAYLOR: That's not necessary right now.

WESLEY: He'll never sell you know.

TAYLOR: Well, he may have to. According to your mother he owes a great deal of money.

EMMA: To who? Who does he owe money to?

TAYLOR: To everyone. He's in hock up to his ears.

EMMA: He doesn't owe a cent! Everything's paid for!

WESLEY: Emma, shut up! Go change your clothes.

EMMA: You shut up! This guy's a creep, and he's trying to sell us all down the river. He's a total meatball!

WESLEY: I know he's a meatball! Just shut up, will you?

EMMA: *(to* TAYLOR*)* My Dad doesn't owe money to anyone!

TAYLOR: *(to* WESLEY*)* I'm really sorry. I thought your mother told her.

    ELLA *enters from left in a dress and handbag with white gloves.* TAYLOR *stands when he sees her.*

ELLA: What's all the shouting going on for? Oh, Mr. Taylor. I wasn't expecting you for another half-hour.

TAYLOR: Yes, I know. I saw the car out in front so I thought I'd stop in early.

ELLA: Well, I'm glad you did. Did you meet everyone?

TAYLOR: Yes, I did.

ELLA: *(noticing lamb)* What's that animal doing in here, Wesley?

WESLEY: It's got maggots.

ELLA: Well, get him out of the kitchen.

WESLEY: It's the warmest part of the house.

ELLA: Get him out!

EMMA: Mom, are you selling this house?

ELLA: Who told her?

TAYLOR: Well, I'm afraid it slipped out.

ELLA: Emma, I'm not going to discuss it now. Go change your clothes.

EMMA: *(coldly)* If you sell this house, I'm never going to see you again.

    EMMA *exits left.* TAYLOR *smiles, embarrassed.*

TAYLOR: I'm very sorry. I assumed that she knew.

ELLA: It doesn't matter. She's leaving anyway. Now, Wes, I'm going out with Mr. Taylor for a little lunch and to discuss our business. When I come back I want that lamb out of the kitchen.

TAYLOR: *(to* WESLEY, *extending his hand again)* It was very nice to have met you.

    WESLEY *ignores the gesture and just stares at him.*

ELLA: *(to* TAYLOR*)* He's sullen by nature. Picks it up from his father.

TAYLOR: I see. *(to* WESLEY*)* Nitroglycerin, too, I suppose? *(chuckles)*

    ELLA *and* TAYLOR *start to exit off right.* ELLA *turns to* WESLEY.

ELLA: Keep an eye out for Emma, Wes. She's got the curse. You know what that's like for a girl, the first time around.

    TAYLOR *and* ELLA *exit.* WESLEY *stands there for a while. He turns and looks at the lamb.*

WESLEY: *(staring at lamb)* "Eat American Lamb. Twenty million coyotes can't be wrong."

He crosses to refrigerator and opens it. He stares into it.

WESLEY: You're out of luck. Santa Claus hasn't come yet.

He slams refrigerator door and turns to lamb. He stares at lamb.

WESLEY: *(to lamb)* You're lucky I'm not really starving. You're lucky this is a civilized household. You're lucky it's not Korea and the rains are pouring through the cardboard walls and you're tied to a log in the mud and you're drenched to the bone and you're skinny and starving, but it makes no difference because someone's starving more than you. Someone's hungry. And his hunger takes him outside with a knife and slits your throat and eats you raw. His hunger eats you, and you're starving.

Loud crash of garbage cans being knocked over off stage right. Sound of WESTON, WESLEY'*s father, off right.*

WESTON'S VOICE: *(off right)* WHO PUT THE GODDAMN GARBAGE CANS RIGHT IN FRONT OF THE GODDAMN DOOR?

WESLEY listens for a second, then bolts off stage left. More crashing is heard off right. General cursing from WESTON, *then he enters from right with a large duffel bag full of laundry and a large bag full of groceries. He's a very big man, middle-aged, wearing a dark overcoat which looks like it's been slept in, a blue baseball cap, baggy pants, and tennis shoes. He's unshaven and slightly drunk. He takes a few steps and stops cold when he sees the lamb. He just stares at the lamb for a minute, then crosses to the table and sets the bag of groceries and the laundry on the table. He crosses back to center and looks at the lamb inside the fence.*

WESTON: *(to Lamb)* What in the hell are you doin' in here? *(he looks around the space, to himself)* Is this inside or outside? This is inside, right? This is the inside of the house. Even with the door out it's still the inside. *(to lamb)* Right? *(to himself)* Right. *(to lamb)* So what the hell are you doing in here if this is the inside? *(he chuckles to himself)* That's not funny.

. *He crosses to the refrigerator and opens it.*

WESTON: Perfect! ZERO! ABSOLUTELY ZERO! NADA! GOOSE EGGS! *(he yells at the house in general)* WE'VE DONE IT AGAIN! WE'VE GONE AND LEFT EVERYTHING UP TO THE OLD MAN AGAIN! ALL THE UPKEEP! THE MAINTENANCE! PERFECT!

He slams the refrigerator door and crosses back to the table.

WESTON: I don't even know why we keep a refrigerator in this house. All it's good for is slamming.

He picks up the bag of groceries and crosses back to the refrigerator, talking to himself.

WESTON: Slams all day long and through the night. SLAM! SLAM! SLAM! What's everybody hoping for, a miracle! IS EVERYBODY HOPING FOR A MIRACLE?

He opens refrigerator as WESLEY *enters from stage right and stops.* WESTON's *back is to him.* WESTON *starts taking artichokes out of the bag and putting them in the refrigerator.*

WESTON: *(to house)* THERE'S NO MORE MIRACLES! NO MIRACLES TODAY! THEY'VE BEEN ALL USED UP! IT'S ONLY ME! MR. SLAVE LABOR HIMSELF COME HOME TO REPLENISH THE EMPTY LARDER!

WESLEY: What're you yelling for? There's nobody here.

WESTON *wheels around facing* WESLEY. WESLEY *stays still.*

WESTON: What the hell are you sneakin' up like that for? You coulda' got yourself killed!

WESLEY: What's in the bag?

WESTON: Groceries! What else. Somebody's gotta' feed this house.

WESTON *turns back to refrigerator and goes on putting more artichokes into it.*

WESLEY: What kind of groceries?

WESTON: Artichokes! What do you think?

WESLEY: *(coming closer)* Artichokes?

WESTON: Yeah. Good desert artichokes. Picked 'em up for half-price out in Hot Springs.

WESLEY: You went all the way out there for artichokes?

WESTON: 'Course not! What do you think I am, an idiot or something? I went out there to check on my land.

WESLEY: What land?

WESTON: My desert land! Now stop talking! Everything was all right until you came in. I was talking to myself and everything was all right.

WESTON *empties the bag into the refrigerator, then slams the door shut. He crunches up the bag and crosses back to the table. He opens up his bag of laundry and starts taking dirty clothes out and stacking them in piles on the table.* WESLEY *crosses to refrigerator and opens it, looks in at artichokes. He takes one out and looks at it closely, then puts it back in. They keep talking through all this.*

WESLEY: I didn't know you had land in the desert.

WESTON: 'Course I do. I got an acre and a half out there.

WESLEY: You never told me.

WESTON: Why should I tell you? I told your mother.

WESLEY: She never told me.

WESTON: Aw, shut up, will ya'?

WESLEY: What kind of land is it?

WESTON: It's not what I expected, that's for sure.

WESLEY: What is it, then?

WESTON: It's just not what I expected. Some guy came to the door selling land. So I bought some.

WESLEY: What guy?

WESTON: Some guy. Looked respectable. Talked a real good line. Said it was an investment for the future. All kinds of great things were going to be developed. Golf courses, shopping centers, banks, sauna baths. All that kinda' stuff. So I bought it.

WESLEY: How much did you pay?

WESTON: Well, I didn't pay the whole thing. I put something down on it. I'm not stupid.

WESLEY: How much?

WESTON: Why should I tell you? I borrowed it, so it's none of your goddamn business how much it was!

WESLEY: But it turned out to be a hoax, huh?

WESTON: A real piece of shit. Just a bunch of strings on sticks, with the lizards blowing across it.

WESLEY: Nothing around it?

WESTON: Not a thing. Just desert. No way to even get water to the goddamn place. No way to even set a trailer on it.

WESLEY: Where's the guy now?

WESTON: How should I know! Where's your mother anyway?

WESLEY: (shutting refrigerator) She went out.

WESTON: Yeah, I know she went out. The car's gone. Where'd she go to?

WESLEY: Don't know.

WESTON: (bundling up empty duffel bag under his arm) Well, when she gets back tell her to do this laundry for me. Tell her not to put bleach in anything but the socks and no starch in the collars. Can you remember that?

WESLEY: Yeah, I think so. No bleach and no starch.

WESTON: That's it. You got it. Now don't forget. *(he heads for stage right)*

WESLEY: Where are you going?

WESTON: Just never mind where I'm going! I can take care of myself. *(he stops and looks at the lamb)* What's the matter with the lamb?

WESLEY: Maggots.

WESTON: Poor little bugger. Put some a' that blue shit on it. That'll fix him up. You know that blue stuff in the bottle?

WESLEY: Yeah.

WESTON: Put some a' that on it. *(pauses a second, looks around)* You know I was even thinkin' a' sellin' this place.

WESLEY: You were?

WESTON: Yeah. Don't tell your mother though.

WESLEY: I won't.

WESTON: Bank probably won't let me, but I was thinkin' I could sell it and buy some land down in Mexico.

WESLEY: Why down there?

WESTON: I like it down there. *(looks at lamb again)* Don't forget about that blue stuff. Can't afford to lose any lambs. Only had but two sets a' twins this year, didn't we?

WESLEY: Three.

WESTON: Well, three then. It's not much.

> WESTON *exits stage right.* WESLEY *looks at lamb. Lights fade to black.*

ACT 2

SCENE:

Same set. Loud hammering and sawing heard in darkness. Lights come up slowly on WESLEY *building a new door center stage. Hammers, nails, saw, and wood lying around, sawdust on floor. The fence enclosure and the lamb are gone. A big pot of artichokes is boiling away on the stove.* WESTON's *dirty laundry is still in piles on the table.* EMMA *sits at the stage left end of the table making a new set of charts for her demonstration with magic markers and big sheets of cardboard. She is dressed in jodhpurs, riding boots, and a western shirt. Lights up full. They each continue working at their*

separate tasks in silence, each of them totally concentrated. WES-
LEY *measures wood with a tape measure and then cuts it on one of
the chairs with the saw. He nails pieces together. After a while they
begin talking but still concentrate on their work.*

EMMA: Do you think she's making it with that guy?

WESLEY: Who, Taylor? How should I know?

EMMA: I think she is. She's after him for his money.

WESLEY: He's after our money. Why should she be after his?

EMMA: What money?

WESLEY: Our potential money.

EMMA: This place couldn't be that valuable.

WESLEY: Not the way it is now, but they'll divide it up. Make lots out
of it.

EMMA: She's after more than that.

WESLEY: More than what?

EMMA: Money. She's after esteem.

WESLEY: With Taylor?

EMMA: Yeah. She sees him as an easy ticket. She doesn't want to be
stuck out here in the boonies all her life.

WESLEY: She shoulda' thought of that a long time ago.

EMMA: She couldn't. Not with Pop. He wouldn't let her think. She just
went along with things.

WESLEY: She can't think. He can't either.

EMMA: Don't be too harsh.

WESLEY: How can they think when they're behind the eight ball all the
time. They don't have time to think.

EMMA: How come you didn't tell me when Pop came in last night?

WESLEY: I don't know.

EMMA: You could've told me.

WESLEY: He just brought his dirty laundry and then left.

EMMA: He brought food, too.

WESLEY: Artichokes.

EMMA: Better than nothing. *(pause, as they work)* They're probably half
way to Mexico by now.

WESLEY: Who?

EMMA: She's snuggling up to him and giggling and turning the dial on
the radio. He's feeling proud of himself. He's buying her hot dogs
and bragging about his business.

WESLEY: She'll be back.

EMMA: She's telling him all about us and about how Dad's crazy and trying to kill her all the time. She's happy to be on the road. To see new places go flashing by. They cross the border and gamble on the jai alai games. They head for Baja and swim along the beaches. They build campfires and roast fish at night. In the morning they take off again. But they break down somewhere outside a little place called Los Cerritos. They have to hike five miles into town. They come to a small beat-up gas station with one pump and a dog with three legs. There's only one mechanic in the whole town, and that's me. They don't recognize me though. They ask if I can fix their "carro," and I speak only Spanish. I've lost the knack for English by now. I understand them though and give them a lift back up the road in my rebuilt four-wheel-drive International. I jump out and look inside the hood. I see that it's only the rotor inside the distributor that's broken, but I tell them that it needs an entire new generator, a new coil, points and plugs, and some slight adjustments to the carburator. It's an overnight job, and I'll have to charge them for labor. So I set a cot up for them in the garage, and after they've fallen asleep I take out the entire engine and put in a rebuilt Volkswagen block. In the morning I charge them double for labor, see them on their way, and then resell their engine for a small mint.

WESLEY: If you're not doing anything, would you check the artichokes?

EMMA: I am doing something.

WESLEY: What?

EMMA: I'm remaking my charts.

WESLEY: What do you spend your time on that stuff for? You should be doing more important stuff.

EMMA: Like checking artichokes?

WESLEY: Yeah!

EMMA: You check the artichokes. I'm busy.

WESLEY: You're on the rag.

EMMA: Don't get personal. It's not nice. You should have more consideration.

WESLEY: Just put some water in them, would you? Before they burn.

EMMA *throws down her magic marker and crosses to the pot of artichokes. She looks in the pot and then crosses back to her chair and goes on working on her charts.*

WESLEY: Are they all right?

EMMA: Perfect. Just like a little boiling paradise in a pot. What're you making anyway?

WESLEY: A new door. What's it look like?

EMMA: Looks like a bunch of sawed-up wood to me.

WESLEY: At least it's practical.

EMMA: We're doing okay without a front door. Besides it might turn off potential buyers. Makes the place look like a chicken shack. *(remembers her chicken)* Oh, my chicken! I could've killed her right then.

WESLEY: You don't understand what's happening yet, do you?

EMMA: With what?

WESLEY: The house. You think it's Mr. and Mrs. America who're gonna' buy this place, but it's not. It's Taylor.

EMMA: He's a lawyer.

WESLEY: He works for an agency. Land development.

EMMA: So what?

WESLEY: So it means more than losing a house. It means losing a country.

EMMA: You make it sound like an invasion.

WESLEY: It is. It's a zombie invasion. Taylor is the head zombie. He's the scout for the other zombies. He's only a sign that more zombies are on their way. They'll be filing through the door pretty soon.

EMMA: Once you get it built.

WESLEY: There'll be bulldozers crashing through the orchard. There'll be giant steel balls crashing through the walls. There'll be foremen with their sleeves rolled up and blueprints under their arms. There'll be steel girders spanning acres of land. Cement pilings. Prefab walls. Zombie architecture, owned by invisible zombies, built by zombies for the use and convenience of all other zombies. A zombie city! Right here! Right where we're living now.

EMMA: We could occupy it. Dad's got a gun.

WESLEY: It's a Jap gun.

EMMA: It works. I saw him shoot a peacock with it once.

WESLEY: A peacock?

EMMA: Blasted it to smithereens. It was sitting right out there in the sycamore tree. It was screaming all night long.

WESLEY: Probably mating season.

EMMA: *(after long pause)* You think they'll come back?

WESLEY: Who?

EMMA: Our parents.

WESLEY: You mean ever?

EMMA: Yeah. Maybe they'll never come back, and we'll have the whole place to ourselves. We could do a lot with this place.

WESLEY: I'm not staying here forever.

EMMA: Where are you going?

WESLEY: I don't know. Alaska, maybe.

EMMA: Alaska?

WESLEY: Sure. Why not?

EMMA: What's in Alaska?

WESLEY: The frontier.

EMMA: Are you crazy? It's all frozen and full of rapers.

WESLEY: It's full of possibilities. It's undiscovered.

EMMA: Who wants to discover a bunch of ice?

> WESTON *suddenly stumbles on from stage right. He's considerably drunker than the last time.* EMMA *stands at the table, not knowing whether to stay or leave.* WESTON *looks at her.*

WESTON: *(to* EMMA*)* Just relax. Relax! It's only your old man. Sit down!

> EMMA *sits again.* WESLEY *stands by awkwardly.* WESTON *looks at the wood on the floor.*

WESTON: *(to* WESLEY*)* What the hell's all this? You building a barn in here or something?

WESLEY: New door.

WESTON: What! Don't talk with your voice in the back of your throat like a worm! Talk with your teeth! Talk!

WESLEY: I am talking.

WESTON: All right. Now I asked you what all this is. What is all this?

WESLEY: It's a new door.

WESTON: What's a new door? What's the matter with the old door?

WESLEY: It's gone.

> WESTON *turns around, weaving slightly, and looks off stage right.*

WESTON: Oh. *(he turns back to* WESLEY*)* Where'd it go?

WESLEY: You broke it down.

WESTON: Oh. *(he looks toward table)* My laundry done yet?

EMMA: She didn't come back yet.

WESTON: Who didn't?

EMMA: Mom.

WESTON: She didn't come back yet? It's been all night. Hasn't it been all night?

EMMA: Yes.

WESTON: Hasn't the sun rised and falled on this miserable planet?

EMMA: Yes.

WESTON: *(turning to* WESLEY*)* So where's she been?

WESLEY: Don't know.

WESTON: Don't pull that one! Don't pull that one on me!

He starts to come after WESLEY. WESLEY *backs off fast.* WESTON *stops. He stands there weaving in place.*

WESLEY: I don't know. Really.

WESTON: Don't try protecting her! There's no protection! Understand! None! She's had it!

WESLEY: I don't know where she went.

EMMA: She went with a lawyer.

WESTON *turns to* EMMA *slowly.*

WESTON: A what?

EMMA: A lawyer.

WESTON: What's a lawyer? A law man? A person of the law? *(suddenly yelling)* WHAT'S A LAWYER?

EMMA: A guy named Taylor.

Long pause, as WESTON *stares at her drunkenly, trying to fathom it. Then he turns to* WESLEY.

WESTON: *(to* WESLEY*)* Taylor? You knew?

WESLEY: I thought she'd be back by now. She said she was going out for a business lunch.

WESTON: You knew!

EMMA: Maybe they had an accident.

WESTON: *(to* EMMA*)* In my car! In my Kaiser-Fraser! I'll break his fucking back!

WESLEY: Maybe they did have an accident. I'll call the hospitals.

WESTON: DON'T CALL ANYBODY! *(quieter)* Don't call anybody. *(pause)* That car was an antique. Worth a fortune.

EMMA: *(after long pause)* You wanna' sit down, Pop?

WESTON: I'm standing. What's that smell in here? What's that smell!

WESLEY: Artichokes.

WESTON: They smell like that?

WESLEY: They're boiling.

WESTON: Stop them from boiling! They might boil over.

WESLEY *goes to stove and turns it off.*

WESTON: Where's that goddamn sheep you had in here? Is that what you're building? A barn for that sheep?

WESLEY: A door.

WESTON: *(staggering)* I gotta' sit down.

He stumbles toward table and sits at stage right end. EMMA *stands.*

WESTON: *(to* EMMA*)* Sit down! Sit back down! Turn off those artichokes!

WESLEY: I did.

WESTON: *(pushing laundry to one side)* She didn't do any of this. It's the same as when I brought it. None of it!

EMMA: I'll do it.

WESTON: No, you won't do it! You let her do it! It's her job! What does she do around here anyway? Do you know? What does she do all day long? What does a woman do?

EMMA: I don't know.

WESTON: You should be in school.

EMMA: It's all right if I do it. I don't mind doing it.

WESTON: YOU'RE NOT DOING IT! *(long silence)* What do you think of this place?

EMMA: The house?

WESTON: The whole thing. The whole fandango! The orchard! The air! The night sky!

EMMA: It's all right.

WESTON: *(to* WESLEY*)* What do you think of it?

WESLEY: I wouldn't sell it.

WESTON: You wouldn't sell it. You couldn't sell it! It's not yours!

WESLEY: I know. But I wouldn't if it was.

WESTON: How come? What good is it? What good's it doing?

WESLEY: It's just here. And we're on it. And we wouldn't be if it got sold.

WESTON: Very sound reasoning. Very sound. *(turns to* EMMA*)* Your brother never was much in the brain department, was he? You're the one who's such a smart-ass. You're the straight-A student, aren't you?

EMMA: Yes.

WESTON: Straight-A's and you're moldering around this dump. What're you going to do with yourself?

EMMA: I don't know.

WESTON: You don't know. Well you better think of something fast, because I've found a buyer. *(silence)* I've found someone to give me cash. Cash on the line! *(he slams table with his hand. Long silence, then* EMMA *gets up and exits off left)*

WESTON: What's the matter with her?

WESLEY: I don't know. She's got her first period.

WESTON: Her what? She's too young for that. That's not supposed to happen when they're that age. It's premature.

WESLEY: She's got it.

WESTON: What happens when I'm gone, you all sit around and talk about your periods? You're not supposed to know when your sister has her period! That's confidential between women. They keep it a secret that means.

WESLEY: I know what "confidential" means.

WESTON: Good.

WESLEY: Why don't you go to bed or something, so I can finish this door.

WESTON: What for? I told ya' I'm selling the joint. Why build a new door? No point in putting money into it.

WESLEY: I'm still living here. I'm living here right up to the point when I leave.

WESTON: Very brave. Very courageous outlook. I envy it in fact.

WESLEY: You do?

WESTON: Sure! Of course! What else is there to envy but an outlook? Look at mine! Look at my outlook. You don't envy it, right?

WESLEY: No.

WESTON: That's because it's full of poison. Infected. And you recognize poison, right? You recognize it when you see it?

WESLEY: Yes.

WESTON: Yes, you do. I can see that you do. My poison scares you.

WESLEY: Doesn't scare me.

WESTON: No?

WESLEY: No.

WESTON: Good. You're growing up. I never saw my old man's poison until I was much older than you. Much older. And then you know how I recognized it?

WESLEY: How?

WESTON: Because I saw myself infected with it. That's how. I saw me carrying it around. His poison in my body. You think that's fair?

WESLEY: I don't know.

WESTON: Well, what do you think? You think I asked for it?

WESLEY: No.

WESTON: So it's unfair, right?

WESLEY: It's just the way it happened.

WESTON: I didn't ask for it, but I got it.

WESLEY: What is it anyway?

WESTON: What do you mean, what is it? You can see it for yourself!

WESLEY: I know it's there, but I don't know what it is.

WESTON: You'll find out.

WESLEY: How?

WESTON: How do you poison coyotes?

WESLEY: Strychnine.

WESTON: How! Not what!

WESLEY: You put it in the belly of a dead lamb.

WESTON: Right. Now do you see?

WESLEY: *(after pause)* No.

WESTON: You're thick! You're really thick. *(pause)* You know I watched my old man move around. I watched him move through rooms. I watched him drive tractors, watched him watching baseball, watched him keeping out of the way of things. Out of the way of my mother. Away from my brothers. Watched him on the sidelines. Nobody saw him but me. Everybody was right there, but nobody saw him but me. He lived apart. Right in the midst of things and he lived apart. Nobody saw that.

Long pause.

WESLEY: You want an artichoke?

WESTON: No.

WESLEY: Who's the buyer?

WESTON: Some guy. Owns the "Alibi Club" downtown. Said he'll give me cash.

WESLEY: How much?

WESTON: Enough to get to Mexico. They can't touch me down there.

WESLEY: Who?

WESTON: None of your goddamn business! Why is it you always drive yourself under my skin when I'm around? Why is that?

WESLEY: We don't get along.

WESTON: Very smart! Very observant! What's the matter with you anyway? What're you doing around here?

WESLEY: I'm part of your offspring.

WESTON: Jesus, you're enough to drive a sane man crazy! You're like having an espionage spy around. Why are you watching me all the time?

WESTON looks at him. They stare at each other for a moment.

WESTON: You can watch me all you want to. You won't find out a thing.

WESLEY: Mom's trying to sell the place, too.

WESTON looks at him hard.

WESLEY: That's who the lawyer guy was. She's selling it through him.

WESTON stands and almost topples over.

WESTON: I'LL KILL HER! I'LL KILL BOTH OF THEM! Where's my gun? I had a gun here! A captured gun!

WESLEY: Take it easy.

WESTON: No, you take it easy! This whole thing has gone far enough! It's like living in a den of vipers! Spies! Conspiracies behind my back! I'M BEING TAKEN FOR A RIDE BY EVERY ONE OF YOU! I'm the one who works! I'm the one who brings home food! THIS IS MY HOUSE! I BOUGHT THIS HOUSE! AND I'M SELLING THIS HOUSE! AND I'M TAKING ALL THE MONEY BECAUSE IT'S OWED ME! YOU ALL OWE IT TO ME! EVERY LAST ONE OF YOU! SHE CAN'T STEAL THIS HOUSE AWAY FROM ME! IT'S MINE!

He falls into table and collapses on it. He tries to keep himself from falling to the floor. WESLEY *moves toward him.*

WESTON: JUST KEEP BACK! I'M NOT DYING, SO JUST KEEP BACK!

He struggles to pull himself up on the table, knocking off dirty laundry and EMMA's *charts.*

WESTON: I don't need a bed. I don't need anything from you! I'll stay right here. DON'T ANYONE TRY TO MOVE ME! NOBODY! I'm staying right here.

He finally gets on table so that he's lying flat out on it. He slowly goes unconscious. WESLEY *watches him from a safe distance.*

WESLEY: *(still standing there watching* WESTON*)* EMMA! *(no answer)* Oh, shit. Don't go out on me. Pop?

He moves toward WESTON *cautiously.* WESTON *comes to suddenly. Still lying on table.*

WESTON: DON'T GET TOO CLOSE!

WESLEY *jumps back.*

WESLEY: Wouldn't you rather be on the bed?

WESTON: I'm all right here. I'm numb. Don't feel a thing. Feels good to be numb.

WESLEY: We don't have to sell, you know. We could fix the place up.

WESTON: It's too late for that. I owe money.

WESLEY: I could get a job.

WESTON: You're gonna' have to.

WESLEY: I will. We could work this place by ourselves.

WESTON: Don't be stupid. There's not enough trees to make a living.

WESLEY: We could join that California Avocado Association. We could make a living that way.

WESTON: Get out of here! Get away from me!

WESLEY: Taylor can't buy this place without your signature.

WESTON: I'll kill him! If I have to, I'll kill myself along with him. I'll crash into him. I'll crash the Packard right into him. What's he look like? *(no answer from* WESLEY*)* WHAT'S HE LOOK LIKE?

WESLEY: Ordinary. Like a crook.

WESTON: *(still lying on table)* I'll find him. Then I'll find that punk who sold me that phony desert land. I'll track them all down. Every last one of them. Your mother too. I'll track her down and shoot them in their bed. In their hotel bed. I'll splatter their brains all over the vibrating bed. I'll drag him into the hotel lobby and slit his throat. I was in the war. I know how to kill. I was over there. I know how to do it. I've done it before. It's no big deal. You just make an adjustment. You convince yourself it's all right. That's all. It's easy. You just slaughter them. Easy.

WESLEY: You don't have to kill him. It's illegal, what he's doing.

WESTON: HE'S WITH MY WIFE! THAT'S ILLEGAL!

WESLEY: She'll come back.

WESTON: He doesn't know what he's dealing with. He thinks I'm just like him. Cowardly. Sniveling. Sneaking around. He's not counting on what's in my blood. He doesn't realize the explosiveness. We don't belong to the same class. He doesn't realize that. He's not counting on that. He's counting on me to use my reason. To talk things out. To have a conversation. To go out and have a business lunch and talk things over. He's not counting on murder. Murder's the farthest thing from his mind.

WESLEY: Just take it easy, Pop. Try to get some sleep.

WESTON: I am sleeping! I'm sleeping right here. I'm falling away. I was a flyer you know.

WESLEY: I know.

WESTON: I flew giant machines in the air. Giants! Bombers. What a sight. Over Italy. The Pacific. Islands. Giants. Oceans. Blue oceans.

Slowly WESTON *goes unconscious again as* WESLEY *watches him lying on table.* WESLEY *moves toward him slightly.*

WESLEY Pop? *(he moves in a little closer)* You asleep?

He turns downstage and looks at the wood and tools. He looks toward the refrigerator. ELLA *enters from down right carrying a bag of groceries. She stops when she sees* WESLEY. WESLEY *turns toward her.* ELLA *looks at* WESTON *lying on the table.*

ELLA: How long's he been here?

WESLEY: Just got here. Where have you been?

ELLA: *(crossing to refrigerator)* Out.

WESLEY: Where's your boyfriend?

ELLA: *(opening refrigerator)* Don't get insulting. Who put all these artichokes in here? What's going on?

WESLEY: Dad. He brought them back from the desert.

ELLA: What desert?

WESLEY: Hot Springs.

ELLA: Oh. He went down to look at his pathetic piece of property, I guess.

ELLA *sets the bag of groceries on the stove, then starts throwing the artichokes out onto the floor from the refrigerator.*

WESLEY: What are you doing?

ELLA: Throwing these out. It's a joke bringing artichokes back here when we're out of food.

WESLEY: How do you know about his desert property?

ELLA: I just know, that's all.

WESLEY: He told you? He never told me about it.

ELLA: I just happen to know he was screwed out of five hundred bucks. Let's leave it at that. Another shrewd business deal.

WESLEY: Taylor.

ELLA: *(turning to* WESLEY*)* What?

WESLEY: Taylor sold it to him right?

ELLA: Don't be ridiculous. *(turns back to refrigerator)*

WESLEY: How else would you know?

ELLA: He's not the only person in the world involved in real estate, you know.

WESLEY: He's been sneaking around here for months.

ELLA: Sneaking? He doesn't sneak. He comes right to the front door every time. He's very polite.

WESLEY: He's venomous.

ELLA: You're just jealous of him, that's all.

WESLEY: Don't give me that shit! It was him, wasn't it? I remember seeing him with his briefcase, wandering around the property.

ELLA: He's a speculator. That's his job. It's very important in this day and age to have someone who can accurately assess the value of land. To see its potential for the future.

She starts putting all the groceries from her bag into the refrigerator.

WESLEY: What exactly is he anyway? You told me he was a lawyer.

ELLA: I don't delve into his private affairs.

WESLEY: You don't, huh?

ELLA: Why are you so bitter all of a sudden?

WESLEY: It's not all of a sudden.

ELLA: I should think you'd be very happy to leave this place. To travel. To see other parts of the world.

WESLEY: I'm not leaving!

ELLA: Oh, yes you are. We all are. I've sealed the deal. It just needs one last little signature from me and its finished. Everything. The beat-up cars, the rusted out tractor, the moldy avocados, the insane horse, the demented sheep, the chickens, the whole entire shooting match. The whole collection. Over.

WESLEY: Then you're free I suppose?

ELLA: Exactly.

WESLEY: Are you going off with him?

ELLA: I wish you'd get your mind out of the garbage. I'm on my own.

WESLEY: Where'd you get the groceries?

ELLA: I picked them up.

WESLEY: *(after pause)* You know, you're too late. All your wheeling and dealing and you've missed the boat.

ELLA: *(closing refrigerator, turning to WESLEY)* What do you mean?

WESLEY: Dad's already sold it.

ELLA: You must be crazy! He couldn't sell a shoestring! Look at him!

Look at him lying there! Does that look like a man who could sell something as valuable as a piece of property? Does that look like competence to you? Take a look at him! He's pathetic!

WESLEY: I wouldn't wake him up if I were you.

ELLA: He can't hurt me now! I've got protection! If he lays a hand on me, I'll have him cut to ribbons! He's finished!

WESLEY: He's beat you to the punch and he doesn't even know it.

ELLA: Don't talk stupid! And get this junk out of here! I'm tired of looking at broken doors every time I come in here.

WESLEY: That's a new door.

ELLA: GET IT OUT OF HERE!

WESLEY: *(quietly)* I told you, you better not wake him up.

ELLA: I'm not tiptoeing around anymore. I'm finished with feeling like a foreigner in my own house. I'm not afraid of him anymore.

WESLEY: You should be. He's going to kill Taylor, you know.

ELLA: He's always going to kill somebody! Every day he's going to kill somebody!

WESLEY: He means it this time. He's got nothing to lose.

ELLA: That's for sure!

WESLEY: He's going to kill you, too.

ELLA *is silent for a while. They look at each other.*

ELLA: Do you know what this is? It's a curse. I can feel it. It's invisible but it's there. It's always there. It comes onto us like nighttime. Every day I can feel it. Every day I can see it coming. And it always comes. Repeats itself. It comes even when you do everything to stop it from coming. Even when you try to change it. And it goes back. Deep. It goes back and back to tiny little cells and genes. To atoms. To tiny little swimming things making up their minds without us. Plotting in the womb. Before that even. In the air. We're surrounded with it. It's bigger than government even. It goes forward too. We spread it. We pass it on. We inherit it and pass it down, and then pass it down again. It goes on and on like that without us.

ELLIS, *the owner of the "Alibi Club," enters from right and smiles at them. He is wearing a shiny yellow shirt, open at the collar, with a gold cross on a chain hanging from his neck. He's very burly, with tattooes all over his arms, tight-fitting pants, shiny shoes, lots of rings. He looks around and notices* WESTON *still lying on the table.*

ELLIS: A few too many "boiler-makers," huh? I keep telling him to go light, but it's like fartin' in the wind. *(laughs at his own joke)* You must be the wife and kids. Name's Ellis, I run the "Alibi Club," down in town. You must know it, huh?

No reaction from ELLA *and* WESLEY.

ELLIS: Well, the old man knows it, that's for sure. Down there pretty near every night. Regular steady. Always wondered where he slept. What's that smell in here?

WESLEY: Artichokes.

ELLIS: Artichokes, huh? Smells like stale piss. *(bursts out laughing; no reaction from others)* Never was big on vegetables myself. I'm a steak man. "Meat and blood," that's my motto. Keeps your bones hard as ivory.

ELLA: I know it may be asking a little bit too much to knock when there's no door to knock on, but do you always make a habit of just wandering into people's houses like you own them?

ELLIS: I do own it. *(pause)* That's right. Signed, sealed, and delivered. Got the cash right here.

He pulls out two big stacks of bills from his belt and waves them in the air.

ELLIS: Fifteen hundred in hard core mean green.

WESLEY: Fifteen hundred dollars! *(looks at* ELLA*)*

ELLIS: That's what he owes. That's the price we agreed on. Look, buddy, I didn't even have to show up here with it. Your old man's such a sap he signed the whole thing over to me without a dime even crossing the bar. I coulda' stung him easy. Just happens that I'm a man of honor.

ELLA: *(to* WESLEY*)* Get him out of here!

ELLIS: *(coldly to* WESLEY*)* I wouldn't try it, buddy boy.

ELLIS *and* WESLEY *stare at each other.* ELLIS *smiles.*

ELLIS: I've broken too many backs in my time, buddy. I'm not a hard man, but I'm strong as a bull calf, and I don't realize my own strength. It's terrible when that happens. You know? Before you know it, someone's hurt. Someone's lying there.

ELLA: This is a joke! You can't buy a piece of property from an alcoholic! He's not responsible for his actions!

ELLIS: He owns it, doesn't he?

ELLA: I OWN IT!

ELLIS: That's not what he told me.

ELLA: I own it and it's already been sold, so just get the hell out!

ELLIS: Well, I've got the deed right here. *(he pulls deed out)* Right
here. Signed, sealed, and delivered. How do you explain that?

ELLA: It's not legal!

WESLEY: Who does he owe money to?

ELLIS: Oh, well, now I don't stick my nose where it doesn't belong. I
just happen to know that he owes to some pretty hard fellas.

WESLEY: Fifteen hundred bucks?

ELLIS: That's about the size of it.

ELLA: Wake him up! We'll get to the bottom of this.

WESLEY: *(to ELLA)* Are you crazy? If he sees you here he'll go off the
deep end.

ELLA: *(going to WESTON and shaking him)* I'll wake him up, then!

WESLEY: Oh, Jesus!

WESTON *remains unconscious.* ELLA *keeps shaking him violently.*

ELLA: Weston! Weston get up! Weston!

ELLIS: I've seen some hard cases in my time, but he's dedicated. That's
for sure. Drinks like a Canadian. Flat out.

WESLEY: You say these guys are tough? What does he owe them for?

ELLIS: Look, buddy, he borrows all the time. He's a borrowing fool. It
could be anything. Payments on a car. Land in the desert. He's always got some fool scheme going. He's just let it slide too long
this time, that's all.

WESLEY: What'll they do to him?

ELLIS: Nothing now. I've saved his hide. You should be kissing my
feet.

ELLA: WESTON! GET UP!

She is tiring from shaking him. WESTON *remains unconscious.*

WESLEY: They'd kill him for fifteen hundred bucks?

ELLIS: Who said anything about killing? Did I say anything about killing?

WESLEY: No.

ELLIS: Then don't jump to conclusions. You can get in trouble that
way.

WESLEY: Maybe you should deliver it to them.

ELLIS: Look, I've carried the ball this far, now he's gonna' have to do
the rest. I'm not his bodyguard.

WESLEY: What if he takes off with it?

ELLIS: That's his problem.

WESLEY: Give it to me.

ELLIS: What?

WESLEY: The money. I'll deliver it.

ELLA: *(leaving WESTON)* Wesley, don't you touch that money! It's tainted! Don't you touch it!

    ELLIS *and* WESLEY *look at each other.*

WESLEY: You've got the deed. I'm his oldest son.

ELLA: You're his only son!

WESLEY: Just give it to me. I'll take care of it.

ELLIS: *(handing money to WESLEY)* All right, buddy. Just don't go off half-cocked. That's a lot a' spendin' change for a young man.

    WESLEY *takes it.*

ELLA: Wesley, it's illegal! You'll be an accomplice!

WESLEY: *(to ELLIS)* Where do I find them?

ELLIS: That's your business, buddy. I'm just the buyer.

    ELLIS *walks around, looking over the place.* ELLA *crosses to* WES‑ LEY *as* WESLEY *counts the money.*

ELLA: Wesley, you give me that money! It doesn't belong to you! Give it to me!

WESLEY: *(looking at her coldly)* There's not enough here to go to Europe on, Mom.

ELLIS: I was thinkin' of turning this place into a steak house. What do you think? Make a nice little steak house, don't you think?

WESLEY: *(still counting money)* Sure.

ELLIS: People stop in off the highway, have a steak, a martini, afternoon cocktail, look out over the valley. Nice and peaceful. Might even put in a Japanese garden out front. Have a few goldfish swimming around. Maybe an eight-hole pitch-and-putt course right out there, too. Place is full of potential.

ELLA: Wesley!

    TAYLOR *appears with attaché case stage right.* ELLA *turns and sees him.* WESLEY *keeps counting money.*

TAYLOR: Oh. I'm sorry. I didn't realize you had company. *(to ELLA)* I've got the final draft drawn up.

    TAYLOR *crosses toward table, sees* WESTON *lying on it, stops, looks for a place to set down his attaché case.*

ELLA: *(to TAYLOR)* It's too late.

TAYLOR: Excuse me? What's too late?

ELLA: The whole thing. Weston's sold it.

TAYLOR: That's silly. I've got the final draft right here in my case. All it needs is your signature.

ELLIS: Who's this character?

ELLA: *(to* TAYLOR*)* He sold it for fifteen hundred dollars.

TAYLOR: *(laughs)* That's impossible.

ELLA: There it is right there! Wesley's got it in his hands! Wesley's taking it!

TAYLOR: He can't sell this piece of property. He's incompetent. We've already been through that.

ELLIS: *(crossing to* TAYLOR*)* Hey, listen, buddy. I don't know what your story is, but I suggest you get the fuck outa' here because this is my deal here. Understand? This is my little package.

TAYLOR: *(to* ELLA*)* Who's this?

ELLA: He's the buyer.

WESLEY: *(to* TAYLOR*)* Too slow on the trigger, Taylor. Took it right out from under you, didn't he?

TAYLOR: Well, it's simply a matter of going to court then. He doesn't have a leg to stand on. Legally he's a ward of the state. He can't sell land.

ELLIS: *(waving deed)* Look, I checked this deed out at city hall, and everything's above board.

TAYLOR: The deed has nothing to do with it. I'm speaking of psychological responsibility.

WESLEY: Does that apply to buying the same as selling?

TAYLOR: *(to* EMMA*)* What's he talking about?

ELLA: Nothing. Wesley, you give that money back!

WESLEY: Does that apply to buying dried up land in the middle of the desert with no water and a hundred miles from the nearest gas pump?

TAYLOR: *(to* WESLEY*)* I think you're trying to divert the focus of the situation here. The point is that your father's psychologically and emotionally unfit to be responsible for his own actions, and, therefore, any legal negotiations issuing from him cannot be held binding. This can be easily proven in a court of law. We have first-hand evidence that he's prone to fits of violence. His license for driving has been revoked, and yet he still keeps driving. He's unable to get insurance. He's unable to hold a steady job. He's absent from his home ninety percent of the time. He has a jail record. It's an open and shut case.

ELLIS: *(to* TAYLOR*)* What are you anyway? A lawyer or something?

Where do you get off talkin' like that in my house!

ELLA: IT'S NOT YOUR HOUSE! THAT'S WHAT HE'S SAYING! CAN'T YOU LISTEN? DON'T YOU HAVE A BRAIN IN YOUR HEAD?

ELLIS: Listen, lady, I sell booze. You know what I mean? A lot a' weird stuff goes on in my bar, but I never seen anything as weird as this character. I never seen anything I couldn't handle.

WESLEY: You best take off, Taylor, before it all catches up to you.

TAYLOR: I refuse to be intimidated any further! I put myself out on a limb for this project and all I'm met with is resistance!

ELLA: I'm not resisting.

TAYLOR: *(to* WESLEY*)* You may not realize it, but there's corporations behind me! Executive management! People of influence. People with ambition who realize the importance of investing in the future. Of building this country up, not tearing it down. You people carry on as though the whole world revolved around your petty little existence. As though everything was holding its breath, waiting for your next move. Well, it's not like that! Nobody's waiting! Everything's going forward! Everything's going ahead without you! The wheels are in motion. There's nothing you can do to turn it back. The only thing you can do is cooperate. To play ball. To become part of us. To invest in the future of this great land. Because if you don't, you'll all be left behind. Every last one of you. Left high and dry. And there'll be nothing to save you. Nothing and nobody.

A policeman appears stage right in highway patrol gear.

SERGEANT MALCOLM: Uh—excuse me. Mrs. Tate?

ELLA: Yes.

MALCOLM: Are you Mrs. Tate?

ELLA: Yes, I am.

MALCOLM: I'm sorry. I would have knocked but there's no door.

ELLA: That's all right.

TAYLOR *begins to move to stage left nervously.* WESLEY *watches him.*

MALCOLM: I'm Sergeant Malcolm, Highway Patrol.

ELLA: Well, what is it?

MALCOLM: You have a daughter, Emma Tate?

ELLA: Yes. What's wrong?

MALCOLM: She's been apprehended.

ELLA: What for?

MALCOLM: It seems she rode her horse through a bar downtown and shot the place full of holes with a rifle.

ELLA: What?

ELLIS: What bar?

MALCOLM: Place called the "Alibi Club." I wasn't there at the time, but they picked her up.

ELLIS: That's my club!

MALCOLM: *(to ELLIS)* Are you the owner?

ELLIS: THAT'S MY CLUB!

MALCOLM: Are you Mr. Ellis?

ELLIS: What kind of damages?

MALCOLM: Well, we'll have to get an estimate, but it's pretty severe. Shot the whole place up. Just lucky there was no one in it at the time.

ELLIS: *(to WESLEY)* Give me that money back!

ELLIS *grabs money out of* WESLEY's *hands.* TAYLOR *sneaks off stage left.*

WESLEY: *(to cop)* Hey! He's getting away! That guy's a crook!

MALCOLM: What guy?

WESLEY: *(moving toward stage left)* That guy! That guy who just ran out of here! He's an embezzler! A confidence man! Whatever you call it. He sold my old man phony land!

MALCOLM: That's not within my jurisdiction.

ELLIS: *(to ELLA)* I know he sent her down there. I wasn't born yesterday, ya' know! He's crazy if he thinks he can put that kind of muscle on me! What does he think he is anyway? I'm gonna' sue him blind for this! I'm gonna' take the shirt right off his back! I was trying to do him a favor! I was stickin' my neck out for him! You just tell him when he wakes up out of his stupor that he's in bigger trouble than he thinks! He ain't seen nothin' yet! You tell him. *(starts to leave)* And just remember that I own this place. It's mine! So don't try any more funny stuff. I got friends in high places, too. I deal directly with them all the time. Ain't that right, Sarge?

MALCOLM: I don't know about that. I'm here on other business.

ELLIS: *(to ELLA)* You just tell him! I'll teach him to mess around with me!

ELLIS *exits. Right.*

ELLA: *(to cop)* He's taking our money!

MALCOLM: Look, lady, your daughter's in jail. I don't know about any of this other stuff. I'm here about your daughter.

WESLEY *runs off right.* ELLA *yells after him.*

ELLA: WESLEY! WHERE ARE YOU GOING?

WESLEY'S VOICE: *(off)* I'M GONNA' GET THAT MONEY BACK!

ELLA: IT'S NOT YOUR MONEY! COME BACK HERE! WESLEY!
(she stops and looks at MALCOLM*)* Everybody's running off. Even
Mr. Taylor. Did you hear the way he was talking to me? He was
talking to me all different. All different than before. He wasn't nice
at all.

MALCOLM: Mrs. Tate, what are we going to do about your daughter?

ELLA: I don't know. What should we do?

MALCOLM: Well, she has to stay in overnight, and if you don't want her
back home she can be arraigned in juvenile court.

ELLA: We're all leaving here though. Everyone has to leave. She can't
come home. There wouldn't be anyone here.

MALCOLM: You'll have to sign a statement then.

ELLA: What statement?

MALCOLM: Giving permission for the arraignment.

ELLA: All right.

MALCOLM: You'll have to come down with me unless you have a car.

ELLA: I have a car. *(pause)* Everyone's run away.

MALCOLM: Will you be all right by yourself?

ELLA: I am by myself.

MALCOLM: Yes, I know. Will you be all right or do you want to come
with me in the patrol car?

ELLA: I'll be all right.

MALCOLM: I'll wait for you down at the station then.

MALCOLM *exits.* ELLA *just stands there.*

ELLA: *(to herself)* Everybody ran away.

WESTON *sits up with a jolt on the table.* ELLA *jumps. They look at
each other for a moment, then* ELLA *runs off stage.* WESTON *just
stays sitting up on the table. He looks around the stage. He gets to
his feet and tries to steady himself. He walks toward the refrigerator and kicks the artichokes out of his way. He opens refrigerator and locks in. Lights slowly fade to black with* WESTON
standing there looking into refrigerator.

ACT 3

SCENE:

Same set. Stage is cleared of wood and tools and artichokes. Fence enclosure with the lamb inside is back, center stage. Pot of fresh coffee heating on the stove. All the laundry has been washed and WESTON *is at the table to stage left folding it and stacking it in neat piles. He's minus his overcoat, baseball cap, and tennis shoes and wears a fresh clean shirt, new pants, shined shoes, and has had a shave. He seems sober now and in high spirits compared to before. The lamb is heard "baaing" in the dark as the lights slowly come up on* WESTON *at the table.*

WESTON: *(to lamb as he folds clothes)* There's worse things than maggots ya' know. Much worse. Maggots go away if they're properly attended to. If you got someone around who can take the time. Who can recognize the signs. Who brings ya' in out of the cold, wet pasture and sets ya' up in a cushy situation like this. No lamb ever had it better. It's warm. It's free of draft, now that I got the new door up. There's no varmints. No coyotes. No eagles. No— *(looks over at lamb)* Should I tell ya' something about eagles? This is a true story. This is a true account. One time I was out in the fields doing the castrating, which is a thing that has to be done. It's not my favorite job, but it's something that just has to be done. I'd set myself up right beside the lean-to out there. Just a little roof-shelter thing out there with my best knife, some boiling water, and a hot iron to cauterize with. It's a bloody job on all accounts. Well, I had maybe a dozen spring ram lambs to do out there. I had 'em all gathered up away from the ewes in much the same kinda' set up as you got right there. Similar fence structure like that. It was a crisp, bright type a' morning. Air was real thin and you could see all the way out across the pasture land. Frost was still well bit down on the stems, right close to the ground. Maybe a couple a' crows and the ewes carrying on about their babies, and that was the only sound. Well, I was working away out there when I feel this shadow cross over me. I could feel it even before I saw it take shape on the ground. Felt like the way it does when the clouds move across the sun. Huge and black and cold like. So I look up, half expecting a buzzard or maybe a red-tail, but what hits me across the eyes is this giant eagle. Now I'm a flyer and I'm used to aeronautics, but this sucker was doin' some downright suicidal antics. Real low down like he's coming in for a landing or something, then changing his mind and pulling straight up again and sailing out away from me. So I watch him going small for a while, then turn back to my work. I do a couple more lambs maybe, and the same thing happens. Except this time he's even lower yet. Like I could almost feel his feathers on my back. I could hear his sound real clear. A giant bird. His wings made a kind of cracking noise. Then up he went again. I watched him longer this time, trying to figure out his intentions. Then I put the whole thing together. He was after those testes. Those fresh little remnants of manlihood. So I decided to oblige him this time and threw a few a' them on top a' the shed roof. Then I just went back to work again, pretending to be preoccupied. I was waitin' for him this time though. I was listening hard for him, knowing he'd be comin', in from behind me. I was watchin' the ground for any sign of blackness. Nothing happened for about three more lambs, when all of a sudden he comes. Just like a thunder clap. Blam! He's down on that shed roof with his talons taking half the tar paper with him, wings whippin' the air, screaming like a bred mare then climbing straight back up into the sky again. I had to stand up on that one. Somethin' brought me straight up off the ground and I started yellin' my head off. I don't know why it was comin' outa' me but I was standing there with this icy feeling up my backbone and just yelling my fool head off. Cheerin' for that eagle. I'd never felt like that since the first day I went up in a B-49. After a while I sat down again and went on workin'. And every time I cut a lamb I'd throw those balls up on top a' the shed roof. And every time he'd come down like the Cannonball Express on that roof. And every time I got that feeling.

WESLEY *appears stage right with his face and hands bloody.*

WESLEY: Then what?

WESTON: Were you listening to me?

WESLEY: What happens next?

WESTON: I was tellin' it to the lamb!

WESLEY: Tell it to me.

WESTON: You've already heard it. What happened to your face anyway?

WESLEY: Ran into a brick wall.

WESTON: Why don't ya' go clean up.

WESLEY: What happens next?

WESTON: I ain't tellin' it again!

WESLEY: Then I ain't cleaning up!

WESTON: What's the matter with you anyway? Are you drunk or something?

WESLEY: I was trying to get your money back.

WESTON: What money?

WESLEY: From Ellis.

WESTON: That punk. Don't waste your time. He's a punk crook.

WESLEY: He ran off with your money. And he's got the house too.

WESTON: I've got the house! I've decided to stay.

WESLEY: What?

WESTON: I'm stayin'. I finished the new door. Did you notice?

WESLEY: No.

WESTON: Well, you shoulda' noticed. You walked right through it. What's the matter with you? I'm fixin' the whole place up. I decided.

WESLEY: You're fixing it up?

WESTON: Yeah. That's what I said. What's so unusual about that? This could be a great place if somebody'd take some interest in it. Why don't you have some coffee and clean yourself up a little. You look like forty miles a' rough road. Go ahead. There's fresh coffee on the stove.

WESLEY *crosses slowly to the stove and looks at the coffee.*

WESTON: I got up and took a walk around the place. Bright and early. Don't think I've walked around the whole place for a couple a' years. I walked around and a funny thing started happening to me.

WESLEY: *(looking at coffee)* What?

WESTON: I started wondering who this was walking around in the orchard at six-thirty in the morning. It didn't feel like me. It was some character in a dark overcoat and tennis shoes and a baseball cap and stickers comin' out of his face. It didn't feel like the owner of a piece a' property as nice as this. Then I started to wonder who the owner was. I mean if I didn't feel like the owner, then who was the owner? I started wondering if the real owner was gonna' pop up out of nowhere and blast my brains out for trespassing. I started feeling like I should be running or hiding or something. Like I shouldn't be there in this kind of a neighborhood. Not that it's fancy or anything, but it's peaceful. It's real peaceful up here. Especially at that time a' the morning. Then it struck me that I actually was the owner. That somehow it was me and I was actually the one walking on my own piece of land. And that gave me a great feeling.

WESLEY: *(staring at coffee)* It did?

WESTON: Yeah. So I came back in here, and the first thing I did was I took all my old clothes off and walked around here naked. Just walked through the whole damn house in my birthday suit. Tried to get the feeling of it really being me in my own house. It was like peeling off a whole person. A whole stranger. Then I walked straight in and made myself a hot bath. Hot as I could stand it. Just sank down into it and let it sink deep into the skin. Let it fog up all the windows and the glass on the medicine cabinet. Then I let all the water drain out, and then I filled the whole tub up again but this time with ice cold water. Just sat there and let it creep up on me until I was in up to my neck. Then I got out and took a shave and found myself some clean clothes. Then I came in here and fixed myself a big old breakfast of ham and eggs.

WESLEY: Ham and eggs?

WESTON: Yeah. Somebody left a whole mess a' groceries in the ice box. Surprised the hell outa' me. Just like Christmas. Just like somebody knew I was gonna' be reborn this morning or something. Couldn't believe my eyes.

WESLEY *goes to refrigerator and looks in.*

WESTON: Then I started makin' coffee and found myself doing all this stuff I used to do. Like I was coming back to my life after a long time a' being away.

WESLEY: *(staring in refrigerator)* Mom brought this stuff.

WESTON: Then I started doing the laundry. All the laundry. I went around the house and found all the piles of dirty clothes I could get my hands on. Emma's, Ella's, even some a' yours. Some a' your socks. Found everybody's clothes. And every time I bent down to pick up somebody's clothes I could feel that person like they were right there in the room. Like the clothes were still attached to the person they belonged to. And I felt like I knew every single one of you. Every one. Like I knew you through the flesh and blood. Like our bodies were connected and we could never escape that. But I didn't feel like escaping. I felt like it was a good thing. It was good to be connected by blood like that. That a family wasn't just a social thing. It was an animal thing. It was a reason of nature that we were all together under the same roof. Not that we had to be but that we were supposed to be. And I started feeling glad about it. I started feeling full of hope.

WESLEY: *(staring in refrigerator)* I'm starving.

WESTON: *(crossing to* WESLEY) Look, go take a bath and get that crap off your face, and I'll make ya' some ham and eggs. What is that crap anyway?

WESLEY: Blood.

WESTON: He took a few swipes at ya', huh? Well go wash it off and come back in here. Go on!

WESLEY: *(turning to* WESTON*)* He wouldn't give me the money, you know.

WESTON: So what. The guy's a knuckle-head. Don't have the brains God gave a chicken. Now go in there and clean up before *I* start swingin' on you.

WESLEY exits off left. WESTON *starts taking ham and eggs out of refrigerator and fixing a breakfast at the stove. He yells off stage to* WESLEY *as he cooks.*

WESTON: *(yelling)* So I was thinkin' about that avocado deal you were talkin' about before! You know, joining up with the "Growers Association" and everything! And I was thinkin' it might not be such a bad deal after all! I mean we don't have to hire Chicanos or nothin'! We could pick 'em ourselves and sell 'em direct to the company! How 'bout that idea! Cut down on the overhead! That tractor's still workin', isn't it? I mean the motor's not seized up or nothin', and we got plenty a' good pressure in the irrigation! I checked it this morning! Water's blastin' right through those pipes! Wouldn't take much to get the whole operation goin' full-tilt again! I'll resell that piece a' land out there! That'll give us somethin' to get us started! Somebody somewhere's gonna' want a good piece a' desert land! It's prime location even if it isn't being developed! Only a three-hour drive from Palm Springs, and you know what that's like! You know the kinda' people who frequent that place! One of 'em's bound to have some extra cash!

ELLA enters from stage right. She looks haggard and tired. She stands there looking at WESTON, *who keeps cooking the eggs. Then she looks at the lamb.* WESTON *knows she's there but doesn't look at her.*

ELLA: *(after pause)* What's that lamb doing back in here?

WESTON: I got him back on his feet. It was nip and tuck there for a while. Didn't think he'd pull through. Maggots clear up into the small intestine.

ELLA: *(crossing to table)* Spare me the details.

She pulls off her white gloves and sits exhausted into the chair at stage right. She looks at the piles of clean laundry.

WESTON: *(still cooking)* Where you been anyway?

ELLA: Jail.

WESTON: Oh, they finally caught ya', huh? *(chuckles)*

ELLA: Very humorous.

WESTON: You want some breakfast? I was just fixin' something up for Wes, here.

ELLA: You're cooking?

WESTON: Yeah. What's it look like?

ELLA: Who did all this laundry?

WESTON: Yours truly.

ELLA: Are you having a nervous breakdown or what?

WESTON: Can't a man do his own laundry?

ELLA: As far as I know he can.

WESTON: Even did some a' yours too.

ELLA: Gee, thanks.

WESTON: Well, I coulda' just left it. I was doin' a load of my own, so I thought I'd throw everybody else's in to boot.

ELLA: I'm very grateful.

WESTON: So where you been? Off with that fancy lawyer?

ELLA: I've been to jail, like I said.

WESTON: Come on. What, on a visit? They throw you in the drunk tank? Out with it.

ELLA: I was visiting your daughter.

WESTON: Oh, yeah? What'd they nab her for?

ELLA: Possession of firearms. Malicious vandalism. Breaking and entering. Assault. Violation of equestrian regulations. You name it.

WESTON: Well, she always was a fireball.

ELLA: Part of the inheritance, right?

WESTON: Right. Direct descendant.

ELLA: Well, I'm glad you've found a way of turning shame into a source of pride.

WESTON: What's shameful about it? Takes courage to get charged with all that stuff. It's not everyone her age who can run up a list of credits like that.

ELLA: That's for sure.

WESTON: Could you?

ELLA: Don't be ridiculous! I'm not self-destructive. Doesn't run in my family line.

WESTON: That's right. I never thought about it like that. You're the only one who doesn't have it. Only us.

ELLA: Oh, so now I'm the outsider.

WESTON: Well, it's true. You come from a different class of people. Gentle. Artists. They were all artists, weren't they?

ELLA: My grandfather was a pharmacist.

WESTON: Well, scientists then. Members of the professions. Professionals. Nobody raised their voice.

ELLA: That's bad?

WESTON: No. Just different. That's all. Just different.

ELLA: Are we waxing philosophical over our eggs now? Is that the idea? Sobered up over night, have we? Awoken to a brand-new morning? What is this crap! I've been down there all night trying to pull Emma back together again and I come back to Mr. Hyde! Mr. "Goody Two-Shoes!" Mister Mia Copa himself! Well, you can kiss off with that crap because I'm not buying it!

WESTON: Would you like some coffee?

ELLA: NO, I DON'T WANT ANY GODDAMN COFFEE! AND GET THAT SON-OF-A-BITCHING SHEEP OUT OF MY KITCHEN!!

WESTON: *(staying cool)* You've picked up on the language okay, but your inflection's off.

ELLA: There's nothing wrong with my inflection!

WESTON: Something doesn't ring true about it. Something deep in the voice. At the heart of things.

ELLA: Oh, you are really something. How can you accuse me of not measuring up to your standards! You're a complete washout!

WESTON: It's got nothing to do with standards. It's more like fate.

ELLA: Oh, knock it off, would you? I'm exhausted.

WESTON: Try the table. Nice and hard. It'll do wonders for you.

ELLA: *(suddenly soft)* The table?

WESTON: Yeah. Just stretch yourself out. You'll be amazed. Better than any bed.

ELLA *looks at the table for a second, then starts pushing all the clean laundry off it onto the floor. She pulls herself up onto it and stretches out on it.* WESTON *goes on cooking with his back to her. She watches him as she lies there.*

WESTON: And when you wake up I'll have a great big breakfast of ham and eggs, ready and waiting. You'll feel like a million bucks. You'll wonder why you spent all those years in bed, once you feel that table. That table will deliver you.

WESLEY *wanders on stage from stage left, completely naked, his hair wet. He looks dazed.* WESTON *pays no attention but goes on preparing the breakfast and talking as* WESLEY *wanders upstage and stares at* ELLA. *She looks at him but doesn't react. He turns downstage and looks at* WESTON. *He looks at lamb and crosses down to it. He bends over and picks it up, then carries it off stage right.* WESTON *goes on cooking and talking.* ELLA *stays on table.*

WESTON: That's the trouble with too much comfort, you know? Makes you forget where you come from. Makes you lose touch. You think you're making headway but you're losing all the time. You're falling behind more and more. You're going into a trance that you'll never come back from. You're being hypnotized. Your body's being mesmerized. You go into a coma. That's why you need a hard table once in a while to bring you back. A good hard table to bring you back to life.

ELLA: *(still on table, sleepily)* You should have been a preacher.

WESTON: You think so?

ELLA: Great voice you have. Deep. Resonates.

WESTON: *(putting eggs on plate)* I'm not a public person.

ELLA: I'm so exhausted.

WESTON: You just sleep.

ELLA: You should have seen that jail, Weston.

WESTON: I have.

ELLA: Oh, that's right. How could you ever sleep in a place like that?

WESTON: If you're numb enough you don't feel a thing. *(he yells off stage to* WESLEY) WES! YOUR BREAKFAST'S READY!

ELLA: He just went out.

WESTON: What?

ELLA: He just walked out stark naked with that sheep under his arm.

WESTON *looks at fence enclosure, sees lamb gone. He's still holding plate.*

WESTON: Where'd he go?

ELLA: Outside.

WESTON: *(crossing right, carrying plate)* WES! GODDAMNIT, YOUR BREAKFAST'S READY!

WESTON *exits carrying plate off stage right.* ELLA *tries to keep her eyes open, still on table.*

ELLA: *(to herself)* Nothing surprises me any more.

She slowly falls asleep on table. Nothing happens for a while. Then WESTON *comes back on from right still carrying plate.* ELLA *stays asleep on table.*

WESTON: *(crossing to stove)* He's not out there. Wouldn't ya' know it? Just when it's ready, he walks out. *(turning to* ELLA*)* Why'd he take the lamb? That lamb needs to be kept warm. *(sees that* ELLA's *sound asleep)* Great. *(turns and sets plate down on stove; looks at food)* Might as well eat it myself. A double breakfast. Why not? *(he starts eating off the plate, talks to himself)* Can't expect the thing to get well if it's not kept warm. *(he turns upstage again and looks at* ELLA *sleeping, then turns back to the plate of food)* Always was best at talkin' to myself. Always was the best thing. Nothing like it. Keeps ya' company at least.

WESLEY *enters from right dressed in* WESTON's *baseball cap, overcoat, and tennis shoes. He stands there.* WESTON *looks at him.* ELLA *sleeps.*

WESTON: What in the hell's goin' on with you? I was yellin' for you just now. Didn't you hear me?

WESLEY: *(staring at* WESTON*)* No.

WESTON: Your breakfast was all ready. Now it's cold. I've eaten half of it already. Almost half gone.

WESLEY: *(blankly)* You can have it.

WESTON: What're you doin' in those clothes anyway?

WESLEY: I found them.

WESTON: I threw them out! What's got into you? You go take a bath and then put on some old bum's clothes that've been thrown-up in, pissed in, and God knows what all in?

WESLEY: They fit me.

WESTON: I can't fathom you, that's for sure. What'd you do with that lamb?

WESLEY: Butchered it.

WESTON: *(turning away from him, disgusted)* I swear to God. *(pause, then turning to* WESLEY*)* WHAT'D YA' BUTCHER THE DUMB THING FOR!

WESLEY: We need some food.

WESTON: THE ICE BOX IS CRAMMED FULL A' FOOD!

WESLEY *crosses quickly to refrigerator, opens it, and starts pulling all kinds of food out and eating it ravenously.* WESTON *watches him, a little afraid of* WESLEY's *state.*

WESTON: WHAT'D YA' GO AND BUTCHER IT FOR? HE WAS GETTING BETTER! *(watches* WESLEY *eating hungrily)* What's a' matter with you, boy? I made ya' a big breakfast. Why didn't ya' eat that? What's the matter with you?

WESTON *moves cautiously, away from* WESLEY *to stage right.* WES-
LEY *keeps eating, throwing half-eaten food to one side and then
digging into more. He groans slightly as he eats.*

WESTON: *(to* WESLEY*)* Look, I know I ignored some a' the chores
around the place and you had to do it instead a' me. But I brought
you some artichokes back, didn't I? Didn't I do that? I didn't have
to do that. I went outa' my way. I saw the sign on the highway and
drove two miles outa' my way just to bring you back some artichokes. *(pause, as he looks at* WESLEY *eating; he glances nervously up at* ELLA, *then back to* WESLEY*)* You couldn't be all that
starving! We're not that bad off, goddamnit! I've seen starving
people in my time, and we're not that bad off! *(pause, no reaction
from* WESLEY, *who continues to eat ravenously)* You just been
spoiled, that's all! This is a paradise for a young person! There's
kids your age who'd give their eyeteeth to have an environment like
this to grow up in! You've got everything! Everything! Opportunity
is glaring you in the teeth here! *(turns toward* ELLA*)* ELLA! ELLA,
WAKE UP! *(no reaction from* ELLA; *turns back to* WESLEY, *still
eating)* If this is supposed to make me feel guilty, it's not working!
It's not working because I don't have to pay for my past now! Not
now! Not after this morning! All that's behind me now! YOU UN-
DERSTAND ME? IT'S ALL OVER WITH BECAUSE I'VE
BEEN REBORN! I'M A WHOLE NEW PERSON NOW! I'm a
whole new person.

WESLEY *stops eating suddenly and turns to* WESTON.

WESLEY: *(coldly)* They're going to kill you.

WESTON: *(pauses)* Who's going to kill me! What're you talking about!
Nobody's going to kill me!

WESLEY: I couldn't get the money.

WESTON: What money?

WESLEY: Ellis.

WESTON: So what?

WESLEY: You owe it to them.

WESTON: Owe it to who? I don't remember anything. All that's over
with now.

WESLEY: No, it's not. It's still there. Maybe you've changed, but you
still owe them.

WESTON: I can't remember. Must've borrowed some for the car pay-
ment. Can't remember it.

WESLEY: They remember it.

WESTON: So, I'll get it to them. It's not that drastic.

WESLEY: How? Ellis has the house and everything now.

WESTON: How does he have the house? This is my house!

WESLEY: You signed it over.

WESTON: I never signed anything!

WESLEY: You were drunk.

WESTON: SHUT UP!

WESLEY: How're you going to pay them?

WESTON: *(pause)* I can sell that land.

WESLEY: It's phony land. The guy's run off to Mexico.

WESTON: What guy?

WESLEY: Taylor. The lawyer. The lawyer friend of Mom's.

WESTON: *(pause, looks at ELLA sleeping, then back to WESLEY)* Same guy?

WESLEY: Same guy. Ripped us all off.

WESTON: This isn't right. I was on a whole new track. I was getting right up on top of it all.

WESLEY: They've got it worked out so you can't.

WESTON: I was ready for a whole new attack. This isn't right!

WESLEY: They've moved in on us like a creeping disease. We didn't even notice.

WESTON: I just built a whole new door and everything. I washed all the laundry. I cleaned up all the artichokes. I started over.

WESLEY: You better run.

WESTON: Run? What do you mean, run? I can't run!

WESLEY: Take the Packard and get out of here.

WESTON: I can't run out on everything.

WESLEY: Why not?

WESTON: 'CAUSE THIS IS WHERE I SETTLED DOWN! THIS IS WHERE THE LINE ENDED! RIGHT HERE! I MIGRATED TO THIS SPOT! I GOT NOWHERE TO GO TO! THIS IS IT!

WESLEY: Take the Packard.

WESTON *stands there for a while. He looks around, trying to figure a way out.*

WESTON: *(after pause)* I remember now. I was in hock. I was in hock up to my elbows. See, I always figured on the future. I banked on it. I was banking on it getting better. It couldn't get worse, so I figured it'd just get better. I figured that's why everyone wants you to buy things. Buy refrigerators. Buy cars, houses, lots, invest. They wouldn't be so generous if they didn't figure you had it comin' in. At some point it had to be comin' in. So I went along with it. Why not borrow if you know it's coming in. Why not make a touch here and there. They all want you to borrow anyhow. Banks, car lots, investors. The whole thing's geared to invisible money. You never hear the sound of change any more. It's all plastic shuffling back and forth. It's all in everybody's heads. So I figured if that's the case, why not take advantage of it? Why not go in debt for a few grand if all it is is numbers? If it's all an idea and nothing's really there, why not take advantage? So I just went along with it, that's all. I just played ball.

WESLEY: You better go.

Pause, as WESTON *looks at* ELLA *sleeping.*

WESTON: Same guy, huh? She musta' known about it, too. She musta' thought I left her.

WESTON *turns and looks at* WESLEY. *Silence.*

WESLEY: You did.

WESTON: I just went off for a little while. Now and then. I couldn't stand it here. I couldn't stand the idea that everything would stay the same. That every morning it would be the same. I kept looking for it out there somewhere. I kept trying to piece it together. The jumps. I couldn't figure out the jumps. From being born, to growing up, to droppin' bombs, to having kids, to hittin' bars, to this. It all turned on me somehow. It all turned around on me. I kept looking for it out there somewhere. And all the time it was right inside this house.

WESLEY: They'll be coming for you here. They know where you live now.

WESTON: Where should I go?

WESLEY: How 'bout Mexico?

WESTON: Mexico? Yeah. That's where everyone escapes to, right? It's full of escape artists down there. I could go down there and get lost. I could disappear. I could start a whole new life down there.

WESLEY: Maybe.

WESTON: I could find that guy and get my money back. That real estate guy. What's his name?

WESLEY: Taylor.

WESTON: Yeah, Taylor. He's down there too, right? I could find him.

WESLEY: Maybe.

WESTON: *(looking over at* ELLA *again)* I can't believe she knew and still went off with him. She musta' thought I was dead or something. She musta' thought I was never coming back.

WESTON *moves toward* ELLA, *then stops. He looks at* WESLEY, *then turns and exits off right.* WESLEY *just stands there.* WESLEY *bends down and picks some scraps of food up off the floor and eats them very slowly. He looks at the empty lamb pen.* EMMA *enters from left, dressed as she was in Act 2. She crosses into center, looking in the direction of where* WESTON *went.* WESLEY *seems dazed as he slowly chews the food.* ELLA *stays asleep on table.* EMMA *carries a riding crop. She taps her leg with it as she looks off right.*

EMMA: Mexico, huh? He won't last a day down there. They'll find him easy. Stupid going to Mexico. That's the first place they'll look. *(to* WESLEY*)* What're you eating?

WESLEY: Food.

EMMA: Off the floor? You'll wind up just like him. Diseased!

WESLEY: *(dazed)* I'm hungry.

EMMA: You're sick! What're you doing with his clothes on? Are you supposed to be the head of the family now or something? The Big Cheese? Daddy Bear?

WESLEY: I tried his remedy, but it didn't work.

EMMA: He's got a remedy?

WESLEY: *(half to himself)* I tried taking a hot bath. Hot as I could stand it. Then freezing cold. Then walking around naked. But it didn't work. Nothing happened. I was waiting for something to happen. I went outside. I was freezing cold out there and I looked for something to put over me. I started digging around in the garbage and I found his clothes.

EMMA: Digging around in the garbage?

WESLEY: I had the lamb's blood dripping down my arms. I thought it was me for a second. I thought it was me bleeding.

EMMA: You're disgusting. You're even more disgusting than him. And that's pretty disgusting. *(looking at* ELLA, *still asleep)* What's she doing?

WESLEY: I started putting all his clothes on. His baseball cap, his tennis shoes, his overcoat. And every time I put one thing on it seemed like a part of him was growing on me. I could feel him taking over me.

EMMA: *(crossing up to table, tapping crop on her leg)* What is she, asleep or something? *(she whacks* ELLA *across the butt with the riding crop)* WAKE UP! *(*ELLA *stays sleeping)*

WESLEY: I could feel myself retreating. I could feel him coming in and me going out. Just like the change of the guards.

EMMA: Well, don't eat your heart out about it. You did the best you could.

WESLEY: I didn't do a thing.

EMMA: That's what I mean.

WESLEY: I just grew up here.

EMMA: *(crossing down to* WESLEY*)* Have you got any money?

WESLEY *starts digging around in the pockets of the overcoat.*

EMMA: What're you fishing around in there for? That's *his* coat.

WESLEY: I thought you were supposed to be in jail?

EMMA: *(crossing back up to table)* I was.

WESLEY: What happened?

EMMA: *(picking up* ELLA's *handbag and going through it)* I used my ingenuity. I made use of my innate criminal intelligence.

EMMA *throws things onto the floor from* ELLA's *pocket book as she searches through it.*

WESLEY: What'd you do?

EMMA: I got out.

WESLEY: I know, but how?

EMMA: I made sexual overtures to the sergeant. That's how. Easy.

She takes a big wad of money out of pocket book and a set of car keys, then throws the bag away. She holds up the money.

EMMA: I'm going into crime. It's the only thing that pays these days.

WESLEY: *(looking at roll of bills in* EMMA's *hand)* Where'd she get that?

EMMA: Where do you think?

WESLEY: You're taking her car?

EMMA: It's the perfect self-employment. Crime. No credentials. No diplomas. No overhead. No upkeep. Just straight profit. Right off the top.

WESLEY: How come I'm going backwards?

EMMA: *(moving in toward* WESLEY*)* Because you don't look ahead. That's why. You don't see the writing on the wall. You gotta learn how to read these things, Wes. It's deadly otherwise. You can't believe people when they look you in the eyes. You gotta' look behind them. See what they're standing in front of. What they're hiding. Everybody's hiding, Wes. Everybody. Nobody looks like what they are.

WESLEY: What are you?

EMMA: *(moving away)* I'm gone. I'm gone! Never to return.

ELLA *suddenly wakes up on the table. She sits up straight.*

ELLA: *(as though waking from a bad dream)* EMMA!!

EMMA *looks at her, then runs off stage left.* ELLA *sits there on table staring in horror at* WESLEY. *She doesn't recognize him.*

ELLA: *(to* WESLEY*)* Weston! Was that Emma?

WESLEY: It's me, Mom.

ELLA: *(yelling off stage but still on table)* EMMA!! *(she jumps off table and looks for a coat)* We've got to catch her! She can't run off like that! That horse will kill her! Where's my coat? *(to* WESLEY*)* WHERE'S MY COAT?

WESLEY: You weren't wearing one.

ELLA: *(to* WESLEY*)* Go catch her, Weston! She's your daughter! She's trying to run away!

WESLEY: Let her go.

ELLA: I can't let her go! I'm responsible!

Huge explosion off stage. Flash of light, then silence. WESLEY *and* ELLA *just stand there staring.* EMERSON *enters from right, giggling. He's a small man in a suit.*

EMERSON: Jeeezus! Did you ever hear a thing like that? What a wallop! Jeezus Christ! *(giggles)*

WESLEY *and* ELLA *look at him.*

EMERSON: Old Slater musta' packed it brim full. I never heard such a godalmighty bang in my whole career.

SLATER, *his partner, enters from right, holding out the skinned lamb carcass. He's taller than* EMERSON, *also in a suit. They both giggle as though they'd pulled off a halloween stunt.*

SLATER: Emerson, get a load a'this! *(giggling)* Did you see this thing? *(to* WESLEY*)* What is this, a skinned goat?

WESLEY: *(blank)* Lamb.

SLATER: Oh, it's a lamb! *(they laugh)* Looks like somebody's afterbirth to me! *(they laugh hysterically)*

WESLEY: What was that bang?

They stop laughing and look at WESLEY. *They laugh again, then stop.*

EMERSON: Bang? What bang?

WESLEY: That explosion.

EMERSON: Oh that! That was just a little reminder. A kind of a post-hypnotic suggestion. *(they laugh)*

ELLA: Who are these men, Weston?

EMERSON: *(to* WESLEY*)* Weston? You're Weston?

WESLEY: My father.

EMERSON: *(to* SLATER*)* Looks a little young, don't ya' think?

SLATER: *(dropping lamb carcass into fence enclosure)* Well, if she says he's Weston, he must be Weston.

ELLA: What are these men doing here? *(she moves away from them)*

EMERSON: *(to* WESLEY*)* So you're Weston? We had a different picture in mind. We had someone altogether different in mind.

WESLEY: What was it that blew up out there?

EMERSON: Something that wasn't paid for. Something past due.

SLATER: Long overdue.

WESLEY: The car. You blew up the car.

EMERSON: Bingo!

They crack up. WESLEY *moves upstage and looks out as though trying to see outside.*

ELLA: Get these men out of here, Weston! They're in my kitchen.

SLATER: *(looking around)* Some mess in here, boy. I couldn't live like this if you paid me.

EMERSON: Well, that's what comes from not paying your bills. You let one thing slide; first thing you know you let everything slide. You let everything go downhill until you wind up in a dungheap like this.

WESLEY: *(looking out, upstage)* There's a fire out there.

SLATER: It'll go out. It's just a gelignite-nitro mixture. Doesn't burn for long. May leave a few scars on the lawn but nothin' permanent.

WESLEY: *(without emotion, still looking out)* Nothing left of the car.

SLATER: That's right. Very thorough. The Irish developed it. Beautiful stuff. Never know what hit ya'.

EMERSON: *(to* WESLEY*)* Well, we gotta' run, Weston. But you can get the general drift. *(they start to leave;* EMERSON *stops)* Oh, and if you see your old man, you might pass on the info. We hate to keep repeating ourselves. The first time is great, but after that it gets pretty boring.

SLATER: *(to* WESLEY*)* Don't forget to give that lamb some milk. He looks pretty bad off.

They both laugh loudly, then exit. ELLA *is facing downstage now, staring at the lamb carcass in the pen.* WESLEY *has his back to her upstage. He looks out. Pause.*

ELLA: *(staring at dead lamb)* I must've slept right through the day. How long did I sleep?

They stay in these positions facing away from each other.

WESLEY: Not so long.

ELLA: And Emma left. She really left on that horse. I didn't think she'd do it. I had a dream she was leaving. That's what woke me up.

WESLEY: She was right here in the kitchen.

ELLA: I must've slept right through it. *(pause, as she stares at lamb carcass)* Oh! You know what, Wes?

WESLEY: What?

ELLA: Something just went right through me. Just from looking at this lamb.

WESLEY: What?

ELLA: That story your father used to tell about that eagle. You remember that?

WESLEY: Yeah.

ELLA: You remember the whole thing?

WESLEY: Yeah.

ELLA: I don't. I remember something about it. But it just went right through me.

WESLEY: Oh.

ELLA: *(after pause)* I remember he keeps coming back and swooping down on the shed roof and then flying off.

WESLEY: Yeah.

ELLA: What else?

WESLEY: I don't know.

ELLA: You remember. What happens next?

WESLEY: A cat comes.

ELLA: That's right. A big tom cat comes. Right out in the fields. And he jumps up on top of that roof to sniff around in all the entrails or whatever it was.

WESLEY: *(still with back to her)* And that eagle comes down and picks up the cat in his talons and carries him screaming off into the sky.

ELLA: *(staring at lamb)* That's right. And they fight. They fight like crazy in the middle of the sky. The cat's tearing his chest out, and the eagle's trying to drop him, but the cat won't let go because he knows if he falls he'll die.

WESLEY: And the eagle's being torn apart in midair. The eagle's trying to free himself from the cat, and the cat won't let go.

ELLA: And they come crashing down to the earth. Both of them come crashing down. Like one whole thing.

They stay like that with WESLEY *looking off upstage, his back to* ELLA, *and* ELLA *downstage, looking at the lamb. Lights fade very slowly to black.*

CURTAIN

Killer's Head

a monologue

Killer's Head was first performed at the American Place Theatre, New York, in 1975. It was directed by Nancy Meckler, with Richard Gere as Mazon.

SCENE: *Bare stage. Center on slightly raised platform,* MAZON *sits in electric chair facing audience. Hands, arms, legs, feet, chest, neck bound with bands of steel to the silver chair. He is barefoot, blindfolded, wears T-shirt and jeans, yellow spot on chair, rest of stage black. Lights rise slow on* MAZON *(speaks in clipped, south-western rodeo accent.)*

MAZON: Oh yeah, today's the day I buy the pick-up. I've decided. Six cylinder, three-quarter ton bed, heavy-duty rear springs, three speed column. Should pull the horses all right. 'Course with the three fifty V-8 you'd get more power. Don't really need it though. Won't be goin' off the road much. Just up to Santa Rosa and back. Maybe sixty miles round trip. Just to take that mare up and get her bred. Jesus! You should see that stud, boy! Does the quarter mile in twenty-one seconds dead. Like to rip the silks right off that jockey. Said they never seen an Appaloosa like him. Should throw a blanket foal, that's for sure. Got a leopard on both sides of the pedigree. Could make a cuttin' horse too, what with that mare. She's almost one-third Quarter Horse herself. She can move, boy. I've seen her doubled in half over a cow. Anyway, that six cylinder should do it. Save us some on gas. Don't plan on doin' much rodeo. That old Tommy Ferguson's got it wrapped up. Might try some halter shows up North. We got those yearling fillies we could show. They got class, boy. That's the ticket, see. You take those Quarter mares and you breed right back to Thoroughbreds, racing stock, and you got yourself an all-purpose type horse. You got refinement when you out-cross like that. You take Three Bars. If it weren't for that damn stud horse the whole Quarter Horse breed would look like Angus steers by now. That's the truth. Refinement, that's what he brought to the breed. Look at the heads he threw. Anyway, the Appaloosa isn't hurtin' from Thoroughbred blood neither. What's that Indian Hemp stud they got now? Forget his name. Good blood. And that Sheljet horse outa' Colorado. Shit man, you never seen a pedigree like that. Jet Deck on the top side. Lady Bug Moon on the bottom. Bright red sorrel horse. Sure to throw colored foals. You take any Appaloosa mare to him and I guarantee you'd get a colored foal. Speed too. He's a flyin' machine. 'Course they all got speed outa' Colorado. It's that mountain air. Must be. Grass ain't bad either. Out here they got that all-purpose pasture. Ain't worth a damn. Too much blue alfalfa. Blows 'em up. Blow a horse inside out with that stuff. Gets inside there and ferments. I've seen it. Swells 'em up like a Goodyear Blimp. That Colorado grass is the real stuff. Rocky Mountain. No wonder they got so many triple-A horses comin' outa' there. Out here they feed pellets and then wonder how come a horse don't put the flesh on. Can't beef a racin' horse up like that. Needs grain and good pasture. I'd send the whole string out there for the summer if I could afford it. I would. 'Course out here you got the money. You got the mares too. Never seen such mares. You take that T-Dok mare. I was ridin' her flat out the other day and I swear to God she wasn't even blowin' at the finish. Musta' done six furlongs at full tilt, and she had everything left. Took all I had to haul her in. We had that gelding out there with her and she left him standin'. Had six lengths on him. He's a tough horse too. Barrel racer. 'Course the shoer said he's got a slight touch a' ring bone. That shouldn't hurt him though if we keep him workin'. I noticed he was a little turned in on his front feet but I took him to be over-muscled. Shoer says he can compensate by filing down the outside horn. You know, that gelding was out to pasture for four months straight, never had a soul on his back, and I took him straight in and cut five calves with him. Right off the dime like that. Five calves. That's what I call cow sense. Too bad he ain't registered. We could make some money off that pony. Put him in the Snaffle Bit Futurity and clean up. I put a snaffle on him the other day and it made all the difference. That curb was puttin' too much pressure on his jaw. You could tell the way he was tossin' his head all the time. Skeeter told me to try a martingale on him but I could tell that wasn't it. It was that damn bit. Too much pressure. Soon's I put that snaffle in his mouth he turned as soft as butter. Just neck reinin' to beat all hell. Dandy horse.

He stops suddenly and just sits silently, no movement, lasting for one full minute, then he begins again.

MAZON: Dude says he can give me a deal on that blue truck. Almost four hundred off the list price. Smells good inside that thing. Sweet. Steers like a damn car. Got that big eight-foot bed. No extras. Got those skinny bicycle tires on it. Comes stock like that. Put some big mags on there and she'll be tough. Should pull that two horse trailer. Furthest I'd take it is down to L.A. Highway Five all the way. Right down through the center. Over the Grapevine. Bakersfield. Should pull that okay. That V-8 would do it better but I can't afford the gas. Damn thing only gets about twelve to the gallon. Ain't worth it in the long run. Only be makin' that long haul once a season. Just to hit that fair circuit. 'Couple a' auctions maybe. It's a full eight hours no matter how ya' cut it. Specially with a double rig. Full day's ride.

He stops suddenly again and sits silently. The lights begin to dim very slowly and take a full minute to come to black. Just as the lights reach black the chair ignites with an electric charge that lights up MAZON's *entire body. He makes no sound. The electric charge is very short, just long enough to take in the illuminated body then back to black.*

CURTAIN

Action

Action was first performed at the American Place Theatre, New York, in 1975. It was directed by Nancy Meckler, with the following cast:

Shooter: *R. A. Dow*
Jeep: *Richard Lynch*
Liza: *Dorothy Lyman*
Lupe: *Marcia Gean Kurtz*

Scene

Upstage center, a small Christmas tree on a small table with tiny blinking lights. Downstage center left, a plain board table with four wooden chairs, one each on the four sides. The table is set very simply for four people. Just plates, forks, and knives. Four coffee cups and a pot of hot coffee in the middle. Running across the middle of the stage above is a clothesline attached to a pulley at either side of the stage. The light on stage is divided exactly in half, so that upstage is in complete darkness except for the blinking lights of the Christmas tree. Downstage is lit in pale yellow and white light which pulses brighter and dimmer every ten minutes or so, as though the power were very weak.

The characters are all in their late twenties to early thirties. SHOOTER *and* JEEP, *the two men, are dressed in long dark overcoats, jeans, lumberjack shirts, and heavy boots. They both have their heads shaved.* LUPE *wears a flowered print dress in the 1940s pearl harbor style. She wears platform heels.* LIZA *wears a long full, Mexican type skirt, plain blouse and an apron. She wears sandals.* LUPE *sits upstage of the table facing* LIZA *across from her.* LIZA's *back is directly to the audience.* JEEP *sits stage right at one end of the table across from* SHOOTER, *who sits at the other end.*

The stage is in darkness for a while with just the tree blinking. The lights come up very slowly downstage. Nothing happens for a while except the slight movements of the actors drinking coffee. JEEP *rocks slightly in his chair.*

All the exits and entrances occur upstage into or out of the darkness.

JEEP: *(leaning back in his chair and rocking gently)* I'm looking forward to my life. I'm looking forward to uh—me. The way I picture me.

SHOOTER: Who're you talking to?

JEEP: Uh— *(pause)* I had this room I lived in. Shall I describe this room? *(pause as the others take a sip of coffee together)* I had a wall with a picture of Walt Whitman in an overcoat. Every time I looked at the picture I thought of Pennsylvania. I had a picture of an antelope on a yellow prairie. Every time I looked at this picture

I saw him running. I had a picture of the Golden Gate Bridge. Every time I looked at it I saw the water underneath it. I had a picture of me sitting on a jeep with a gun in one hand.

He lets the chair come to rest on the floor again. Pause as they all sip coffee. Suddenly LIZA *jumps up and makes a big gesture with her hands melodramatically.*

LIZA: Oh my God! The turkey!

She goes running off upstage and disappears into the darkness.

LUPE: *(to herself)* It's funny the way the snow is.

SHOOTER: *(pulling a book out from his lap and placing it on the table)* Maybe we should read.

LUPE: We'll have to wait for Liza.

SHOOTER: Yeah. But we could be looking for the place. Do you remember where it was?

LUPE: I thought we marked it.

SHOOTER: I lost the place.

LUPE: *(taking the book and thumbing through it)* Here, let me look.

JEEP: Shooter, can you do a soft shoe?

SHOOTER: Naw. I don't think so.

JEEP: I was wondering if we could both do it sitting down. Without getting up. Just our legs.

SHOOTER: Just like this you mean?

JEEP: Yeah.

LUPE: Was it chapter sixteen?

SHOOTER: Uh—Maybe. (LUPE *continues thumbing*)

JEEP: Just try. Put your hands on the table.

They both put their hands on the table.

JEEP: One, two, three, quatro!

They both break into an attempt at a soft shoe patter as they stare blankly at each other in their seats. LUPE *keeps looking through the book. This lasts for about thirty seconds and ends with* LIZA *coming back into the light sucking on her fingers and wiping her hands on her apron. She sits back down in her chair.*

LIZA: *(noticing* LUPE *with the book).* Oh. Are we gonna read?

LUPE: I can't find the place.

LIZA: Let me take a look.

LUPE *shoves the book across the table to* LIZA, *who takes it and starts thumbing through it. She keeps sucking on her fingers in between turning the pages.*

LUPE: Shooter lost the place.

JEEP: Uh—I saw this picture of a dancing bear. Some gypsies had it on a leash. They were all laying by the side of the road and the bear was standing on all fours. Right in the middle of the road. In the background was this fancy house.

SHOOTER *pulls his overcoat over his head and holds his hands up in front of him like bear paws. Slowly he pushes his chair back and rises. He takes short staggering steps like a bear on his hind legs.* LIZA *keeps looking through the book.*

JEEP: *(to* SHOOTER*)* Don't act it out. (SHOOTER *keeps on*)

LIZA: *(referring to book)* Were we past the part where the comet exploded?

JEEP: *(to* SHOOTER*)* You don't have to act it out. (SHOOTER *pays no attention*)

LUPE: I never saw a dancing bear. That was before my time. I guess they made it illegal. Too cruel or something.

SHOOTER *goes back and forth downstage like a trained bear, looking out at the audience.*

SHOOTER: It doesn't feel cruel. Just humiliating. It's not the rightful position of a bear. You can feel it. It's all off balance.

LUPE: Well, that's what I mean.

JEEP: What?

LUPE: That's cruel. For a bear that's cruel.

SHOOTER: No. It's as though something's expected of me. As though I was human. But it puts me in a different position. A different situation.

JEEP: How?

SHOOTER: Performing. Um— Without realizing it. Um— I mean I realize it but the bear doesn't. He just finds himself doing something unusual for him. Awkward.

JEEP: You're not the bear.

LIZA: I found it! They've returned to earth only to find that things are exactly the same. Nothing's changed.

JEEP: That's not it. Let me try.

JEEP *takes the book from* LIZA *and goes through it.* SHOOTER *drops his bear routine and pulls his overcoat down on his shoulders. He looks blankly at the audience, then strolls back to his seat and sits. They all sip their coffee. After a long pause.*

SHOOTER: I think I'll take a bath.

LIZA: The turkey's almost ready.

SHOOTER: I'm too scared to eat. *(not showing it)*

LUPE: *(to LIZA)* Let him take a bath. It'll calm him down.

SHOOTER: Is there any hot water left?

JEEP: *(thumbing through the book)* There was the last time I was up there.

SHOOTER: I don't want to go up there alone.

LUPE: If you could remember the last time when you got scared it might help you this time.

SHOOTER: I know. It's the same. It's the snow. Being inside. Everything's so shocking inside. When I look at my hand I get terrified. The sight of my feet in the bathtub. The skin covering me. That's all that's covering me.

LIZA: *(pulling out a hip flask from her apron)* You want some rum?

SHOOTER *takes the flask and has a drink*

LUPE: I can remember the last time I got scared. I thought I'd poisoned myself. I thought I'd eaten something. I imagined it working its way into me. I went outside in my bare feet and forced myself to throw up. It was that kind of a night.

LIZA: I remember that night. We were watching the stars.

The two girls start laughing, covering their mouths, then stop.

SHOOTER: I know I'll get over this. It just sorta' came on me.

He hands the flask back to LIZA, who puts it in her apron.

LIZA: *(without giving it back)* You can keep it.

SHOOTER: *(blankly)* I've got this feeling that females are more generous. I've always felt that.

JEEP: *(pushing the book away from him)* OH THIS IS RIDICULOUS!! I CAN'T FIND THE PLACE!!

He stands suddenly, picks up his chair and smashes it to the floor. The chair shatters into tiny pieces. Pause. None of the others are shocked.

LIZA: *(standing)* I think there's another one out on the back porch.

LIZA leaves. She disappears in the darkness upstage. JEEP pulls his overcoat up over his head and raises his hands like SHOOTER did. He goes through the same bear motions as SHOOTER did before. LUPE takes the book again and looks through the pages.

SHOOTER: *(to himself)* That's what I do. I get this feeling I can't control the situation. Something's getting out of control. Things won't work. And then I smash something. I punch something. I scream. Later I find out that my throat is torn. I've torn something loose.

My voice is hoarse. I'm trembling. My breath is short. My heart's thumping. I don't recognize myself.

LUPE: Shooter, weren't you the last one to read?

SHOOTER: Was I?

LUPE: Yeah. It was you.

SHOOTER: It doesn't matter does it?

LUPE: Only if you can remember where you left off.

SHOOTER: Well, let me look. I'll see if I can find it.

He takes the book and looks through it. LUPE *starts into a soft shoe sitting down.* JEEP *has his back to her, but as he hears her feet tapping he stops his bear routine and turns to look at her. She continues with a smile.* JEEP *pulls his overcoat down on his shoulders and just stares at her.*

JEEP: *(flatly)* There's something to be said for not being able to do something well.

LUPE *stops. Her smile disappears.*

JEEP: No, I mean it's all right. It takes a certain amount of courage to bring it out into the open like that.

LUPE: It's no worse than the one you guys did.

JEEP: No, I know. I'm not trying to insult you or anything.

LUPE *starts up the soft shoe again in defiance*

JEEP: I mean we've got this picture in our head of Judy Garland or Gene Kelly or Fred Astaire. Those feet flying all over the place. That fluid motion. How can we do anything for the first time. Even Nijinksy went nuts.

LUPE: *(continuing with her feet)* What about it?

JEEP: It's hard to have a conversation.

He sits down on the floor. LUPE *continues dancing for a while after* JEEP's *seated. She slowly stops.* SHOOTER *thumbs through the book. They sip their coffee.*

LUPE: *(to* JEEP*)* When you're in a position of doing something like that it's hard to talk about it. You know what I mean? I mean while I was doing it—while I was in the middle of actually doing it—I didn't particularly feel like talking about it. I mean it made me feel funny. You know what I mean. It was like somebody was watching me. Judging me. Sort of making an evaluation. Chalking up points. I mean especially the references to all those stars. You know. I mean I know I'm not as good as Judy Garland. But so what? I wasn't trying to be as good as Judy Garland. It started off like it was just for fun you know. And then it turned into murder. It was like being murdered. You know what I mean.

JEEP: Didn't mean to piss you off.

Pause. LIZA *enters from upstage with a new chair in one hand and a broom and dustpan in the other. She sets the chair down.* JEEP *gets up off the floor and sits in the new chair, folding his arms across his chest.* LIZA *starts sweeping up the pieces of the old chair.* JEEP *watches her.*

JEEP: *(to* LIZA*).* I'm not going to offer to clean it up because you're already doing it.

LIZA *continues sweeping in silence.*

SHOOTER: *(looking up from the book, directed at everyone)* I know that feeling of being out of control. Powerless. You go crazy. In a second you can go crazy. You can almost see it coming. A thunderstorm.

JEEP: *(to* SHOOTER*)* It's not that.

SHOOTER: Oh.

SHOOTER *goes back to thumbing through the book.*

JEEP: I mean sometimes it's like that but this time it wasn't.

LIZA: *(still sweeping)* Did you find the place yet?

SHOOTER: Nope.

LUPE: I'm starving. (SHE *licks her lips)*

JEEP: This time it came from something else. I had an idea I wanted to be different· I pictured myself being different than how I was. I couldn't stand how I was. The picture grew in me, and the more it grew the more it came up against how I really was. Then I exploded.

SHOOTER: *(without looking up from the book)* That's what I meant.

LUPE: Oh, when are we gonna EAT! *(hitting the table once with her fist)*

LIZA: It's almost ready.

LIZA *exits upstage with the pieces of the old chair leaving the broom on stage.*

JEEP: I couldn't take it. Just thumbing through the book. Not even looking. Not even seeing the papers. Just turning them. Acting it out. Just pretending.

Suddenly LUPE *starts gnawing ravenously on her own arm.* JEEP *and* SHOOTER *pay no attention.*

SHOOTER: *(still looking through the book)* I know.

JEEP: Is that what you're doing? Is that what you're doing right now?

SHOOTER: *(without looking up)* I'm looking for the place.

JEEP: I admire your concentration. I couldn't concentrate. I kept thinking of other things. I kept drifting. I kept thinking of the sun. The Gulf of Mexico. Barracuda.

SHOOTER: *(still into the book)* That's okay.

JEEP: *(standing suddenly and yelling)* I KNOW IT'S OKAY!! THAT'S NOT WHAT I'M SAYING!

He picks up the new chair and smashes it to the ground just like the other one. LUPE stops chewing on her arm and licks it like a cat licking a wound. SHOOTER keeps looking for the place in the book. JEEP stands there looking at the damage.

SHOOTER: *(after a short pause, referring to book)* Was it just after the fall of the Great Continent?

LUPE: Oh my stomach!

She clutches her stomach with both hands and holds it like a baby. LIZA enters with a huge golden turkey on a silver platter with the steam rising off it. She sets it down on the table in front of LUPE.

LUPE: I'll carve.

LUPE picks up a knife and begins to slice the turkey in a calm way, very formally, and laying the slices on plates for everyone. LIZA walks over to JEEP, who is still looking at the broken chair. They look at the chair together as though seeing it as an event outside themselves.

LIZA: *(to JEEP but looking at the broken chair)* You'll have to stop doing that. We've only got one left.

LIZA picks up the broom. JEEP grabs it. They both hold it together.

JEEP: I'll do it.

LIZA: That's okay.

A short pause as they look at each other, then JEEP yanks the broom out of LIZA's hand and starts sweeping up the broken chair. LIZA goes to the table and sits folding her hands in her lap while LUPE continues to carve standing up. SHOOTER sticks with the book.

LUPE: We're lucky to have a turkey you know.

LIZA: Yes, I know.

LUPE: It was smart thinking to raise our own. To see ahead into the crisis.

LIZA: Whose idea was it anyway?

SHOOTER: *(not looking up)* Mine.

JEEP: *(still sweeping)* I think it was mine.

SHOOTER: *(not looking up)* It was your idea, and then I went and bought it.

JEEP: That's right.

LIZA: That's right.

LUPE: We're sure lucky.

LIZA: Do you know what they say is the best way to prepare a turkey? They say that before you kill it—about two weeks before—you start feeding it a little corn meal and some sherry. About a teaspoon full of sherry, three times a day. Then in the second week you force a whole walnut down its throat once a day and keep up the sherry dosage. When it comes time for the kill you'll have a turkey with a warm, nutty flavor.

LUPE: Is that what you did?

LIZA: Partly. I started out the first week with the sherry, but by the time the second week rolled around I couldn't bring myself to do it. I mean the walnut thing. I couldn't do that.

JEEP: *(as* HE *exits upstage with the broken pieces of the chair)* It's not cruel.

LUPE: Who killed it anyway?

LIZA: I did.

SHOOTER: I can't find the place.

SHOOTER *folds the book and puts it on the floor, opens his napkin and tucks it into his shirt, picks up his knife and fork and waits to be served*

SHOOTER: Aren't we going to have any vegetables?

LIZA: No. We had a late frost remember?

LUPE: We're lucky to have a turkey.

SHOOTER: I know we are. I was just wondering about the vegetables. The creamed onions and stuff. The candied yams.

LUPE: *(to* SHOOTER*)* Dark or light?

SHOOTER: White.

She hands SHOOTER *a plate of turkey. He digs in.*

LIZA: No wine either, I suppose?

LUPE: You were in the kitchen.

She hands LIZA *a plate of turkey.* LIZA *eats.* LUPE *serves herself and sits down to eat.*

LIZA: Yes. I've never cooked over an open fire before. I mean a big fire blazing like that. It's hard to keep from cooking yourself. Your arms start roasting. You get afraid the kitchen's going to burn down.

LUPE: I can imagine.

LIZA: The heat is tremendous.

SHOOTER: I thought turkeys were supposed to cook slow.

LIZA: Well, you let the flames die down. It's just the embers you're cooking on. But the heat!

SHOOTER: Yeah, it's hot in here for a change.

JEEP enters from upstage into the light, shivering and rubbing his arms. LIZA stops him.

LIZA: Oh Jeep, could you get us all some water?

JEEP: *(standing still, shivering)* Right now?

LIZA: Yeah, if you don't mind.

JEEP: From the well? It's a lot of work you know. We can't just turn on a tap.

LUPE: We're lucky to have a turkey.

JEEP turns upstage and exits.

SHOOTER: It *is* freezing out there. I don't envy him. Hauling up water. Spilling it on his hands. It's freezing.

LIZA: It's all right.

SHOOTER: In the dark. Feeling your way around. He might fall in.

LIZA: We'll hear him.

LUPE: It's all right, Shooter.

SHOOTER: *(standing suddenly)* I KNOW IT'S ALL RIGHT!

The two women continue eating, paying no attention. SHOOTER *sits down after a while.*

SHOOTER: *(quietly to himself;* LUPE *and* LIZA *eat quietly)* Just because we're surrounded by four walls and a roof doesn't mean anything. It's still dangerous. The chances of something happening are just as great. Anything could happen. Any move is possible. I've seen it. You go outside. The world's quiet. White. Everything resounding. Not a sound of a motor. Not a light. You see into the house. You see the candles. You watch the people. You can see what it's like inside. The candles draw you. You get a cold feeling being outside. Separated. You have an idea that being inside it's cosier. Friendlier. Warmth. People. Conversation. Everyone using a language. Then you go inside. It's a shock. It's not like how you expected. You lose what you had outside. You forget that there even is an outside. The inside is all you know. You hunt for a way of being with everyone. A way of finding how to behave. You find out what's expected of you. You act yourself out.

JEEP enters from upstage with a bucket full of water and four cups in the other hand. Each cup dangling from one of his fingers by the handle. He sets the bucket down on the table with the cups. He picks up a cup and dips it into the bucket. He does the same with each cup and serves everyone at the table with a cup of water. Then he sits down on the floor. This all happens in silence, except for the sounds of the others eating and the water.

LIZA: *(standing)* There's one chair left.

SHOOTER: *(standing and moving upstage)* I'll get it.

SHOOTER *exits.* LIZA *sits again.*

LUPE: Dark or light, Jeep?

JEEP: White.

LUPE *serves him a plate of turkey.* JEEP *eats, sitting on the floor.*

JEEP: I was thinking. If things get worse we should get a cow.

LIZA: Nobody's selling.

JEEP: You've asked around?

LIZA: Nobody's selling.

LUPE: I was thinking chickens would be better.

LIZA: Nobody's selling.

JEEP: That's all right.

LUPE: A goat might be good.

LIZA: There's no way of actually preparing. We'll have to do the best with what we've got. We're all eating now. At least we're eating. We'll have to gauge our hunger. Find out if we actually need food when we think we need it. Find out how much it takes to stay alive. Find out what it does to us. Find out what's happening to us. Sometimes I think I know, but it's only an idea. Sometimes I have the idea I know what's happening to us. Sometimes I can't see it. I go blind. Other times I don't have any idea. I'm just eating.

SHOOTER *comes back on from upstage empty-handed. They all stop eating and look at him.*

SHOOTER: I forgot what it was I went for. I got out there and forgot.

JEEP: *(still on the floor)* The chair.

SHOOTER: Oh yeah.

SHOOTER *turns upstage and exits again. They go back to eating.*

JEEP: *(to himself)* It doesn't really matter. I'm okay on the floor.

LIZA: I made a move to go get it, and then he beat me to it.

JEEP: It doesn't matter.

LUPE: Was he being polite?

LIZA: I guess.

LUPE: *(to* LIZA*)* Just to keep you from going out there?

LIZA: I guess so.

LUPE: But he's getting the chair for Jeep, and Jeep doesn't even care.

LIZA: It's all right.

JEEP: *(suddenly, to himself)* Walt Whitman was a great man. He kissed soldiers. He held their hands. He saw mounds of amputated limbs.

LUPE: I don't know anything about him.

SHOOTER *comes on from upstage pulling a very heavy, stuffed red armchair. He huffs and puffs with it, pulling it by inches downstage as the others stay sitting and eat their turkey.*

JEEP: He expected something from America. He had this great expectation.

LUPE: I don't know. I never heard about it.

JEEP: He was like what Tolstoy was to Russia.

LIZA: I don't know much about it either.

JEEP: A father. A passionate father bleeding for his country.

LIZA: *(staying seated)* Do you want some help, Shooter?

SHOOTER: *(between heavy breaths)* No— I'm uh— okay. It's— not much— further. I'll be all right.

JEEP: Almost a hundred years ago to the day. The same thing happened. Everybody at each other's throats. Walt was there. He could tell you.

LIZA: I thought he was dead.

JEEP: *(conversationally)* "Manahatta," it was called then. Indian. They had big, open tents on the Bowery with sawdust on the floor. German beer. Juggling acts. Dancing bears. The Civil War was just beginning.

LUPE: When was this?

JEEP: He'd tip his hat to Abe, and Abe would tip his hat back.

LIZE: They liked each other.

JEEP: *(in a Walter Cronkite newscaster voice)* The poet and the President. The poet all gray and white standing on his feet. The President all dark and somber, glooming down from his horse. The face of war in his eyes. The two of them seeing each other from their respective positions. The entire nation in a jackknife. This all happened on Vermont Avenue near L Street. The street itself was raining. Blue soldiers were lying wounded in every doorway; some having slept there all night with gaping wounds. Soaked through to the bone. Walt was a witness to it.

SHOOTER *finally gets the chair downstage right and stands by it try-*

ing to catch his breath. He looks at JEEP, *who stays seated on the floor.* SHOOTER *makes a motion toward the chair with his hand. He tries to speak, but he's out of breath. He tries again.*

SHOOTER: *(motioning to chair)* There it is.

JEEP: I'm okay here.

SHOOTER *looks at him for a while*

SHOOTER: You don't want it? *(no answer from* JEEP, *who keeps eating)* Don't you want it?

Still no answer from JEEP. SHOOTER *moves in front of the armchair and collapses into it, staring out at the audience.*

SHOOTER: Aaaaaaaah! This is the life. Now I'm glad I went through all that.

LIZA: *(to* SHOOTER*)* Aren't you hungry?

SHOOTER: No. I'm glad.

He folds his arms behind his head and smiles.

LIZA: *(standing)* Well, time to wash up.

She starts gathering all the dishes together very quickly, whipping the plates out from under everyone. JEEP *and* LUPE *pick their teeth and smack their lips loudly.*

JEEP: *(with his back to* SHOOTER*)* Do you want some water, Shooter? There's plenty of water.

SHOOTER: Nope. This is it for me. I'm never leaving this chair. I've finally found it.

JEEP: *(standing and moving to the bucket on the table)* I'm gonna have some water. I'd be glad to get you a cup if you want.

LUPE: He just said he doesn't want any.

JEEP *stands by the bucket with a cup in one hand. He dips the cup into the bucket, raises the cup slowly, and tips the water back into the bucket, watching the trickle of water as he does it. He keeps doing this over and over as though hypnotized by his own action. When* LIZA *has all the dishes she exits upstage leaving the remains of the turkey on the table.*

LUPE: Does anyone want to read? *(pause)*

SHOOTER: I'm never leaving again.

LUPE: I don't mind looking for the place.

She goes and picks up the book on the floor and sits back down in her chair. She looks through it.

SHOOTER: I could conduct all my business from here. I'll need a bed pan and some magazines.

JEEP: *(looking at the remains of the turkey)* We should save the bones for soup.

SHOOTER: This is more like it. This is more in line with how I see myself. I picture myself as a father. Very much at home. The world can't touch me.

JEEP: Shooter? You remember when you were scared? Shooter? You remember? Oh, Shooter?

SHOOTER: Naw. I don't remember that. Better to leave that. People are washing dishes now. Lupe's looking for the place again. Things are rolling right along. Why bring that up?

LUPE: *(in the book)* Wasn't it around where the space ship had collided with the neutron?

JEEP: Shooter, I remember. I remember you were so scared you couldn't go up to take a bath.

SHOOTER: Naw. That's not me at all. That's entirely the wrong image. That must've been an accident.

JEEP: Oh.

JEEP *keeps pouring the water over his hand.*

SHOOTER: I've never been afraid of baths. I've always been brave in those situations. I've plunged right in.

JEEP: Oh, I thought it was you.

SHOOTER: I knew a guy once who was afraid to take a bath. Something about the water. Stank to high heaven. "High Heaven." That's a good one. He stank, boy. Boy, how he stank. Boy, did he ever stink.

JEEP: Was it the water?

SHOOTER: Yeah. Something about how it distorted his body when he looked down into it.

JEEP: Then, it wasn't the water.

SHOOTER: Yeah. The water. The way it warped his body.

JEEP: But that's just the way he saw it. That was him, not the water.

SHOOTER: Then, he began to fear his own body.

JEEP: From that? From seeing it in the water?

SHOOTER: He began to feel like a foreign spy. Spying on his body. He'd lie awake. Afraid to sleep for fear his body might do something without him knowing. He'd keep watch on it.

JEEP: Was he a close friend?

SHOOTER: I knew him for a while.

JEEP: What happened to him?

SHOOTER: His body killed him. One day it just had enough and killed him.

JEEP: What happened to the body?

SHOOTER: It's still walking around I guess. *(pause)* Would somebody tell Liza to bring me the flask?

LUPE: *(not looking up from the book)* She's washing the dishes.

JEEP: *(still pouring)* That's an interesting story, Shooter.

SHOOTER: Thank you.

JEEP: How did it get started?

SHOOTER: What?

JEEP: I mean how did he get into this relationship?

SHOOTER: Who knows. It developed. One day he found himself like that.

LUPE: *(without looking up)* Remember the days of mass entertainment?

JEEP: No.

LUPE: *(not looking up)* This could never have happened then. Something to do every minute. Always something to do. I once was very active in the community.

JEEP: What's a community?

LUPE: *(looking up)* A sense of— A sense um— What's a community, Shooter?

SHOOTER: Oh uh— You know. You were on the right track.

LUPE: Something uh—

JEEP: I know.

LUPE: Yeah. You know. It doesn't need words.

She goes back into the book.

JEEP: I know what you mean.

LUPE: Just a kind of feeling.

JEEP: Yeah, I know what you mean.

SHOOTER: I think we're beginning to get it a little. To get it back. I mean you can feel it even in the dead of winter. Sort of everybody helping each other out.

JEEP: Did he suspect his body of treason? Was that it?

SHOOTER: I'm not sure. It was a touchy situation.

SHOOTER *rolls both his pants legs up above his knees and starts scratching his legs as he talks.*

JEEP: He must've had a hard time. I mean he couldn't reach out. I mean he wouldn't expect anyone else to be in the same boat probably.

SHOOTER: Probably not.

LUPE: *(without looking up)* Well it *is* rare.

JEEP: Was it in a particular time of hardship?

SHOOTER: I can't rightly say.

JEEP: I mean were things crumbling?

SHOOTER: I suspect he couldn't see it. I mean I suspect he had his ideas. His opinions. Certain stiff attitudes.

LUPE: *(not looking up)* When was this?

JEEP: And his body's still walking around?

SHOOTER: That's right. A walking stiff.

JEEP: Can anyone tell? I mean if we ran into this body could we tell it was vacant?

SHOOTER: I'm not sure.

LUPE: *(still thumbing through the book)* Well how *could* you tell?

JEEP: *(to* LUPE*)* There must be a way. I mean something must be missing. You could tell if he wasn't all there.

SHOOTER: I don't know.

LUPE: *(still in book)* How? How could you tell?

JEEP: You'd know. I'd know. I mean with us, we know. We know. We hear each other. We hear our voices. We know each other's voice. We can see. We recognize each other. We have a certain— We can tell who's who. We know our names. We respond. We call each other. We sort of— We— We're not compltely stranded like that. I mean— It's not— It's not like that. How that would be.

Pause as JEEP *slowly pours the water over his hand.* SHOOTER *scratches his legs.* LUPE *thumbs through the book. After a short while* SHOOTER *sits back in the armchair with a jerk and holds his stomach.*

SHOOTER: I'm starving. Did we eat already?

LUPE: *(still in book)* You weren't here.

SHOOTER: I was here. I was here all along.

LUPE: *(in book)* Not at the right time.

SHOOTER *stands suddenly in the chair with his pants legs still rolled up.* LUPE *and* JEEP *pay no attention.*

SHOOTER: You mean you ate without me!

Pause as SHOOTER *looks around the space slowly.*

SHOOTER: *(to himself)* Now I'm beginning to regret my decision.

LUPE: What.

SHOOTER: *(gazing around him in amazement)* To stay in the chair.

LUPE: Oh.

SHOOTER: It was short-sighted. I'd give anything just to travel around this space. Just to lick the corners. To get my nose in the dust. To feel my body moving.

LUPE: *(referring to book)* Was it near the place where the sky rained fire?

SHOOTER: I can picture it. I give in to it. I let my body go. It moves out. It sniffs the board. My head imagines forests! Chain saws! Hammers and nails in my ears! A whole house is being built!

LUPE: *(in book)* Keep it to yourself.

SHOOTER: My nose finds things. Everything's churning with new pictures. Then suddenly it all ends again, and I'm back in the chair. But now I've ruined it. Now I've had my cake. Now neither one is any good. The chair doesn't get it on, and neither does the adventure. I'm nowhere.

LUPE: I'm trying to concentrate.

SHOOTER: Shall I tell a story?

LUPE: *(looking up from book)* O God! If I could find the place we could *read* a story!

SHOOTER: *(still standing)* I'll tell a story. I feel like a story. Jeep? How 'bout it?

JEEP: *(still pouring water, blankly)* You bet.

LUPE: *(back into book)* Oh, Jesus!

Through the story which SHOOTER *tells standing on the armchair,* JEEP *keeps pouring the water slowly over his hand into the bucket, and* LUPE *keeps looking through the book.* SHOOTER *tells it directly to the audience.*

SHOOTER: One night there was some moths. A bunch of moths. In the distance they could see a candle. Just one candle in a window of a big house. The moths were tormented by this candle. They longed to be with this candle but none of them understood it or knew what it was. The leader of the moths sent one of them off to the house to bring back some information about this light. The moth returned and reported what he had seen, but the leader told him that he hadn't understood anything about the candle. So another moth went to the house. He touched the flame with the tip of his wings but the heat drove him off. When he came back and reported, the leader still wasn't satisfied. So he sent a third moth out. This moth approached the house and saw the candle flickering inside the window. He became filled with love for this candle. He crashed against the glass and finally found a way inside. He threw himself on the flame. With his forelegs he took hold of the flame and united himself joyously with her. He embraced her completely, and his whole body became red as fire. The leader of the moths, who was watching from far off with the other moths, saw that the flame and the moth appeared to be one. He turned to the other moths and said: "He's learned what he wanted to know, but he's the only one who understands it."

JEEP *suddenly slaps the water in the bucket with his free hand and pulls a large dead fish out of the bucket and throws it on the floor.* SHOOTER *looks down on it from the chair.* LUPE *sticks with the book.*

JEEP: I've about had it with this bucket! I can't figure out what I've been doing here all this time.

SHOOTER: *(still standing and looking down at the fish)* How deep is our well anyway?

JEEP: *(to* LUPE*)* What's happened to Liza?

LUPE: Washing dishes.

JEEP: *(to* LUPE*)* Have I been standing here all this time?

LUPE: *(looking up)* I don't know! I've been looking for the place! I wish people would just leave me alone!

SHOOTER: I'm not standing up here because I'm afraid of fish, I'll tell you that much. I was standing up here before the fish ever arrived. It's just a coincidence. It's not the way it looks.

JEEP: Shooter, could you create some reason for me to move? Some justification for me to find myself somewhere else?

SHOOTER: Only if you promise that you're not thinking that I'm afraid of fish just because I'm standing up here on the chair and there happens to be a fish in the house.

JEEP: I'm not thinking about you!

Suddenly LUPE *gives an exasperated exhale of air, slams the book shut, glares at the two men, stands, and exits upstage.* SHOOTER *and* JEEP *are stuck in their respective positions. Short pause as they look at each other.*

SHOOTER: Go and pick up the fish.

JEEP *goes to the fish and picks it up.*

SHOOTER: Go and put the fish on the table.

JEEP *goes upstage of the table, facing audience, moves the turkey carcass to one side and lays the fish down on the table.*

SHOOTER: *(still standing)* Take your jacknife out of your pocket.

JEEP *does it.*

SHOOTER: Open your jacknife. The big blade.

JEEP *does it.*

SHOOTER: Cut open the belly of the fish, starting from the pee-hole and slicing toward the head.

JEEP *cuts open the fish.*

SHOOTER: Now clean it like you would any other fish.

JEEP *goes about cleaning the fish in silence.* SHOOTER *sits back down slowly in the chair. He looks at his bare legs.*

SHOOTER: What's been going on in here? *(to* JEEP*)* Was there a party?

JEEP *keeps cleaning the fish.* SHOOTER *looks at his legs again.*

SHOOTER: Was someone taking liberties?

He leans back in the chair with a sigh.

SHOOTER: It's agonizing. All this time I could've swore I was getting something done. I can't even remember eating. *(back to* JEEP*)* Did we eat already? Wasn't there a turkey? *(turns front again and leans back)* Somebody's gonna have to bring me some food, you know. I've made this decision not to leave the chair and I'm gonna stick with it. Come hell or high water. It's not my fault. *(back to* JEEP*)* I could have the fish. When you're finished with it, could you fry it up and bring it to me? If it's not too much trouble? *(no response from* JEEP, SHOOTER *turns front again and leans back in the chair)* This isn't the worst. It's just that my stomach is growling. I COULDN'T STAY HERE FOREVER! I don't know what possessed me. *(back to* JEEP*)* Didn't I say that I'll never leave the chair? *(back front again)* If I get up, it would be a sign of my weakness. Jeep? If I got up would you think I was weak? *(no answer)* This isn't the worst thing that could happen. *(short pause)*

JEEP: The table's littered with carcasses. Guts. Bones. The insides. I'm in the middle of all this.

SHOOTER: Who are you talking to?

JEEP: I'm swimming in it.

SHOOTER: *(still front)* It's nobody's fault you know.

JEEP: I can't help eating. I'll eat to my dying day.

SHOOTER: Oh, brother!

SHOOTER *gives a heave and a groan and pushes with his feet so that the armchair tips over backwards with him in it. The bottom of the chair conceals* SHOOTER *from the audience. Only his voice is heard.* JEEP *continues with the fish methodically.*

JEEP: *(looking at the fish)* If you were alone would you have done that?

SHOOTER: I'm still in the chair. I'm sticking to my promise.

JEEP: You wouldn't call it showing off?

SHOOTER: I'm at my wit's end. The whole world could disappear.

The two women enter from upstage. Each one holds a handle on either end of a large wicker basket full of wet laundry. LUPE *is now wearing* LIZA's *apron with the pockets full of clothes pins. They haul the basket down left center where the clothesline is. They set the basket down on the floor, and* LUPE *grabs one of the chairs and stands up on it to reach the clothesline.* LIZA *starts handing her the wet clothes, one piece at a time from the basket, while* LUPE *pins them onto the line and pulls the line out, making room for the next piece. Gradually the clothes are strung clear across the stage but high enough so as not to block too much of the action.* JEEP *keeps working on the fish, cutting the head off, scaling it, fileting it, cleaning it off in the bucket of water, etc. He is very meticulous about it and gets more involved as he goes along.* SHOOTER *remains hidden behind the armchair. The two girls remain closed off in their activity.*

JEEP: I'm starting to feel better already. You remember before when I was getting the fears?

SHOOTER: No. When was that?

JEEP: When I was asking you if you remembered when you were scared to go up and take a bath.

SHOOTER: That was a long time ago.

JEEP: I'm getting better now. Even in the middle of all this violence.

SHOOTER: You should've told me you were scared. I would've done something about it. I didn't realize you were scared.

JEEP: I'm in a better position now. Now I've got something to do.

SHOOTER pulls the armchair over on top of himself so that his arms stick out the sides like a headless turtle. He moves the chair slightly from side to side with his back. The women continue in silence with the laundry.

JEEP: I can even imagine how horrifying it could be to be doing all this, and it doesn't touch me. It's like I'm dismissed.

SHOOTER: Am I completely hidden?

JEEP: More or less.

SHOOTER: Maybe I'm gone.

JEEP: Maybe.

SHOOTER: That's what it's like.

JEEP: Maybe that's it, then. Gone.

SHOOTER starts moving the armchair slowly around like a giant tortoise. The girls pay no attention.

SHOOTER: That's it all right. Flown the coop. Is there anyone to verify? To check it out?

JEEP: *(looking at the girls)* Are you sure you want to?

SHOOTER: Maybe it's better like this. We can keep it a secret.

JEEP: Are you sure you're not there?

SHOOTER: More or less. Something creeps back, now that you mention it.

JEEP: Oh.

SHOOTER: What's the matter?

JEEP: I don't know. I got no references for this. Suddenly it's shifted.

SHOOTER: What's the matter? You have to clue me in.

JEEP: Once, I was in a family. I had no choice about it. I lived in different houses. I had no choice. I couldn't even choose the wallpaper.

SHOOTER: Are you getting to the point?

JEEP: I found myself in schools. In cars. I got arrested. That was when it changed. The second I got arrested.

SHOOTER: Have you forgotten about me?

JEEP: The second I got arrested I understood something. I remember the phrase "getting in trouble." I remember the word "trouble." I remember the feeling of being in trouble. It wasn't until I got in trouble that I found out my true position.

SHOOTER: What was that?

JEEP: I was in the world. I was up for grabs. I was being taken away by something bigger.

SHOOTER: The cops?

JEEP: Something bigger. Bigger than family. Bigger than school. Bigger than the 4-H Club. Bigger than Little League Baseball. This was Big Time. My frame of reference changed.

SHOOTER: Did you go to jail?

JEEP: I went everywhere. Cop car, court, jail, cop car, jail, court, cop car, home, cop car, jail. And everywhere I noticed this new interest in my existence. These new details. Every scar was noted down. Every mark. The lines in my fingers. Hair. Eyes. Change in the pocket. Knives. Race. Age. Every detail.

SHOOTER: Who was interested?

JEEP: A vast network. A chain of events. I entered a new world.

SHOOTER: Weren't you scared?

JEEP: I used to have this dream that would come to me while I was on my feet. I'd be on my feet just standing there in these walls, and

I'd have this dream come to me that the walls were moving in. It was like a sweeping kind of terror that struck me. Then something in me would panic. I wouldn't make a move. I'd just be standing there very still, but inside something would leap like it was trying to escape. And then the leap would come up against something. It was like an absolutely helpless leap. There was no possible way of getting out. I couldn't believe it. It was like nothing in the whole wide world could get me out of there. I'd relax for a second. I'd be forced to relax because if I didn't, if I followed through with this inward leap, if I let my body do it I'd just crash against the wall. I'd just smash my head in or something. I had to relax. For a second I could accept it. That I was there. In jail. That I wasn't getting out. No escape. For a second. Then these thoughts would come. "How long? How long was I there for? A day. Maybe I could last a day. A week. A month? I'd never last a month! FOREVER!" That's the thought that did it. FOREVER! And the whole thing would start up again. Except worse this time. As though it wasn't just a thought. As though it really was. And then I'd start to move. I couldn't help myself. My body was shaking.

JEEP *begins to move around the stage. The words animate him as though the space is the cell he's talking about but not as though he's recalling a past experience but rather that he's attempting his own escape from the space he's playing in. The other actions continue in their own rhythm.*

I'd start to make sounds. It just came out of me. A low moan. An animal noise. I was moving now. I was stalking myself. I couldn't stop. Everything disappeared. I had no idea what the world was. I had no idea how I got there or why or who did it. I had no references for this.

JEEP *just stands there. The others continue their actions. Lights fade slowly to black. The Xmas tree keeps blinking.*

CURTAIN

The Mad Dog Blues

A Two-Act Adventure Show

The Mad Dog Blues was first presented by Theatre Genesis at St. Mark's Church in the Bowery on March 4, 1971. It was directed by Robert Glaudini and designed by Ralph Lee, with the following cast:

Kosmo: *Morris Lafon*
Yahoodi: *Jim Storm*
Waco Texas: *John Bottoms*
Marlene Dietrich: *Kathleen Cramer*
Mae West: *O-Lan Johnson-Shepard*
Captain Kidd: *Leroy Logan*
Paul Bunyan: *Robert Glaudini (later replaced by Beeson Carroll)*
Ghost Girl: *Nina Glaudini*
Jesse James: *Ralph Lee*
Musicians: *Sam Shepard, Lamar Alford, Robin Remaily,*
Michael Winsett

KOSMO: A rock-and-roll star. Dressed in a green velvet satin cape with tight blue velvet pants, teased hair and no shirt. He carries a conga drum.

YAHOODI: His sidekick. Dressed slick like a big-city dope dealer. Shades, short-brimmed black hat, and black suit with black patent-leather shoes. He carries an Indian flute.

WACO: A drifter from Texas. Dressed in raggedy pants and shirt, a long overcoat, and a cowboy hat and boots. Carries around a broken guitar.

MARLENE DIETRICH: Dressed in short shorts with teased hair, lots of makeup, high heels, and a whip.

MAE WEST: Dressed in a long sequined evening gown with a feather boa.

CAPTAIN KIDD: Dressed like a swashbuckler with saber, boots, and the whole bit.

PAUL BUNYAN: Dressed in giant proportions, with an ax.

GHOST GIRL: Dressed like a South Sea island girl. Carries a spear.

JESSE JAMES: Dressed like Jesse James, with a long raincoat.

SCENE: *An open, bare stage. All the places the characters move through are imagined and mimed. Some minor props can be used, but the production should stay away from heavy scenery. The lighting should designate where the characters are in time and space, following the rhythm of the action. The characters, costumes, and lights should be the main focus. All the offstage sound effects should be performed live, like those on oldtime radio shows (a large sheet of metal being shaken for thunder, and so on). The music should also be live, with the band in a pit below the stage as for a vaudeville show. Maybe the piano player could follow some of the action like they did with the old silent movies.*

The play opens with the theme music which KOSMO *keeps hearing throughout the play. This music is heard at different times, but not necessarily when* KOSMO *says he hears it in the script. After the music, lights come up on* KOSMO *and* YAHOODI *on opposite sides of the stage.* THEY *speak directly to the audience.*

PROLOGUE

KOSMO: Kosmo. Tall, lean, angular, wolflike. Leads with his cock. Intuitive decisions based on a leaking-roof brain. Lots of dashing images. Taken with himself as a man with the ladies. Has a sado-masochist hid in his closet. Fights him off in favor of a more heroic pose. Has no control over his primeval violence. Hates politics, philosophy, and religion. Asks for God's help. Gropes in the dark without a game. Invents one without no meaning. Gives the impression from the outside that he's winning. Moves from spot to spot across the planet hoping to find a home.

YAHOODI: Yahoodi. Short, dark, strikes like a serpent. Perfected a walk that cuts through the pavement. Loves how the brain works. Sucks in the printed word. Prefers isolation. Hates to be lonely. Has a weakness for soft things but hates to have them seen. Walks around the block five times preparing to cop. Passes himself off as a nigger. Watches for men in trenchcoats. Trades his mojo for a bag of coke and disappears in the night.

Blackout. Theme music, fading as the lights come up.

ACT I

Lights up. KOSMO *and* YAHOODI *still at opposite sides of the stage. Music fades.*

KOSMO: *(calling across a vast expanse)* Yahoodi! Hey, Yahoodi!

YAHOODI: Yeah!

KOSMO: I've had a vision!

YAHOODI: Here I come! *(traveling through different terrain)* Here I is.

KOSMO: I've had a vision.

YAHOODI: Yeah?

KOSMO: It came to me in music. It was like old rhythm-and-blues and gospel, a cappella, sort of like The Persuasions but with this bitchin' lead line. Like a Hendrix lead line. Like a living Hendrix lead line right through the middle of it.

YAHOODI: What about the visuals? Did ya see any pictures?

KOSMO: A tall golden woman like Marlene Dietrich or something. In short shorts and teased blonde hair. Carrying a whip.

SHE *appears and cracks her whip.*

YAHOODI: Sing it.

KOSMO: I can't. I can't get my head straight. I have to take a trip. I have to go somewhere else.

YAHOODI: Me too.

KOSMO: The city's gettin' me down. Too many tangents. It's no place to collaborate.

YAHOODI: Maybe we could do it by mail. I'll go to the jungle and write you.

KOSMO: Good idea. I'll go to San Francisco and do the same.

YAHOODI: Good luck, brother.

KOSMO: Same here.

THEY *travel in different directions.* YAHOODI *winds up in the jungle and* KOSMO *in Frisco.* MARLENE *comes down to the audience.* SHE *sings "Jungen Mensch."*

MARLENE:

Silly boys just young men
Go away and then they come again
They don't yet know who they are
Silly boys just young men following a star

They hurry here and they hurry there
Eager with their empty hands
Their heads are full their hearts are too
Oh hurry how hurried my lovely fools

End and then begin and end again
Like reflections in a pool
And loneliness comes like a dart
There's nothing to find till you find your heart

KOSMO: *(calling across a great expanse)* Yahoodi!

YAHOODI: *(calling back)* Yeah!

KOSMO: I've had another vision!

YAHOODI: Already!

KOSMO: Yeah! It's Mae West singing the blues like Janis Joplin!

YAHOODI: No shit! Should I come back?

KOSMO: Not yet. I haven't been able to give it any form. She's just sort of strutting around. There's so much cigarette smoke you can barely see her.

YAHOODI: What's it like there?

KOSMO: Full of inspiration! Jack Kerouac country! The Grateful Dead. The Airplane, Quicksilver. The air is full of grist for the mill. The Pacific is blue as hell. How 'bout you?

YAHOODI: Steaming jungle! Coconut girls! Giant pythons! Swinging in my hammock all day long.

KOSMO: Are you off the needle?

YAHOODI: Don't put me down.

KOSMO: I can't help it. I get concerned.

YAHOODI: How about you! How's your depressions?

KOSMO: They come and go like the wind. Here today, gone tomorrow. If I could just put something together. I keep feeling like I'm getting closer and closer to the truth.

MAE WEST *enters and saunters around* KOSMO.

YAHOODI: That's good. It's nighttime here and all the stars are out. The jungle makes the weirdest sounds. Jaguars are running wild. The little kids are sucking on mangoes. Suck, suck, suck, all night long.

KOSMO: *(to* MAE WEST*) Could you take me for a trolley ride?*

MAE WEST: I'll take ya for everything ya got.

KOSMO: Outa sight.

THEY *go for a trolley ride.*

YAHOODI: Ever since I was a little boy I used to watch the subway come up out of the ground and wonder about all those people. How all those people were just living their lives and couldn't care less about me. About how separate we were. Them on the train and me watching them. Them in their life and me in mine. I could see them and hear them and smell them but they didn't even know I existed. Good for them I'd say. Good for me. Hurray for life.

KOSMO: (to MAE, *still riding the trolley*) You're much smaller than the image I have in my head of you. You seemed so big in the movies.

MAE WEST: Big surprises come in small packages.

KOSMO: I could really fall for someone like you.

MAE WEST: You're not exactly a dog yourself.

KOSMO: I had this vision of you, and you were singing like Janis Joplin.

MAE WEST: Never heard of her.

KOSMO: She's dead.

MAE WEST: Maybe that's why.

KOSMO: She was a lot like you. Lots of balls. She could really belt it out.

MAE WEST: Yeah, well, beltin's not exactly my specialty.

KOSMO: She was lying face down between two double beds with her right hand holding the phone so hard that the veins were standing out on her thumb. She had a squirrel fur wrapped around her neck with little black eyes that stared out at me. There were ostrich feathers lying around on the rug and blowing into the air conditioning. The air conditioner made this high, whining sort of sound. The sound went right through me as though it were her voice talking to me, even though she was dead. Then it started to sing. Not like she sang when she was alive, but another kind of voice. A crystal voice. It passed right through me and then the window broke behind me. Like her voice went right through the window. I ran outside into the parking lot of the hotel. I could see her voice sailing over the parked cars. Sailing out over Sunset Boulevard. I ran after the voice. I tried to catch up, but each time I got nearer it took off again, like trying to catch a runaway kite. It sailed higher and higher, and then I saw you.

MAE WEST: Me? What was I doing there?

KOSMO: You were dancing to the voice. You were all dressed in red and you swayed back and forth. You swallowed the voice with the most delicious gulp and then you started to sing. You sang "When a man loves a woman." And right then everything stopped. I saw the whole world come to a dead stop and everyone was listening. Just listening. It was the most beautiful dream I've ever had.

MAE WEST: What do ya say we get us a bottle of hooch and find us a nice cozy place?

KOSMO: Okay by me.

THEY *get a bottle and find a nice cozy place.*

YAHOODI: *(calling across a great expanse, but* KOSMO *doesn't hear)* Kosmo! It's starting to hit me! Like a sledgehammer! Right in the chest! I need to get off! Kosmo! I need some Doliphine at least! Just a little something to tide me over! This jungle's tearing me apart! The bugs are driving me bats!

MARLENE *enters and goes to* YAHOODI.

MARLENE: You put too much emphasis on the pain. Take your mind off the pain. Take your mind off the pain. Your friend is safe and sound in San Francisco.

YAHOODI: Fuck him! Fuck my friend! What good's he do me now? *(to* MARLENE*)* What are you doing here? You got any money? If only I was better known! If only I was famous! I could fly back to the city and put a needle in my arm! I could buy a farm in the country and raise a family and be a happily married man.

MARLENE: It's a good thing to dream.

YAHOODI: What do you know? What do you know about my suffering? What's your suffering compared to mine?

MARLENE: I could take it away. I could steal it from you.

YAHOODI: I don't need sex! I need some dope! Dope! I need some dope!

MARLENE: I need, you need, we all need some ice cream.

THEY *go into a heavy clinch and slurp each other up. Then* THEY *fall asleep.* KOSMO *and* MAE WEST *are now riding in a limousine.*

KOSMO: I keep hearing music. Where are we?

MAE WEST: I took the liberty of having my chauffeur pick us up. You were gettin' a little feisty back at the Blue Onion.

KOSMO: Blue Onion? Where are you taking me? I want to go home.

MAE WEST: Just a little cruise down to Big Sur. Thought we'd watch the waves crash against the rocks and all the seals makin' whoopee.

KOSMO: I gotta get back. The revolution's on.

MAE WEST: What channel?

KOSMO: No, no. It's now or never. If I miss my moment in history it may never happen again. I've got to become involved.

MAE WEST: You were doin' all right by me.

KOSMO: I've gotta make bombs and speeches and mobilize the people. I've gotta work for the party. I've gotta see to it that justice is done. It's now or never. Now is real!

MAE WEST: You said it, brother.

KOSMO: Lemme outa the car! Lemme out! Lemme out!

HE *falls out of the car and rolls across the stage into* PAUL BUN-YAN.

PAUL BUNYAN: You seen Babe? I been lookin' all over.

KOSMO: I don't know what you're talking about.

PAUL BUNYAN: My ox. Babe. He's blue. You seen him?

KOSMO: I don't know. Look, do you know how to get back to New York City? I do believe I've had enough. What highway is this?

PAUL BUNYAN: This is the North Woods. Ain't no highway for miles. Just lumber camps and diners and trucks and chain saws. Sell ya a good ax if ya need one. That's all I use. These new fellas they use the chain saws, but not me. I can outchop the fastest chain saw around.

KOSMO: I believe it. Just point me in the direction of home, okay?

PAUL BUNYAN: I need to find my ox or I'm up shit creek without a paddle. There's nothin' like a good ox. Worth their weight in gold. Especially old Babe.

KOSMO: My mind's going a mile a minute! I've got to slow down.

PAUL BUNYAN: This is the best place for it. Nothing like the North Woods for a little peace and quite. Just chew on some acorns. Hum a little tune. Whittle your fingernails.

KOSMO: But I'm a musician! I've got to create! I've got to get back to the city. Back to my band. Back to my roots. I've lost touch with my roots.

PAUL BUNYAN: You city folks are all alike. Always tryin' to make a buck.

KOSMO: No. I'm not in it for the money. I'm an artist.

PAUL BUNYAN: Me, I'm a lumberjack. See ya around.

HE *exits.* YAHOODI *wakes up.* MARLENE *stays asleep.*

YAHOODI: *(calling across a great expanse)* Kosmo! I had a dream! I dreamed I was Crazy Horse! I was leading a raiding party against the Crows. I wore a small yellow stone under my left ear, and a hawk circled over me as I rode into battle. I felt what it was like to have no fear. To be completely free from fear. Nothing could touch me. The arrows flew all around me but none of them touched me. It was like I had an understanding of space in another dimension. I knew where the arrows would land. I knew—(HE *notices* MARLENE*)* Hey! Hey, Marlene! Hey. Wake up. Stupid broad. What are ya gonna do, sleep the day away? Hey, Kosmo, I think she's o.d.'d or something. Kosmo!

KOSMO: I was on a Greyhound bus out of Carlsbad heading for Loving, New Mexico. Back to see my dad. After ten years. All duded out in a double-breasted suit with my shoes all shined. The driver calls out "Loving" and I get off the bus. The bus takes off and leaves me in a cloud of dust. Nothing but dust. The dust clears and there I am. Standing right in the middle of a ghost town. Nothing. The stores all boarded up. The windows all busted out. I pick up my bags and start hoofin' it down the street. There's the old Bijou Theatre with Anita Ekberg's name still on it from 1959. And Rose's Cafe where I used to have enchiladas and tamales. And there, way down at the end of the road, rising up like a beautiful vision is my old man's bar. The Palace Saloon! I walk in and all this music comes blasting out at me. It's Pedro Enfantes on the juke box. And my old man behind the bar. His shoulder holster bulging out underneath his coat. I order a beer. And he says sure, son, have a beer. And I say don't call me son. And he says why not and I say because I *am* you son. And he says sure. And I say I am! And he says fuck off. So I say fuck off. Don't you recognize me? It's me, your son!

YAHOODI: *(calling across a great expanse)* Kosmo!

KOSMO: Yeah!

YAHOODI: I've had a vision!

KOSMO: Here I come! (HE *travels through different terrain and arrives at* YAHOODI)

YAHOODI: I had a vision you were coming.

KOSMO: Here I am.

YAHOODI: How was your trip?

KOSMO: I lost my way. It's no fun being on the road.

YAHOODI: I know what ya mean. Still, it's good to get away for a while. This city's a real drag. All I ever do is shoot doogie.

KOSMO: What about your vision?

YAHOODI: A giant American bald eagle flying through a smoke-filled sky with the world clutched in his talons. He flies higher and higher until he can't fly anymore and then he lets the world drop. The world falls faster and faster through the smoke-filled sky and plunges into the ocean and explodes sending a huge tidal wave up to the surface.

KOSMO: I'm getting fucking tired of apocalypses. All I ever hear anymore is apocalypse, apocalypse. What about something with some hope?

YAHOODI: It's up to you, boy.

WACO *enters. An old cowboy in an overcoat, boots, hat, with a beat-up guitar.* HE *sings:*

WACO:

I been fightin' like a lion.
But I'm 'fraid I'm gonna lose.
I been fightin' like a lion.
But I'm 'fraid I'm gonna lose.
'Cause there ain't been nobody can whip these old TB blues.*

Old Jimmie. Jimmie Rodgers. Good old Jimmie Rodgers. He had heart. That's what he had. Heart. I'm gonna put him back on the street. 'Cause I love him. Gonna put him right back on the street. You boys know him?

KOSMO: Jimmie Rodgers? Sure.

WACO: Not the young one. The old one. Old Jimmie.

KOSMO: Yeah. I know Jimmie Rodgers.

WACO: You know old Jimmie? Good old boy. That was his last song. "The TB Blues." TB's a motherfucker, boy. It'll tear you up. He knew he was goin' out. He knew it. You got a cigarette?

KOSMO: Yeah, sure.

WACO: Thanks, boy.

YAHOODI: Well look, Kosmo. I'm gonna take a trip.

KOSMO: Again? You just got back.

YAHOODI: I can't stand it anymore. I gotta get out of here.

KOSMO: You're always running out on me. Every time something gets rough you walk out.

YAHOODI: I got to, man.

KOSMO: Okay. Split.

YAHOODI: Well, don't get mad. It's got nothing to do with you.

KOSMO: Just split!

WACO: He knew he was goin' out and he was singin' just the same. *(sings)* "I been fightin' like a lion . . ."

YAHOODI: You're cracking up.

KOSMO: Me! It's not me, boy! You're the one that's fucked. You're the junkie! You're the morbid little nihilistic junkie! Not me! I got my whole life in front of me. And I'm not going down in your hole with you just because you can't see the sun in the morning.

---

*"The TB Blues" by Jimmie Rodgers. Copyright © 1931 by Peer International Corporation. Copyright renewed by Peer International Corporation. Used by permission.

YAHOODI: Fuck you!

KOSMO: Fuck you!

WACO: He had heart. That's what he had. A man's gotta have heart. Go where the heart goes.

YAHOODI: Shut up!

KOSMO: Don't tell him to shut up. He's a friend of mine.

WACO: That's right. Name's Waco. Waco Texas. That's where I was born.

YAHOODI: Who gives a rat's ass?

KOSMO: You turn everything into shit.

YAHOODI: You're really cracking up. Look at you. Shaking all over. Your mind's blowing up. You got no patience. If you could just slow down. You're going to burn yourself up.

KOSMO: I gotta play some music. I gotta find my band. I gotta find a guru or something. Go to the country and eat brown rice and hoe my own garden and plant my own seeds. Listen to the music. I keep hearing the music.

YAHOODI: It's all in your head.

KOSMO: Get away from me! Get out of here! Go on! Take your trip! Go as far away as you can! Get out of my sight!

YAHOODI *takes off and winds up by* MARLENE. HE *doesn't hear* KOSMO.

KOSMO: No! Yahoodi! I'm sorry! Come back! I need you! We're brothers! Yahoodi! I love you.

WACO: Just follow your heart. That's what a man's supposed to do. The only thing a man can do. Just follow your heart.

KOSMO: Maybe you're right.

WACO: Sure.

KOSMO: But look where it got you. You're from Texas?

WACO: Born and raised.

KOSMO: How'd you wind up here?

WACO: I'm just here. That's all. I'm just here.

KOSMO: I know what you mean. It doesn't seem right to suffer. You know? I'm going to stop suffering right now. I'm going to have some bacon and eggs and stop suffering. The air tastes really good. Come on, Waco Texas. We're gonna live!

WACO *and* KOSMO *move to another part of the stage to have some bacon and eggs.*

WACO: *(sings)*

I been fightin' like a lion.
And I do believe I'm gonna win.
I been fightin' like a lion—

Song fades out.

YAHOODI: Marlene? Marlene? You all right?

MARLENE: *(waking up)* I feel, how do you say, "A-OK."

YAHOODI: What happened?

MARLENE: I lost another man. It's a long sad story. My heart is very heavy.

YAHOODI: How about a mango? Could ya go for a mango?

MARLENE: Sure. A mango in the morning is sometimes better than a man.

YAHOODI: Sure feels good to be outa the States. Ya know? I was getting so uptight up there I couldn't see straight.

THEY *take a stroll.*

MARLENE: You're a very sensitive man. You're an artist.

YAHOODI: Maybe I could get a job as a short-order cook or something. Maybe working in the oil fields. Or gold! How about gold! Did you ever think of that?

MARLENE: No. You did.

YAHOODI: Yeah. Sure. Gold! Why not. If I could just find Humphrey Bogart we'd be in business.

MARLENE: But he's so crude. You need a man with finesse.

YAHOODI: To hunt for gold?

MARLENE: You need a man who knows the ropes.

YAHOODI: We could buy the mules in Nogales. Plenty a cheap mules in Nogales.

THEY *run into* PAUL BUNYAN.

PAUL BUNYAN: You seen Babe? He's my ox. A blue ox.

YAHOODI: That's it! We'll use oxen instead. Hey, where could I buy some cheap oxen? You got any for sale?

PAUL BUNYAN: You city slickers are always looking to buy and sell things. I've lost my Babe. That's all I know.

MARLENE: It's hard to lose a loved one.

PAUL BUNYAN: It's even harder to find one.

YAHOODI: Listen, I'm gonna wire Kosmo for some money. We could really strike it rich out here. I'll be right back. You two get acquainted while I'm gone. I won't be long. *(*HE *goes to the telephone and calls* KOSMO)*

MARLENE: You've got such mysterious eyes.

PAUL BUNYAN: Listen, ma'am, I've lost my ox and I can't do a thing without him.

MARLENE: Your eyes. Such mysterious eyes.

THEY *go into a long clinch.*

YAHOODI: *(on the phone)* Kosmo! That you?

KOSMO: *(on the phone)* Yahoodi? Where you been?

YAHOODI: Listen, I've run into a hot deal down here in the jungle and I need some fast money. Say a couple G's.

KOSMO: A couple G's? I'll check out my royalties. I think I can swing it. What is it, dope?

YAHOODI: No, gold! Lots and lots of gold!

KOSMO: Out of sight! I'll send it right away!

YAHOODI: Thanks, pal. *(HE hangs up)*

KOSMO: *(to WACO)* That was Yahoodi. He's struck gold.

WACO: Gold? In the Yukon?

KOSMO: Nope. Somewhere in the jungle.

WACO: Hot diggity.

KOSMO: We gotta get down there, Waco.

WACO: Not me, boy. I'm allergic to mosquitoes.

KOSMO: Come on, it's now or never.

THEY *travel south.* YAHOODI *goes to* MARLENE *and* PAUL BUNYAN.

YAHOODI: Listen, I just contacted my man. He's sending us a couple of G's. So we're all set. All we need now is the mules.

CAPTAIN KIDD *enters.*

CAPT. KIDD: What do ya wanna play around with mules for, limey? I got a treasure all hid away to make the likes a gold seem like dogshit.

YAHOODI: Who're you?

CAPT. KIDD: The name's Kidd, Captain Kidd.

YAHOODI: How do. This is Marlene Dietrich and Paul Bunyan. My name's Yahoodi. That's what they call me anyway. What's this about a treasure?

CAPT. KIDD: Spanish bullion tucked away in a neat little island protected by the prettiest cove ye ever laid eyes on.

YAHOODI: Must be gone by now. Somebody musta run across it.

CAPT. KIDD: No sir. It's protected by a ghost. An Indian girl who hides deep in the cave where it's buried.

MARLENE: Sounds pretty risky, darling.

PAUL BUNYAN: Yeah, you can count me out. All I want is my Babe. I'll see you around. (HE *exits*)

YAHOODI: Wait a minute! That always happens. Just as things are beginning to look up everybody cops out.

MARLENE: Listen, darling, it does sound a little farfetched. It could be, how do you say, a "wild goose chase."

YAHOODI: You too? Everybody's turning against me. Go then! Go!

MARLENE: Now don't be so hasty, darling.

YAHOODI: Ya got a map of this island, Kidd? I guess we'll have to take a boat, right?

CAPT. KIDD: Right. Here is the map.

HE *pulls out a huge map.* YAHOODI, MARLENE *and* CAPTAIN KIDD *examine it. We go to* WACO *and* KOSMO. *As* THEY *travel along,* THEY *sing "Travelin' Shoes."*

WACO AND KOSMO:

I'm just travelin' along in my shoes
Payin' my dues, travelin' along

When I get that hold down blues
I get on the move with my travelin' shoes

La da la da la da da la da la da la

THEY *sing this through twice.*

WACO: Say listen, ain't we gone quite a fer piece? This is gettin' a little tiring.

KOSMO: Let's just sit down here by the side of the stream and take a little breather.

THEY *sit and drink from the stream.* MAE WEST *sneaks up behind* WACO. HE *sees her reflection in the water.*

WACO: Sure is a long trip. I never woulda come if I'd a knowed it was gonna take so long.

KOSMO: It'll be worth it once we're there. All that gold! Just think of it! We'll be able to go anywhere and do anything and be anyone we want to.

WACO: Could I be Jimmie Rodgers?

KOSMO: Sure, why not?

WACO: Who're you gonna be?

KOSMO: I don't know. A different me.

WACO: Why don't you be somebody else. Somebody different from you. You could be Gene Autry or somebody like that. That's great! You be Gene Autry and I'll be Jimmie Rodgers and we'll form a singing team. How 'bout it?

KOSMO: No thanks. I got my own music to sing.

WACO: Boy, your feet sure do smell. Don't you ever take yer boots off?

KOSMO: *My* feet? I was gonna say the same about your feet.

WACO: Well, I know my feet smell but that ain't no excuse for lettin' yer feet go to pot. You gotta take care a yer feet, boy. That's what gets ya around.

KOSMO: I got other things to worry about besides my feet.

WACO: Maybe that's yer whole problem. If ya worried more about yer feet smellin' so bad and less about things that don't exist you'd be a happier fella. Take me as a case in point. I've spent my whole life worrying about things that might happen that never did happen.

KOSMO: Sure is nice country out here. Too bad we have to move on.

WACO: Yeah, well that's the thing about travelin'. Ya never get to see the things in between where yer comin' from and where yer going to. Say, you been noticin' any change in my appearance lately?

KOSMO: No. Why?

WACO: Well, my reflection sure does remind me of this beautiful broad I used to know back in Omaha.

MAE WEST: Coulda been Pensacola for all the attention ya gave me.

HE *turns around and grabs* MAE *by the waist and dances around with her.*

WACO: Mae! Well, I'll be a snaggle-toothed hog-whomper! If it ain't old Mae!

MAE WEST: Easy on the merchandise, big boy.

HE *puts her down.*

WACO: Last time I seen you, you was holdin' four kings to my four queens.

MAE WEST: You never was much with the ladies.

KOSMO: What made you show up at such an opportune moment?

MAE WEST: I can smell a gold mine a mile off. Same as a man, only sweeter.

KOSMO: I suppose you figure we're going to cut you in on this deal.

MAE WEST: Listen, I know how to wrap that Yahoodi character around my little finger. I'll have him eatin' outa the palm a my hand. All you fellas have to do is step in and take things over.

WACO: Sounds good to me.

KOSMO: I don't know. He's a friend of mine.

MAE WEST: Listen, big boy, what do ya think he's doin' down there in that Mexican jungle with Marlene? Sellin' lottery tickets? He's gonna rip you off for your two G's, grab the gold, and head West.

KOSMO: Yahoodi? He wouldn't do that.

MAE WEST: I've seen suckers, but you take the bananas.

WACO: What're you gettin' at, Mae?

MAE WEST: We play it cool. We go down in disguises and infiltrate into the village where they're camped out. One of us finds out the lowdown. Then we give them the money.

KOSMO: But he doesn't even know I'm coming.

MAE WEST: That's why the disguise. Soon as we find out what the plan is we step in and take the whole thing over.

WACO: Just like that?

MAE WEST: Just like that.

KOSMO: Wouldn't it be better to follow them to the mines to make sure we can find them?

MAE WEST: We'll play it by ear.

KOSMO: Let's go.

> THEY *travel south, singing a snatch of "Travelin' Shoes." Meanwhile, back to* MARLENE *and the* BOYS.

YAHOODI: This is a hard map to follow, Captain.

CAPT. KIDD: Leave it to me, me lad. It's clear sailin' all the way.

YAHOODI: We still gotta wait for the money. Kosmo promised he'd send it. I've been thinkin' we oughta divvy up the loot with him, too.

CAPT. KIDD: What's this! Another party! I hadn't bargained for another party, laddie.

YAHOODI: Now wait a minute. He's my friend. I can't just cut him out of the deal.

MARLENE: But darling, he's so rich. He's a famous pop star.

YAHOODI: That don't cut no ice. A friend is a friend. We took the oath. We drank each other's blood.

MARLENE: That's disgusting.

YAHOODI: Besides, what do we need his money for, anyway? We've got a boat.

CAPT. KIDD: We have to travel. We have to eat.

YAHOODI: I'm beginning to have my doubts about this whole thing. How come you need us to go and get your treasure? I mean, you have the map and everything. You know where it is. Why are you so all fired up to cut us in on the deal?

CAPT. KIDD: You have no idea how much there is. Chest after chest piled so high you can barely see the top. A treasure so vast it would take one man a lifetime to bring it up to the surface. Besides, I'm getting old. I'm not long for this earth, and it would do my heart joy to see two young people such as yerselves partake of such riches.

YAHOODI: I don't know. I don't like doin' my friend dirty like that. I mean just taking his money and running away.

MARLENE: But think of our life together, Yahoodi. We could go to San Francisco, Paris, Rome, Berlin. Ah, Berlin!

YAHOODI: What do I wanna go to Berlin for? I'm an American.

CAPT. KIDD: Then forget the whole thing. I'll go find some peasants. (HE *rolls up the map in a huff*)

YAHOODI: No! Wait. I'll do it. I'll do it.

MARLENE: That's more like it, darling.

CAPT. KIDD: Now the first thing we gotta do is wait for the money.

YAHOODI: Right.

MARLENE: I'll handle your friend when he comes. Just leave him to me.

Back to MAE WEST *and the* BOYS. THEY *have on ridiculous disguises—beards and masks and stuff. False noses would be good.*

MAE WEST: Now listen, Kosmo, what you gotta do is pretend you're a peasant that's working for Western Union. You got a special cablegram to deliver this money to Mr. Yahoodi. You got that?

KOSMO: Got it.

WACO: What do we do?

MAE WEST: Just sit tight. We'll think a something. Okay, now go to it.

KOSMO *sneaks over to* MARLENE *and the* BOYS *in his special disguise, with a black satchel full of money.*

KOSMO: Cablegram for Meester Yahoodi!

YAHOODI: That's me.

KOSMO: Oh. Well I got thees money for Mr. Yahoodi. Special delivery from Meester Kosmo.

YAHOODI: Good. Hand it over.

HE *hands over the satchel.* YAHOODI *looks inside.*

Thank you very much.

MARLENE: Darling, tip the boy.

YAHOODI: Oh, yeah. (HE *pulls out a bill and hands it to* KOSMO) This is for you.

KOSMO: Thank you, señor.

YAHOODI: Oh, and send a cable back to Mr. Kosmo telling him thank you very much we got your money.

KOSMO: I don't got a pencil.

YAHOODI: Okay, forget it.

KOSMO: Okay, gracias, señor.

YAHOODI: Yeah. Gracias.

CAPT. KIDD: Adios.

> KOSMOS *goes back to* MAE *and* WACO. YAHOODI *and the* OTHERS *break into cheers.*

YAHOODI: We got it! We got it! We're gonna be rich!

KOSMO: *(to* MAE*)* I think the dirty rat was plannin' on cutting me out of the deal all along.

MAE WEST: It's all right. We got him where we want him. It's only a matter of time now.

WACO: Well, let's build us a fire and have some hot fritters.

MAE WEST: No. We let them build the fires. We let them make the moves. We just follow along in their footsteps. We're gonna shadow them right to that treasure, boys.

> MARLENE *and the* BOYS *build a fire and sit around eating and talking.*

YAHOODI: What about this boat, Captain? Don't we need a crew or something?

CAPT. KIDD: Naw. As worthy a vessel you've never seen. The three of us can handle her easy.

MARLENE: Darling, where exactly is the treasure located?

CAPT. KIDD: A little island near the Aleutian group. It shouldn't be hard to recognize. I'll remember it once we get there.

YAHOODI: What's the treasure like, Captain Kidd? I mean what is it, jewels and stuff?

CAPT. KIDD: Aaah, laddie. 'Tis a treasure to make a man's eyes dance out of his head. There's a ruby ring as big as your fist plucked from the hand of a young maiden who boldly resisted. I was forced to sever her finger from her hand with my saber while her lover stood helplessly by. Those were the days before my conversion, before I saw the light. The cruel days.

YAHOODI: What made you become a pirate in the first place?

CAPT. KIDD: Everyone was doing it. I was sent by the king to put a stop to all this swashbuckling nonsense. But after several days at sea I realized I was working for the wrong side. No one was a bigger pirate than the king himself. So I decided to beat him at his own game. I would become as ruthless, as fearsome and as cruel as all the fancy-dressed snuff-sniffers riding their gilded carriages to and from the palace.

MARLENE: What other treasures are there, darling?

CAPT. KIDD: Sapphires, topaz, diamonds, and pearls. A gold watch with emerald hands on inlaid ivory and ebony, snatched from a poor lad as he was walking the plank. Pouches of gold and silver. Coins of every description. Shimmering platters and vases. Crystal chandeliers. Gold fillings from those who disobeyed. Deeds to land in faraway places. Hand-carved muskets with mother-of-pearl handles.

YAHOODI: It's amazing! All that just waiting for us. Just waiting for the taking. All of my dreams are going to come true. Sure wish Kosmo was here.

MARLENE: Just listen to those nightingales.

CAPT. KIDD: Them is katydids, ma'am. Katydids.

YAHOODI: In the jungle? Katydids in the jungle?

CAPT. KIDD: Or maybe crocodiles.

YAHOODI: That's more like it.

MARLENE: Darling, I think I'll turn in. The night chill is creeping into my bones.

CAPT. KIDD: Same here, lady. Tomorrow's a big day.

THEY *turn in. Back to* MAE *and the* BOYS, *trying to get to sleep.*

KOSMO: Can't we build a fire, Mae? We're gonna freeze our buns off out here.

WACO: Yeah, besides there's big cats out there. Tigres. They liable to eat us alive.

MAE WEST: You ain't in the Boy Scouts. This is real life.

KOSMO: I was thinking. Maybe we oughta give up on this whole thing. I mean I'm rich and famous. What do I need a bunch of gold for?

MAE WEST: Gettin' butterflies already, huh?

WACO: I could sure go for a little nest egg myself. Get me a little cattle ranch out in Arizona. Raise a family.

MAE WEST: Go to sleep.

THEY *fall asleep. Both camps are sleeping. The night sounds of crickets and small jungle creatures.* YAHOODI *and* KOSMO *talk to each other in their sleep. The* OTHERS *stay asleep.* YAHOODI *tosses about as though having a nightmare.*

YAHOODI: Kosmo! It isn't really me. Not my voice. It's you. No. That doesn't make sense. We'll meet up sooner or later. You've taken my place. That's an awful thing to lay on someone. I'm so many different people at once. I keep running away from unseen executioners. You dig where I'm coming from? My feet are caught in the quicksand.

KOSMO: I don't want to die in my sleep. I just want to know I was here. I have an awful memory of places I never was. I was never there. Yahoodi! It's me. It's me again in a different place.

YAHOODI: I can hear you. We've developed a telepathy. You don't have to explain.

KOSMO: I'm following you. I'm dogging your trail. You'll never get away. This is the end of the trail, buckaroo.

YAHOODI: And how long is this night supposed to last? Not nearly as long as the one coming up. The big night in the sky.

KOSMO: Don't get poetic. You'll wake up with a shock. Don't worry. The sun is coming for you, boy.

A loud roar offstage. THEY *jump up.*

What was that?

WACO: One a them tigres. I knew it. We're gonna die. We're all gonna die.

MAE WEST: Don't get your panties in a bunch. It's just the call a the wild.

Back to MARLENE *and the* BOYS.

YAHOODI: Marlene?

MARLENE: Yes, darling?

YAHOODI: Did you hear something?

MARLENE: No, my pet. Go to sleep. You need your rest.

YAHOODI: You know, ever since we started this treasure thing I've had the strangest feeling we're being followed.

MARLENE: It's just your imagination. The jungle does that to you.

YAHOODI: I'm going to wake up Captain Kidd.

MARLENE: But darling—

YAHOODI: Hey! Captain! Captain Kidd!

CAPTAIN KIDD *snores loudly and turns over.* YAHOODI *kicks him.*

Wake up!

MARLENE: Darling, let him sleep. We have a big day ahead of us.

YAHOODI: Hey, Captain! Wake up!

CAPTAIN KIDD *jumps to his feet, saber at the ready.*

CAPT. KIDD: Scuttle the mainsail! Swab the port bow! Every man for himself!

YAHOODI: Hold on. Wait a minute.

CAPT. KIDD: Oh, it's you. What do you mean waking me out of a sound sleep?

YAHOODI: Listen, I think we oughta take off tonight. I think we're being followed.

CAPT. KIDD: Followed?

YAHOODI: Yeah. I've been hearing all these weird noises.

CAPT. KIDD: Followed! We're being followed!

MARLENE: It's just his imagination.

CAPT. KIDD: Well, if it's true then you're right. By all means. We leave tonight! We leave this instant! Pack up your gear.

Music THEY *take off on a march and wind up at the boat.* THEY *climb in the boat and set sail. Meanwhile back to* MAE *and the* BOYS.

KOSMO: Listen, Mae. I think I'm going to go check their camp out. Just to make sure they're not pulling any funny stuff.

WACO: I think we oughta stick together. Them tigres can be mighty fierce.

MAE WEST: You think they're up to something, huh? All right, but be quick about it. Me and Waco here'll hold down the camp.

KOSMO: I'll be right back.

KOSMO *sneaks off through the jungle to where* MARLENE *and the* BOYS *were camped.*

WACO: Listen, Mae, to tell you the truth I'm scared shitless. I mean I ain't used to the jungle. The open prairie's my stompin' grounds.

MAE WEST: Yeah, well just cool yourself out. The worst is yet to come. I wonder what's keeping Kosmo.

WACO: The tigres probably got him. I knew it! I knew it! We're all gonna die!

KOSMO *discovers that* MARLENE *and the* BOYS *have split.* HE *goes running back to* MAE *and* WACO *with the news.*

MAE WEST: Just take it easy. SHHH! I think I hear someone comin'.

KOSMO *comes running up to them out of breath.*

KOSMO: They've left! They're gone!

MAE WEST: Are ya sure?

KOSMO: Positive.

MAE WEST: Why the dirty double-crossers. So they flew the coop on us. Well, let's get a move on.

WACO: Right now? We're leaving right now? In the dark? We're goin' out there in the dark?

MAE WEST: We gotta catch up to 'em before they get too much of a head start.

KOSMO: Right. Let's go.

THEY *move out into the jungle. Back to* MARLENE *and the* BOYS *riding the high seas in their boat.* CAPTAIN KIDD *sings "Fadin'."*

CAPT. KIDD:

I once was the master of the torrid high seas
I pillaged the king's ships, I stole what I pleased
My heart was full sail tattooed with sin
You could rest my good deeds on the head of a pin

I raged and men feared me, they called me black heart
Gold tooth and black patch and tongue like a dart
The women all wanted me and called me a louse
Though tempted by treasure and my black pirate mouth

With visions of white ships I crawled through the night
A victim of penitence and clean-living light
I traded my dark deeds for an angel's good word
My soul fled the devil like a trembling bird

My masthead throws a shadow black as a spade
On the torrid high seas where Captain Kidd fades
On the torrid high seas where Captain Kidd fades

I deceive all that's evil, offer gifts from the sea
The navigator saints all smile on me
And the Book I once branded a book black as hell
Floats broken and damaged in the earth's briny cell

Yet I once was the master of the torrid high seas
A skull and crossbones draped around me
I wear my past proudly tight like a glove
My terrible deeds twist me like love

My masthead throws a shadow black as a spade
On the torrid high seas where Captain Kidd fades
On the torrid high seas where Captain Kidd fades

YAHOODI: This is the life. What a life. How 'bout it, Marlene? Ain't this the life!

MARLENE: *(hanging over the side of the boat)* I think I'm going to be sick.

YAHOODI: What a life. Say, Captain, I wouldn't mind taking that treasure and sailing around the world. Just taking a nice long cruise. What do ya say?

CAPT. KIDD: No, laddie, I think I'll be settling down somewhere off the coast of Spain. Me and the high seas have seen too much of each other.

YAHOODI: Sharks! Look! There's sharks!

CAPT. KIDD: No, me lad. Them's dolphins. Hard to tell the difference at first. But they're a friend of man. If ya listen real close they sing a certain song. Us old sea dogs can hear it a mile off.

YAHOODI: I think I hear it.

CAPT. KIDD: No, you can't hear it. Only us old sea dogs can hear it.

YAHOODI: But I hear it. I swear I can hear it.

CAPT. KIDD: Well, I can't hear it, so how could you be hearin' it?

MARLENE *keeps puking over the side.*

YAHOODI: Then it is my imagination. Like last night. I was hearing something last night too. I am hearing something. We *are* being followed. Faster, Captain Kidd! Faster!

CAPT. KIDD: Just settle down, me lad. There's nothin' around for miles. Take a look for yerself. Nothin' but the deep blue sea.

YAHOODI: Gimme your telescope. I'm going to take a look.

CAPTAIN KIDD *hands him a telescope.* YAHOODI *looks behind him.*

CAPT. KIDD: Well, what do ya see?

YAHOODI: I see a bunch of Mexicans waving a flag and dancing around a fire.

CAPT. KIDD: What else do ya see?

YAHOODI: I see two men on a raft eating Tootsie Rolls.

CAPT. KIDD: What else do ya see?

YAHOODI: I see the whole world going up in smoke and everybody's asleep. There's one old man with a long gray beard trying to wake everybody up but nobody can hear him. They just keep sleeping and sleeping.

CAPT. KIDD: Give me back the telescope. You've gone mad, me lad. It happens to the best of us. But this old ocean does funny things to the mind of man.

YAHOODI: You really think I'm crazy?

CAPT. KIDD: No crazier than the likes of me.

YAHOODI: I wish she'd stop throwing up. It makes me sick.

Back to MAE *and the* BOYS *caught in a storm on the high seas.* THEY'*re in a rowboat.*

WACO: I knew it! We're gonna die! We're all gonna die!

KOSMO: Will you shut up. It's just a storm. It'll pass.

MAE: Watch the port bow, boys. There's a real crusher wave coming up.

WACO: I think I'm gonna be sick.

SHE WACO *throws up over the side.*

MAE WEST: I've seen useless men in my day, but he takes the cake.

KOSMO: He's all right, Mae. He's just used to dry land. He's a cowboy. Cowboys don't go to sea.

MAE: Cowboy, my eyeball. He's a useless twerp. We shoulda canned him right from the start.

KOSMO: Now don't start that. Just because we're in a crisis doesn't mean we can't get along.

MAE: Man the starboard keel! Bring her about! Bring her about!

KOSMO: Where'd you learn all that lingo?

MAE: I've been around, sonny.

KOSMO: Looks like it's gonna clear up.

MAE: Just like that?

KOSMO: Looks like it. Looks like it's going to be a beautiful day.

MAE: All right, you can stop being sick, mister. The storm's over.

KOSMO: Yeah, it looks like it's going to be clear as a bell.

MAE: Here, take a look through this thing and see if you can spot their boat.

SHE *hands him a telescope.* KOSMO *looks through it.*

MAE: You see anything?

KOSMO: Wild dogs.

MAE: What do you mean?

KOSMO: Wild dogs. Circling around. Tracking something down.

MAE: You must be going crazy. Gimme that thing.

HE *hands it to her.* SHE *looks through it.*

MAE: It's them. I can see them.

KOSMO: Really?

WACO *pukes over the side.*

MAE: Looks like they're having trouble. Marlene's sick. She's puking over the side. Looks like one of their sails is broken. There's sharks circling all around the boat. They're in real trouble. Looks like we're gonna catch up to 'em after all.

KOSMO: Lemme see. (HE *takes the telescope and looks*)

MAE: Can you see them?

KOSMO: Nope. I keep hearing music. Jimi Hendrix.

MAE: You can't see them? You must have cotton in your eyeballs.

KOSMO: Oh, yeah. Now I see them. Paul Bunyan's pulling them ashore with his ox.

MAE: Are you kidding?

KOSMO: No. Look.

SHE *takes the telescope and looks.*

MAE: I can't see them anymore. Where'd they go? Full steam ahead. Come on! Let's get a move on! Row! Row! Row! Faster! Faster! We're losing them!

THEY *all start rowing like crazy. Back to* CAPTAIN KIDD.

YAHOODI: Hey, Captain, how many months have we been out here?

MARLENE: Oh, don't say it. It makes me sick to think of it. What a waste of a good life. I could be in Berlin having a good time. Or Copenhagen. Anywhere but here in this awful ocean.

CAPT. KIDD: I'd say maybe six or seven months as the crow flies.

YAHOODI: That long, huh?

MARLENE: It's awful. My makeup has faded. My furs are all wilted. My stockings are torn. And I'm starving to death.

YAHOODI: Shut up, will you? All you ever do is bitch, bitch, bitch. Just be thankful we're still alive.

CAPTAIN KIDD *spots land.*

CAPT. KIDD: Land ho! Land ho!

YAHOODI: Really! Land! It is! It's land, Marlene! We're safe! Look!

MARLENE: Oh, thank God. Land. At last.

YAHOODI: Well, what are we waiting for? Let's go ashore.

CAPT. KIDD: Not so fast. The natives could be dangerous.

YAHOODI: Fuck the natives. I'm going ashore.

THEY *all pile out of the boat and go ashore.* CAPTAIN KIDD *gets out his map.*

CAPT. KIDD: Now if me memory serves me right it should be right in this vicinity.

YAHOODI: Let's go, let's go. Stop fucking around with the map.

MARLENE: Don't be so impatient, darling.

YAHOODI: I wanna get the treasure. Let's go.

THEY *march off into the boondocks. Back to* MAE *in the boat, looking through the telescope.*

MAE: I think I see them. They've landed or something.

KOSMO: Landed! They've found land!

WACO: Water! I need some water.

KOSMO: Lemme take a look.

   SHE *hands him the telescope.*

KOSMO: They have! They've landed. They're heading right for the treasure.

WACO: Water, water.

KOSMO: I keep hearing music. Like distant drums.

MAE: It must be the natives.

KOSMO: No, like Janis Joplin. Like Big Brother.

MAE: You're just getting paranoid.

KOSMO: Thousands of people screaming. More! More! More!

MAE: Gimme the telescope.

   SHE *grabs it away from him and looks through it.*

WACO: Water, water.

MAE: Looks like the natives have spotted them. They're circling around them. They're killing off the natives.

KOSMO: Well, let's get ashore. What are we waiting for?

MAE: We can't let them see the boat. We'll have to swim.

KOSMO: Swim ashore?

MAE: That's right. You think you're up to it?

KOSMO: *I* am. I don't know about him, though.

WACO: Water, water.

MAE: We'll just dump him overboard. He'll have to sink or swim.

KOSMO: All right. Let's go.

   THEY *dump* WACO *over the side and* THEY *all start swimming ashore.*

WACO: I can't swim! I'm going to drown!

MAE: Grab ahold of him. Get him by the neck. Swim, you fool! Swim!

WACO: I can't! I'm going to drown!

KOSMO: What's that! It looks like sharks! Heading this way! It is! It's sharks!

MAE: Swim! Swim for your lives!

   Back to CAPTAIN KIDD. HE *unfolds his map. The* OTHERS *sit down exhausted.*

CAPT. KIDD: I think this is the spot. Right about in here.

YAHOODI: That's what you said before.

MARLENE: These mosquitoes are eating me alive.

CAPT. KIDD: Come on. The cave should be right behind these bushes.

MARLENE: Oh, can't we just rest for a while, darling? I can't take another step.

YAHOODI: Come on. We're being followed, I tell ya. We can't waste any more time.

CAPT. KIDD: Here it is. The cave. I've found it. I knew it was here.

YAHOODI: We found it! We found it!

MARLENE: Thank God!

An Indian GHOST GIRL appears with a spear.

GHOST GIRL: That's far enough.

CAPT. KIDD: It's the Indian ghost girl I told you about. *(HE speaks to her in an ancient tongue)* Santo lala gronto. Muchamo no le santiamo.

GHOST GIRL: Buzz off, buster. This is Captain Kidd's treasure. He told me to watch it for him while he was gone.

CAPT. KIDD: But I am Captain Kidd. Don't you recognize me?

GHOST GIRL: He warned me of impostors. And you're about as phony as they come.

CAPT. KIDD: Wait a minute. I'm real. I'm the real Captain Kidd.

YAHOODI: He is. He's the real one.

GHOST GIRL: Oh yeah? And I suppose she's supposed to be Marlene Dietrich or something?

MARLENE: I don't have to stand here and be insulted.

GHOST GIRL: That's right, sister. If you don't like it you know what you can do about it.

MARLENE: Are you challenging me, darling?

GHOST GIRL: Choose your weapons.

MARLENE: Fingernails and teeth.

GHOST GIRL: Okay by me.

The GHOST GIRL and MARLENE square off for a fight. MARLENE takes off her boa and her furs.

MARLENE: Here, darling, hold these for me.

SHE hands them to YAHOODI. MARLENE and the GHOST GIRL tear into each other and fight all over the stage.

YAHOODI: Hold her off, Marlene! We'll be right back with the treasure.

CAPTAIN KIDD and YAHOODI go offstage for the treasure while MARLENE and GHOST GIRL fight. MAE and the BOYS make it up onto the shore. WACO is waterlogged. KOSMO gives him artificial respiration as MAE watches the fight.

MAE: Musta been a real hunk a man to get them two so all fired up.

Probably one a the natives.

KOSMO: Mae, I don't think he's gonna make it.

MAE: Okay, we'll leave him for the buzzards. He's been a real drag right from the start.

KOSMO: We can't just leave him here.

MAE: We'll come back and pick him up later. After we get that treasure.

KOSMO: I don't know. He's been a real friend.

MAE: This ain't the time to be gettin' sentimental. Let's get a move on.

KOSMO: Okay. So long, Waco, old buddy. Hope you find Jimmie Rodgers in heaven.

MAE: He ain't dead yet.

KOSMO: All right. Let's go.

THEY *follow* CAPTAIN KIDD *and* YAHOODI *offstage. At this point the fight has reached its climax, and* MARLENE *is winning.* SHE *has* GHOST GIRL *by the throat.* GHOST GIRL *collapses in a heap.* MARLENE *pulls herself together.* SHE *looks around the stage.*

MARLENE: It's always been this way. Right from the start. Always left behind. Always left in the lurch. I guess I'm just a born loser.

PAUL BUNYAN *enters.*

Oh, it's you again. You with the mysterious eyes. Have you found your Babe?

PAUL BUNYAN: Nope. I've just about given up hope.

MARLENE: Oh, no. Never give up. Never say no to life. Come with me. We'll find your Babe. I promise you.

PAUL: You think we can?

MARLENE: I'm sure of it.

PAUL: Boy, lady, you sure are one hunk a woman. I could almost forget my ox for you.

MARLENE: Let's go away together.

THEY *exit.* WACO *starts to come to.* HE *shakes his head and sits up, feeling drunk.* HE *looks out over the audience.*

WACO: *(sings)*

I been fightin' like a lion.
But I'm 'fraid I'm gonna lose.

What happened to my hat? I had me a hat. Given to me special. Can't see nothin' but ocean. Nothin' but the deep blue sea. Can't figure out this life. Here one minute, gone the next. Just a space traveler. Just a driftin' fool. Wake up in the mornin' and find yerself in the ocean. Now ain't that the damn truth. *(HE notices the GHOST GIRL and goes to her)* Well now, lookit that. A fair young maiden. Lookit that. Hey! This here's Waco talkin'. Listen to me. I'm so lonely and hungry for love that my stomach is stranglin' my backbone. And that's the truth. Feel like a mule driver eatin' nothin' but borax for a mile. Listen to me, honey. *(HE sits down next to her and strokes her hair)* Oh, my heart's just about ripped wide open just from the sight of somethin' like you. Yessir. Good thing yer unconscious to this babble. You wouldn't believe the journeys I've made. You wouldn't believe. Say, if I told ya a secret you wouldn't tell nobody, would ya? It's somethin' I've been savin' up fer a long, long time. I never told it to nobody before. I'm the real Jimmie Rodgers. That's right. It's me. He lives in me, that's how I figure I'm him. Same thing as though he'd never died at all. I can feel him breathin' down deep inside me. You know how that is. A man gets into yer soul. Same as a woman or a piece a land. He's alive in me. And that's how I'm gonna put him back on the street. He died too fast. A man like that just doesn't come and go. He lives on. He lives in yer heart. He's alive right now. Can ya hear him? Listen: "I been fightin' like a lion. / But I'm 'fraid I'm gonna lose." Ya hear that? He's in there. I know it's him. It's gotta be him. It ain't me, that's for sure. It sure ain't me. *(HE takes off his boots)* My mind's as raggedy and tore up as this old pair a boots. Nothin' holdin' it together no more. Not even the desire left. Just follow yer heart. That's what I say. Follow the heart. It'll lead ya right outa this world right into the next. I got no expectations. The world's a motherfucker, boy. I got nowheres to go and nothin' to see. Nowheres. And that's the truth.

The lights dim out.

ACT II

The lights come up on YAHOODI *and* CAPTAIN KIDD *sitting by a campfire with two big bags full of gold.*

CAPT. KIDD: I can't understand it. How they coulda found it in the first place. How they coulda got past the ghost girl. And how come they left two bags behind. I just can't understand it.

YAHOODI: You sure you ain't holding out on me now?

CAPT. KIDD: Now laddie, why would I even have asked ye to come along with me in the first place if I was plannin' on doublecrossin' ye?

YAHOODI: Yeah. Well, I'm thankful that we got out of there with our skins. Those natives were getting pretty fierce. These two bags should last us quite a while if we play our cards right.

CAPT. KIDD: I'm not a greedy man by nature. There's enough in this bag to see out the rest of my days.

YAHOODI: Yeah, well, you're an old man. Me, I got my whole life in front of me. I wanna live high. I wanna live real high.

CAPT. KIDD: Sure puzzles me what coulda happened to Miss Marlene. Unless that ghost girl dragged her off into the woods.

YAHOODI: Maybe the natives got her.

CAPT. KIDD: She was such a fine woman.

YAHOODI: She was all right.

CAPT. KIDD: But I thought you loved her.

YAHOODI: We had an understanding. That's all. Just an understanding.

CAPT. KIDD: Boy, if I had a woman like that I'd tie her to my waist and never let her out of my sight.

YAHOODI: Shhh! What's that! (HE *stands and listens to the space. Silence*)

CAPT. KIDD: You hearin' things again? There ain't nothin' out there but the wilds.

YAHOODI: There's something out there, I tell ya. There's something been following us ever since we left the jungle. I can feel it. A presence. Something real. Maybe it's Kosmo. Maybe he's been dogging my trail all this time. (HE *calls across a vast expanse*) Kosmo!

CAPT. KIDD: Listen, son. I got an idea. How 'bout if the two of us broke up and went our separate ways? We got nothin' more to do with each other. It's time we followed our own paths.

YAHOODI: Broke up? Oh, no. I get it. You wanna get me out there alone in the jungle. You know the jungle and I don't. That's it, isn't it? You wanna come sneaking up on me and bump me off and take my half of the treasure. Isn't that the truth?

CAPT. KIDD: After all we been through? After all that, you can say something like that to me?

YAHOODI: Maybe you got a deal worked out with Kosmo. The two of you. You sneak off and meet him, and then the two of ya do me in. Maybe that's it. Maybe he's out there right now. Just waiting for your signal. Just waiting for me to fall asleep.

CAPT. KIDD: Now slow down, kid. You've got the fever. Yer mind's been twisted up.

YAHOODI *pulls a gun on* CAPTAIN KIDD.

YAHOODI: Oh no! Not this time. This time the tables are turned. It's me who's gonna take over. It's me who's gonna take your half and leave you in the lurch. Now hand it over! Come on! Hand it over!

CAPTAIN KIDD *hands over his bag of the treasure.*

CAPT. KIDD: You're makin' a big mistake, laddie. I have no evil in my heart for you.

YAHOODI: You think I'm falling for that goodness and kindness routine, you're crazy. This is my show and I'm running it my way. Now turn around! Turn around!

CAPT. KIDD: You can't just shoot me in the back and leave me here to die.

YAHOODI: I can't, huh? Just watch me. You haven't got the guts to do it. You're so moral and self-righteous you couldn't pull the trigger. Isn't that right? Well, not me, Captain Kidd. I'm gonna blow your brains out.

KOSMO'*s voice comes from offstage as if from many miles away.* YAHOODI *turns toward the sound.*

KOSMO'S VOICE: Yahoodi?

YAHOODI: Kosmo? That you? You're out there. I know you're out there. You're trying to drive me crazy. But I'm too smart for that. I got the upper hand. You're not going to get away with it. I'm going to win!

CAPTAIN KIDD *springs on* YAHOODI. THEY *struggle with the gun.* CAPTAIN KIDD *finally grabs it away from him and points it in his face.*

CAPT. KIDD: Now get up!

YAHOODI *stands.* CAPTAIN KIDD *covers him with the gun.*

YAHOODI: Looks like the tables are turned again, eh, Captain Kidd?

CAPT. KIDD: Looks that way, doesn't it?

YAHOODI: What're ya gonna do now? You can't shoot me 'cause you haven't got the guts. You can't leave me here to die in the jungle because your conscience wouldn't let you. So it looks like you'll have to take me with you.

CAPT. KIDD: It looks that way.

YAHOODI: And sooner or later you're gonna have to sleep. Sooner or later the tables will turn again.

CAPT. KIDD: Time will tell that tale. Now come on, we're movin' out into the desert.

THEY *travel to the desert.* KOSMO *and* MAE *enter from the opposite side.* KOSMO *yells across a great expanse.*

KOSMO: Yahoodi!

MAE: Pipe down. What do you wanna do, let the whole jungle know we're here?

KOSMO: I don't care anymore. I don't care about the treasure or the natives or anything. I just wanna find my roots.

MAE: Well, ya ain't gonna find 'em by screaming your head off.

KOSMO: *(calling)* Waco! Hey, Waco!

MAE: Will you shut up? That old buzzard's long gone by now.

KOSMO: But where'd he go? Where's my friend? Where's Yahoodi? Where's all the people I love? I can't hear the music anymore. I can't hear the band.

MAE: Stop blubbering. Once we get that treasure I'll buy you a dozen bands.

KOSMO: I want *my* band. I don't want a dozen bands. I just wanna play my music. My own special music.

MAE: Oh, if I just had me a man. A real man. We could rip off this treasure and have us a ball. But now I get strapped with a kid. A rock-and-roll punk.

KOSMO: *(calling across a great expanse)* Yahoodi! I had a vision! Jimi Hendrix and Janis Joplin and Buddy Holly and Sam Cooke and Big Bopper and Otis Redding and Brian Jones and Jimmie Rodgers and Blind Lemon Jefferson! They're all in heaven and they've started a band! Yahoodi! Can you hear me?

MAE: You've flipped your cake, buster. You've really gone bananas.

KOSMO: I wanna go home. I wanna see my wife and kids again.

MAE: So, now you're a married man.

KOSMO: Sure, what's so strange about that?

MAE: What about all them groupies? All them group gropes? The string of broken hearts from here to Tupelo?

KOSMO: You're making that up. You're trying to drive me crazy. Once I thought I loved you.

MAE: You ain't the first man to spit out them words. Listen, honey, I wanna live high. I mean really high. You think I wanna spend the rest of my life in the jungle?

KOSMO: Look at me. I was living high. I was living in wall-to-wall car-
pets with color TVs and all the dope I could want and girls climbing all over me and my name in all the papers. Look where I am
now. The same place as you. So what's the difference? You want
what I have and I want what you have and we both have each
other.

MAE: You're confusin' my mind. I'm a simple gal. I don't like talkin'
in riddles.

KOSMO: What's gonna happen when we do find Yahoodi? We steal his
treasure and then what?

MAE: We hit all the big ones. St. Louis, New Orleans, San Francisco,
Baton Rouge. We wine and dine with the best of 'em. We knock
'em dead with our glitter. Folks'll say, "Who's that couple? They
sure do know how to live."

KOSMO: But I'm a country boy.

MAE: Then go back to the country. Quit draggin' my time. I'll take that
treasure myself. I've done it before without no help from a man,
and I'll do it again.

KOSMO: But which way is home? I don't know where to start. We don't
even have a compass. I'm lost. We're both lost.

MAE: I know exactly where I'm going, honey. And it ain't to the
poorhouse. If ya wanna tag along you're welcome to. Just stop confusin' my ambitions. (SHE *sings "Back Street Boy"*)

There's a back street boy that comes around
I know he'd like to take me out on the town
But I'd lay odds he doesn't have a cent
And after all I'm a doll who's lookin' for a gent

He sure do have a mournful air
We sure would make a handsome pair
But fate ain't plannin' on takin' that route
'Cause what the hell, I'm a gal who's looking for some loot

I'm a gal who goes for high high livin'
Breakfast served in the afternoon
I'm the type can take whatever's given
And though I'm partial to honey, I ain't askin' for the moon

There'll always be room in my memory

For that back street boy and how he looked at me
But I ain't dwellin' on what never could be
'Cause it's for sure scrubbin' floors ain't my fantasy

Cut to PAUL BUNYAN *and* MARLENE *under the shade of an apple tree, munching on apples and snuggling in each other's arms.*

MARLENE: You know something, Paul?

PAUL: What, honey bunch?

MARLENE: It sure is too bad about your ox.

PAUL: Yeah, old Babe was the only thing I had in life until I met you.

MARLENE: You're such a gentle man. So strong and gentle.

PAUL: I try to be just like I am, ma'am. That's the best way I've found.

MARLENE: Those poor darlings back in the jungle. Searching for treasure. What a silly thing.

PAUL: Yeah, I figure what's the use in striving for things when all ya gotta do is sit back and have 'em come to ya. Except old Babe. I don't know if he'll ever come back.

MARLENE: What made him leave in the first place?

PAUL: I guess I was just workin' him too hard. You know how it is with an ox. Same as a woman. You can't drive 'em too hard or they start yearnin' for a way out.

MARLENE: I know what you mean.

PAUL: That's what I like about you.

MARLENE: What?

PAUL: You know what I mean. I don't have to go through a whole lot of explainin'.

MARLENE: What wonderful music.

PAUL: Music?

MARLENE: In the air. Spring music. Mountain music. Music that sounds like golden leaves.

PAUL: I'm sorry, ma'am, but I don't hear nothin' but the breeze.

MARLENE: You can call me Marlene if you want.

PAUL: All right, Marlene. You sure are swell.

MARLENE: You're pretty swell too, darling.

PAUL: *(sings "Marlene")*

Marlene Dietrich, you took my breath away
If I was born in another day
The dogs couldn't keep me away from your door

Marlene you're so fine
Marlene you're so fine

Some say the stars up in the skies
Are there just because we got eyes
But I could see your star up on the screen
If I was blind as a bean

Marlene you're so fine
Marlene you're so fine

I'd bury my nose in your furs
I'd swallow you whole with your pearls
I'd fight off the dukes and the earls
I'd even give up on all of my girls for you

Marlene you're so fine
Marlene you're so fine

THEY *go into a clinch. Cut to* WACO *and* GHOST GIRL *on another part of the stage.*

GHOST GIRL: *(waking up)* What happened to that bitch? I'm gonna kick her ass.

WACO: Now hold on there, tootsie roll. The war's over. Why don't ya just sit down here beside me and give me a little squeeze?

GHOST GIRL: Who're you anyway? Where'd you come from?

WACO: I'm just here. That's all. Name's Waco. Waco Texas. Born and raised.

GHOST GIRL: Were you hooked up with that broad?

WACO: Not me. I'm my own man. Or God's man. Whatever way ya wanna look at it.

GHOST GIRL: Looks like they got what was left of the treasure. Dirty pigs. I knew they were phonies. Right from the start. A bunch a phonies. Boy, is Captain Kidd gonna be pissed.

WACO: You shouldn't worry about him. You got your own life.

GHOST GIRL: Yeah, I guess you're right. I don't know what I'm doing anymore. Hangin' around this dumb island. Pickin' coconuts. Kickin' sand all day long.

WACO: What a life.

GHOST GIRL: What do you do for a living?

WACO: Me, I'm a drifter. Just follow the breeze. One place is just as good as another for me.

GHOST GIRL: Sounds kinda lonely.

WACO: You get used to it.

GHOST GIRL: What do you say we get outa here? We could go to the States.

WACO: I just came from there. Besides, I just took my travelin' shoes off.

GHOST GIRL: I wanna see all those famous people up there. That must be really something, to see a famous person. You know what I mean?

WACO: Like who, for instance?

GHOST GIRL: Like Elvis Presley. I'd really like to see him. He really turns me on.

WACO: Never heard of him. I like Jimmie Rodgers myself.

GHOST GIRL: I never heard of him either.

WACO: How come a native island girl like you knows about famous people in the States?

GHOST GIRL: He's not from the States, he's from Memphis. And I'm not a native island girl. I was dropped off here by Captain Kidd. He was on his way to Bimini and he just dropped me off and told me to take care of his treasure.

WACO: Where'd he pick you up in the first place?

GHOST GIRL: Some bar in Frisco. That was back in the seventeen hundreds.

WACO: What're you tryin' to do, drive me crazy or something?

GHOST GIRL: I'm a ghost, stupid.

WACO: Yeah, well, I know just how ya feel. I feel that way myself sometimes. Just a ghost. Stuck somewheres between livin' and dyin'.

GHOST GIRL: But I'm really a ghost.

WACO: Okay, okay. How's about some lovin'?

GHOST GIRL: No thanks. I'm saving myself up for Elvis. I'm going to meet him some day. Some day soon. We'll just be walking down the street and we'll run into each other. It'll be an accident. A real accident.

WACO: Guess I'm too old fer ya, huh?

GHOST GIRL: No, it's not that. It's just that you want something special to happen the first time around, you know what I mean?

WACO: You mean to tell me you're a virgin?

GHOST GIRL: Are you kidding? I'm just dreaming. A girl can dream, can't she?

WACO: Sure. Sure.

Cut back to CAPTAIN KIDD *and* YAHOODI. CAPTAIN KIDD *is trying to sleep sitting up, his gun trained on* YAHOODI, *who sits across from him with his hands tied behind his back.*

YAHOODI: It's hard, ain't it, Captain Kidd? Hard to sleep and keep your eyes peeled at the same time. How long do you think you can keep it up? How much longer? Sooner or later you're gonna have to fall asleep. Then it's gonna be my turn. Then the tables are gonna turn again.

CAPT. KIDD: Just keep yer trap shut, limey.

YAHOODI: Not much longer. Not too much longer. You're a real fool, Captain Kidd. A real fool. Why don't you kill me? You know I'm gonna do it to you once I get the chance. Why don't you kill me now and get it over with? You could just leave my body for the buzzards. They'd pick me clean. Nobody'd know the difference.

CAPTAIN KIDD *falls fast asleep.* YAHOODI *slips out of his ropes, sneaks over to him, and takes the gun out of his hand.* HE *kicks* CAPTAIN KIDD *in the ribs.*

YAHOODI: All right! On your feet! I warned you the whole time. You can't say I wasn't fair. On your feet!

CAPTAIN KIDD *struggles to his feet, dead tired from exhaustion.*

Now turn around! Turn around!

CAPTAIN KIDD *turns around.* YAHOODI *kicks him viciously.*

Now march!

THEY *march all over the stage, with* CAPTAIN KIDD *falling down from exhaustion and* YAHOODI *kicking him up on his feet. Finally* THEY *get to a lonely spot.*

All right, here. Right here is good.

CAPT. KIDD: I'm so tired. Can't you let me sleep for a while? Just a little while?

YAHOODI: You're gonna sleep forever, Captain Kidd.

CAPT. KIDD: Thank God.

YAHOODI *fires and hits* CAPTAIN KIDD *in the back.* HE *falls to the ground, dead.* YAHOODI *rushes back and picks up the bags of treasure. As* HE's *doing this* CAPTAIN KIDD, *who turns out to be only wounded, starts pulling himself across the stage until finally* HE's *completely off.* YAHOODI *talks to himself.*

YAHOODI: Thought they could fool me. Ha! Now look who's on top. Thought they could outfox the Yahoodi. Ha! Now I have it all. It's all mine. Guess I'll head for Nogales and cash it in for dollar bills.

No, maybe I'll cash half and keep the other half hid away some-place. No, then they'd find it. They're still out there. I can feel them out there. *(calling)* Kosmo! That you? I know you're out there somewhere. Kosmo! *(to himself)* Maybe it's not him. Maybe it's Captain Kidd. Maybe I didn't really get him good. Maybe I only wounded him. Maybe I'm going crazy. Maybe it's just me. It could be me. My imagination. My imagination running wild. No. There's someone out there. *(calling)* Marlene! Marlene! Is that you? *(to himself)* Couldn't be. She's long gone by now. Maybe she's dead. Maybe they're all dead. That's it. They're all dead. It's just me. It could be their ghosts. Maybe they're haunting me or something. *(calling out)* Is that it? You're all dead and you've come back to haunt me! *(to himself)* No. It must be Captain Kidd. I'm going to go check. Just to make sure. I'll put a few more shells in him just to make sure. No harm in that.

HE *travels back through all the space* THEY *marched through before and arrives at the spot where* HE *shot* CAPTAIN KIDD. HE *discovers that* CAPTAIN KIDD's *gone.*

Couldn't be. It just couldn't be. I drilled him good. No man could walk away from that. *(calling out)* Captain Kidd! Captain Kidd! It's me! Yahoodi! I've decided I was wrong! I'm willing to go fifty-fifty again! Can you hear me? *(to himself)* He's going to track me down like an animal. He knows the jungle and I don't. Why didn't I think of that before? How am I going to get out of here? I don't know the ropes. *(calling out)* Kosmo! Marlene! Is anybody out there? Help me! You can't let me die! Not now! Now that I'm rich! You can't! *(to himself)* There's nobody out there, you fool. Stop wasting your energy. It's what they want you to do. Can't you see they're trying to drive you crazy. They want to drive you to suicide. That's it. *(calling out)* That's it, isn't it? You're trying to make me kill myself! Well, I won't do it! I'm too smart for that! I have my pride! I'm going to fight this jungle! I'm going to fight it! And I'm going to win! Do you hear me? I'm going to win!

HE *collapses in a ball. Cut to* MAE *and* KOSMO *sneaking through the jungle toward* YAHOODI.

MAE: It's this direction. I heard it. I distinctly heard it. We're gettin' warm now, brother.

KOSMO: You sure it was him? It could be a tiger or one of those wild parrots. They screamed sometimes.

MAE: It wasn't no parrot.

KOSMO: You sure you wanna go through with this? I'm getting kind of nervous.

MAE: Shut up. It was right around here someplace.

YAHOODI *sits up and puts the gun to his head and pulls the trigger. A loud gunshot.* HE *topples over on the treasure.*

KOSMO: What was that!

MAE: It must be him. Come on!

THEY *arrive at* YAHOODI.

KOSMO: Yahoodi! Yahoodi. You went and did it. I knew it. I knew he was gonna do it. I knew this was gonna end up like this. Yahoodi, why'd you have to do it?

MAE: Quit blubbering. We got the treasure now. Help me get him off of it.

THEY *pull* YAHOODI *off the treasure.*

KOSMO: He didn't have to do it. There was other ways. He didn't have to off himself. Why'd he do it?

MAE: We're rich! We're rich!

KOSMO: All you care about is the money. I've lost a friend.

MAE: Come on, let's get out of here before the Federales come. Grab one of these sacks and let's get out of here.

JESSE JAMES *enters, with a black bandanna over his face and both his guns drawn.*

JESSE: Not so fast, lady.

MAE: Oh, brother. I suppose you're supposed to be Jesse James or something.

JESSE: That's right, lady. Now hand it over.

MAE: Looks like you got the upper hand, don't it?

JESSE: Sure looks that way.

MAE: Maybe we could make a deal, big boy.

JESSE: No deals. Just hand over the treasure.

KOSMO: Just like that you'd run out on me. After all we been through.

MAE: I go where the action is. What do ya say, Jesse? We split the dough fifty-fifty, and I'll let ya come up and see me sometime. How's that sound?

JESSE: What're ya gonna do with him?

MAE: Who, Kosmo? He'll find something. He's a very enterprisin' young man. Back in the States he packs 'em in. Don't ya, Kosmo?

KOSMO: Sure, sure. You two go ahead and have yourselves a ball. I'm going to stay and bury my friend.

JESSE: I don't know. I been ridin' alone recently, and a woman might slow me down.

MAE: Not this woman, doll. I got the fastest action this side a the Delaware Water Gap.

JESSE: That just might come in handy. All right. Let's get outa here then.

MAE: *(to* KOSMO*)* So long, honey. I'll drop you a line, let ya know how things are cookin'.

SHE *kisses* KOSMO *and grabs the treasure.* MAE *and* JESSE *exit.*

KOSMO: Yeah, take it easy. Don't buy any wooden nickels. (HE *takes a moment and looks around the stage. Then, to* YAHOODI*)* All right, all right. You can get up now. Come on. Look, it's not going to work out if you go and off yourself right when everything gets going so good. You just bring the whole fucking thing to a dead end. We got all these characters strung out all over the place in all these different lives and you just go and rub yourself out. What a fucking drag. Is that responsible? Now I ask you, is it? Yahoodi! If you don't want to go through with this thing then just tell me. Just come right out and tell me. But don't kill yourself off in the middle of the plot.

YAHOODI *comes to and slowly sits up.*

YAHOODI: Well, it seemed like the right moment.

KOSMO: What do you mean? If you die, then everything comes to an end.

YAHOODI: No, it doesn't. There's other parts to the story.

KOSMO: Like what? The love life of Marlene Dietrich and Paul Bunyan? What's so interesting about that?

YAHOODI: It's a beautiful relationship. I thought it was going good.

KOSMO: Until you decided to commit suicide it was great.

YAHOODI: It was driving me crazy. I was driven to do it. I can't help it. It was an intuitive decision. I needed to get off. I can't see doing something unless you're going to get off.

KOSMO: I know, but there's other ways besides suicide.

YAHOODI: I'm a dark person. I do it my way, you do it yours. What's the big deal?

KOSMO: Then, there's no way to continue.

YAHOODI: I wouldn't say that. You could do it yourself.

KOSMO: Where would you go?

YAHOODI: I'll take a trip. I need to get away anyway. This city's driving me crazy.

KOSMO: And just leave me with all the loose ends.

YAHOODI: All right, then you take a trip and I'll stay.

KOSMO: But I've got no place to go.

YAHOODI: Go to Mexico. Go to San Francisco. There's plenty of places.

KOSMO: Oh no. I get it. You just want to get me out there alone somewhere. Out on the open highway so you can run me down in your Mustang and take all the treasure. Well, I'm not falling for it.

YAHOODI: You're crazy. I don't give a shit about your treasure. There is no treasure. What is all this pot of gold shit at the end of the rainbow? You're ripped in the head, boy.

KOSMO: You wanna come sneaking up on me in the Badlands somewhere and knife me in the back.

YAHOODI: I'm splitting. I can't even talk to you anymore.

KOSMO: Okay, go! Go then! Take the treasure with you!

YAHOODI: I don't want the fucking treasure!

KOSMO: But you invented it! It was your idea!

YAHOODI: It was not! It doesn't exist!

KOSMO: You called me on the phone! You asked me for money!

YAHOODI: That was a long time ago!

KOSMO: I don't care! When are you going to pay me back?

YAHOODI: You can have all the treasure!

KOSMO: I don't want the treasure! Mae West took it, anyway!

YAHOODI: That's your problem! I'm leaving!

KOSMO: No, wait a minute. It's gone too far. We're both infected with the same disease. If you leave now, it's all over. I can't keep chasing around with an open wound.

YAHOODI: Well, what'll we do then?

KOSMO: I don't know.

YAHOODI: Look. Look at me!

KOSMO: I am.

YAHOODI: Can you recognize my demon?

KOSMO: Sometimes.

YAHOODI: Do you believe I can recognize yours?

KOSMO: Sometimes.

YAHOODI: Do you believe it's the same demon?

KOSMO: No.

YAHOODI: Then there's nothing to do but—split up. Right?

KOSMO: How did we come together in the first place?

YAHOODI: We have something in common.

KOSMO: We support each other's inability to function. That's no friendship.

YAHOODI: You can't see my demon and you think you're alone. That's the truth, isn't it! You think you're all alone.

KOSMO: Fuck your demon! What about your angel?

YAHOODI: I don't get along with angels.

KOSMO: What about *my* angel then? If you see my demon you must be able to see my angel.

YAHOODI: I don't look for angels. I don't like angels! I'm struggling with something in me that wants to die!

KOSMO: And I'm struggling with something that wants to live.

YAHOODI: I guess that sums it up.

KOSMO: I guess so.

A long pause.

YAHOODI: Good-bye, Kosmo. I'll see you sometime.

KOSMO: Good-bye.

YAHOODI *splits.* KOSMO *looks around the stage, then calls out to* WACO *across a vast expanse.*

Waco! Waco!

Cut to WACO *and* GHOST GIRL.

WACO: Shhh! You hear something?

GHOST GIRL: Nothin'. What're you talkin' about?

WACO: Sounded like my old friend.

GHOST GIRL: You're nuts. This is a desert island. Nobody but you and me.

WACO: What about the natives?

GHOST GIRL: Killed off by treasure hunters.

KOSMO: *(calling)* Waco! Waco!

WACO: There! You hear it? It's him, I tell ya.

GHOST GIRL: Listen, mister, don't try and scare me. I don't scare easy. I been through a lot of tough scrapes and it takes a lot to get me freaked.

WACO: I've gotta go and find him. Maybe he's in trouble.

GHOST GIRL: What am I supposed to do?

WACO: I don't know. It's every man for himself.

WACO *splits and starts searching for* KOSMO. KOSMO *is searching for* WACO, *but* THEY *never meet. Meanwhile* YAHOODI's *at another part of the stage calling out to* MARLENE.

YAHOODI: Marlene! Marlene! It's me! Yahoodi! It's me! I want you back, Marlene! I'm sorry for running out on you and everything! Marlene! Can you hear me?

Cut to MARLENE *and* PAUL BUNYAN.

PAUL BUNYAN: What's the matter? You've been acting awful edgy lately, Marlene.

MARLENE: I keep hearing a voice. Something far away. Like an old friend. Listen, can you hear it?

YAHOODI: Marlene! Marlene!

PAUL BUNYAN: It ain't nothing but the wind. Come on, let's neck some more.

MARLENE: Can't you hear it? So lonely. So distant.

PAUL BUNYAN: Who cares? We're together. What difference does it make?

MARLENE: But it's like my own voice. My own voice calling me back. Back to where I belong.

PAUL BUNYAN: Don't be silly. You belong right here with me.

MARLENE: No. It never would have worked. We're from different worlds. I belong somewhere else.

PAUL BUNYAN: Well, so do I, but that don't mean we can't love each other. I thought we were having a good time together.

MARLENE: We were, but it's useless to go on.

PAUL BUNYAN: What're you talkin' about? First it's my Babe and now you. You can't leave me, Marlene. You're the only thing I've got.

MARLENE *wanders off in search of* YAHOODI, YAHOODI *in search of* MARLENE, *but* THEY *never meet.* PAUL *tries to follow her but* HE *gets lost.*

PAUL BUNYAN: Marlene! Come back! You can't leave me now! Marlene!

MARLENE: Yahoodi! Is that you? Can you hear me?

PAUL BUNYAN: Marlene!

KOSMO: Waco! It's me! Kosmo! Are you out there?

GHOST GIRL: Waco! Waco!

WACO: I hear ya, boy! Just keep yellin'! I'll find ya!

KOSMO: Waco!

YAHOODI: Marlene!

Cut to MAE WEST *and* JESSE JAMES. THEY *enter another part of the stage with the treasure. The* OTHERS *keep searching for each other but never meet, even though at times* THEY *may pass right by each other.* THEY *keep calling out each other's names.* MAE WEST *stops and sits down, exhausted.*

JESSE: Now listen, you promised when we started out that you wouldn't hold me up.

MAE: I know, I know. I just gotta take a little breather. What happened to your horses, anyway?

JESSE: They drowned in the damn river. Piranhas got 'em. It was awful. You ever seen a piranha devour a horse before?

MAE: Can't say as I've had the pleasure.

JESSE: It was awful.

MAE: What's that sound?

JESSE: What? I don't hear nothin'.

MAE: Sounds like voices.

JESSE: You're crazy.

MAE: Listen, mister, a woman don't have to be insulted just 'cause she's of the opposite sex. I hear voices, I tell ya.

JESSE: It might be the Federales. Maybe they've picked up our trail.

MAE: It ain't likely. Sounds like all the people I used to know. Back in the States.

JESSE: Come on. We're wastin' time. We gotta get this stuff back across the border.

MAE: Such a mournful sound.

JESSE: Are you comin' or not?

MAE: Just hold your horses.

JESSE: Let's go.

THEY *move out.* THEY *travel right through all the other characters, who keep on calling and searching.*

KOSMO: Yahoodi! It's gotten worse! It's like a nightmare! I can't keep it up much longer!

YAHOODI: *(calling out to* KOSMO*)* Just let go! Let everything go! It'll take care of itself! I'll meet you in L.A.!

KOSMO: But what about the smog and the cops and the earthquakes and the tidal waves and all that stuff! It's too dangerous! There must be a safer place!

YAHOODI: You worry too much! Everything'll work out for the best!

KOSMO: I can't hear the music anymore! I'm going deaf!

YAHOODI: It'll come back! Everything takes time!

KOSMO: No! Yahoodi!

GHOST GIRL: Waco! I'm sorry for what I said! Waco! You're not too old for me! You're just right! You've got heart! Fuck Elvis! I want you! Waco! You're real! You're a real man! I love you, Waco!

PAUL: Marlene! Forget about Babe! She never meant that much to me anyway. All I want is you! Marlene! Answer me! I've got a cozy little cabin all tucked away in the woods. We could hide out there. We could have coffee and toast in the morning. I'd chop wood all day long. We could make it, Marlene! Marlene!

WACO: Hold on, son! Just a little bit longer! Kosmo boy! Take it easy now! You saved me from drownin'! I'll never forget that! I'll save you, boy! Just keep yellin'! I'll find ya, boy! Just keep callin' out! Don't ever give up!

KOSMO: Yahoodi! It's out of control! The whole thing's crashing in on me! Yahoodi!

MARLENE: Yahoodi! Is that you, darling! I can't see! The trees are so dark. So close together! The moss keeps the sun out! We have to get away from here! We have to go someplace warm. Someplace where the sun always shines and the people dance. Someplace where there's music in the air. We could be so happy! Yahoodi! I know we could be happy!

THEY *all keep up their search, calling out to each other across a vast expanse. The lights go to another part of the stage where* CAP-TAIN KIDD *is pulling himself across the floor in agony, clutching his wounds.*

CAPT. KIDD: If only I was on the Ivory Coast. I know that area. This is strange to me. I feel like a dead man. Dead for a million years. Dying forever. I can't call out or he'll hear me and come back and finish off the job. I've got to keep low to the ground. Be part of the jungle. A low animal. Part of the swamps. The swamps will take me. The snakes will take me. They'll crawl through my bones. Only I will know how I died. Only me. There'll be lies. There'll be legends. But only I will know. Why can't I stop? I keep crawling. What am I crawling for? I could stop. Right here. It could end right here. The motion keeps me alive. Life keeps me moving. The blood keeps on pumping. The brain keeps on working. And where does the mind go? All the visions in space. All the things dreamed and seen in the air. Where do they go? Something flies away. I can see it flying. Taking off like a flamingo. Soaring higher and higher. A beautiful pink bird flying alone. Out over the everglades. Out over the swamps. Higher and higher, straight into the sun. If only I could sing.

Cut to MAE *and* JESSE. *The* OTHERS *keep calling and searching.*

JESSE: Faster, woman! Faster! I can almost see the border.

MAE: You can? The good old US of A? We're really going to make it.

JESSE: If you get your ass in gear.

MAE: I'm trying, I'm trying. I keep hearing the voices. They keep calling me back.

JESSE: Forget about the voices. The Federales are closin' in.

Sound of horses' hooves approaching.

MAE: What about the Customs? What if they check in the bags?

JESSE: Never thought about that. Maybe we should just take what we can carry in our pockets and leave the rest hid. Then we can come back and pick it up some other time.

MAE: Are you crazy? After lugging these things for miles.

JESSE: Well, they're bound to catch us if we try to take the bags across.

MAE: If we only had us a horse. Just a good horse.

BABE THE BLUE OX *enters and wanders over to* MAE *and* JESSE.

JESSE: Wait a minute. What the hell.

MAE: Looks like an ox to me.

JESSE: Maybe we could just ride this critter right across the border. Crash right through the damn Customs. What do ya think?

MAE: Looks pretty slow to me. Think we could get up enough steam to do it?

JESSE: We could sure as hell try. If we backed him up for maybe a quarter mile and whipped him real good, he just might make it.

MAE: Let's give it a whirl.

THEY *climb up on* BABE's *back with the bags of treasure.*

JESSE: Steady now. Steady.

MAE: Gimme a hand.

JESSE: Come on, come on. The Federales should be here any minute.

MAE: All right, I'm on.

JESSE: Good. Now kick the shit out of him and let's see what he can do.

THEY *start kicking* BABE *in the ribs.* HE *takes off at a gallop.* MAE *and* JESSE *let out the rebel yell.* THEY *crash through Customs and get safely to the other side.* THEY *dismount, and kiss and hug each other.*

We made it! We done it, girl!

MAE: Yeah! We made it! We made it!

JESSE: Did you see the look on that Custom guy's face? He never saw nothin' like that before.

MAE: That was a custom he wasn't accustomed to.

THEY *have a good laugh.*

Look, I think it's about time we divvied up the loot. What do ya say?

JESSE: Fine by me. I thought we'd just split it fifty-fifty like you said. You take one bag and I'll take the other.

MAE: Yeah, but there might be more in one than there is in the other.

JESSE: Well, let's take a look.

MAE: Okay by me.

THEY *dump the contents of the bags out on the floor. Tons of bottle caps come crashing out.* MAE *and* JESSE *stare at the bottle caps for a minute, then at each other.*

JESSE: Bottle caps. Millions of bottle caps.

MAE: Well, like they say. Don't carry all your eggs in one basket. What're ya gonna do now, Jesse?

JESSE: Guess I'll head back to Missouri and see my family. Ain't been back there for quite a spell.

MAE: Ain't that kinda dangerous. I mean, ain't they lookin' for ya?

JESSE: Sure, they're lookin' for me. Everybody's lookin' for me.

MAE: Wish someone was lookin' for me.

JESSE: Well, look, seein' as how you got no place to go, why don't you come on back with me? We'd treat ya just like family.

MAE: Gee, that'd be swell, Jesse, but I ain't much of a family gal. Never was.

JESSE: No time to start like the present.

MAE: What about all the others? Maybe we could round them up, too. Maybe we could all go back home together.

JESSE: Sure, why not?

MAE: Wouldn't that be something though? All of us comin' into town. All of us together. All of us singin' and dancin' and carryin' on. What a party we could have. What an extravaganza! Just like the old days. Just like the new days! Just like any old day! Let's do it, Jesse! Let's go on home! Back where we belong!

JESSE *and* MAE *start singing "Home." One by one the* OTHERS *join in until* THEY'*re all singing.*

Hitchin' on the Rio Bravo
Pick me up, won'tcha driver
'Cause ya know that I'm a true believer
In
Home
Home

I'll chance every hand that you deal
Ride behind your drivin' wheel
'Cause home is any place you feel
Like
Home
Home

Home is in the stranger's bones
Home is like a rolling stone
Home is holding something you own
Your own
Home

Crack up in the old ice age
Zoomin' in the super space age
Home got no rules, it's in the heart of a fool
Home is in the coach of a stage

Runnin' the length of a river
Slide me in your sailboat, sailor
My spinnin' brain is a failure
With no
Home
Home

Ride me in a silver airplane
Ride me in a passenger train
Move me against the grain
Move me
Home
Home

THEY *join hands and dance and march together around the stage, through the audience, and out into the street.*

CURTAIN

Cowboy Mouth

Cowboy Mouth was first performed at the Traverse Theatre, Edinburgh, on April 12, 1971. It was directed by Gordon Stewart, with the following cast:

>Slim: *Donald Sumpter*
>Cavale: *Brenda Smiley*
>Lobster Man: *Derek Wilson*

It was subsequently given its American premiere in a special performance at the American Place Theatre, New York, on April 29, 1971, as an afterpiece to Mr. Shepard's *Back Bog Beast Bait*. This performance was directed by Robert Glaudini, with the following cast:

>Slim: *Sam Shepard*
>Cavale: *Patti Smith*
>Lobster Man: *Robert Glaudini*

SCENE: *A fucked-up bed center stage. Raymond, a dead crow, on the floor. Scattered all around on the floor is miscellaneous debris: hubcaps, an old tire, raggedy costumes, a boxful of ribbons, lots of letters, a pink telephone, a bottle of Nescafe, a hot plate. Seedy wallpaper with pictures of cowboys peeling off the wall. Photographs of Hank Williams and Jimmie Rodgers. Stuffed dolls, crucifixes. License plates from Southern states nailed to the wall. Travel poster of Panama. A funky set of drums to one side of the stage. An electric guitar and amplifier on the other side. Rum, beer, White Lightning, Sears catalogue.*

CHARACTERS

CAVALE: a chick who looks like a crow, dressed in raggedy black.

SLIM: a cat who looks like a coyote, dressed in scruffy red. They are both beat to shit.

LOBSTER MAN

CAVALE *has kidnapped* SLIM *off the streets with an old .45.* SHE *wants to make him into a rock-and-roll star, but* THEY *fall in love. We find them after one too many mornings.* THEY'*re both mean as snakes.* SLIM *is charging around screaming words;* CAVALE *is rummaging through junk, yelling with a cracked throat. The lights come up on them in this state.*

SLIM: Wolves, serpents, lizards, gizzards, bad bladders, typhoons, tarantulas, whipsnakes, bad karma, Rio Bravo, Sister Morphine, go fuck yourself!

CAVALE: Fucking dark in here. Fucking old black dog. You fucking. Where's Raymond? Where's Raymond, goddammit? Shit. Raymond, Raymond, where's my crow, old black tooth?

SLIM: Your Raymond! My wife! My kid! Kidnapped in the twentieth century! Kidnapped off the street! Hot off the press! Don't make no sense! I ain't no star! Not me! Not me, boy! Not me! Not yer old dad! Not yer old scalawag! This is me! Fucked! Fucked up! What a ratpile heap a dogshit situation!

CAVALE: Shit, man . . . Raymond, come on, baby, where are you? Come on, honey, is your beak hurt? Raymond? Raymond, don't be scared, honey, come on, he's an old snake, a water moccasin, a buffalo, an old crow . . . No, I'm jes' fooling. Raymond! Fuck them, fuck you.

SLIM *goes to the drums and starts beating the shit out of them, yelling at the top of his voice through a microphone.*

SLIM: *(wailing)*

> You cheated, you lied, you said that you loved me.
> You cheated, you lied, you said that you need me.
> Oh what can I do but just keep on loving you?
> Oooooooooooooooooh what can I do but just keep on loving you?*

Fuck it.

HE *stops.* CAVALE *finds Raymond the dead crow and talks to him.*

CAVALE: Oh, here's my baby. Here's my little crow. He's no crow, I was jes' fooling. We're the crows, me and you, Raymond. (SHE *sings him something like the theme from* Lilith)

SLIM: Will you stop fucking around with that dead crow? It makes me sick! It's morbid and black and dark and dirty! It makes me sick! Can't you see what's happening here? Here we are stuck in some border town, some El Paso town, and you're fucking around with a dead crow. I should just leave and go back to my family. My little family. My little baby. I should, shouldn't I? Shouldn't I!

CAVALE: Fuck you. Fuck you. Fuck, fuck. Can't you see what's happening here? A dream I'm playing. I love Raymond, I love you, Raymond. You don't talk about yesterday stuff. Yeah, you fucking coyote, Slim, always howling after yesterday. Raymond don't squawk 'bout his ole nests, do you, baby? He sleeps on my belly 'cause my belly's today. Yesterday yesterday, that's you, sulking shitface—Mr. Yesterday.

SLIM: Tell me about Johnny Ace.

CAVALE: I already told you about Johnny Ace.

SLIM: I know, but I want to hear it again. Okay?

CAVALE: Okay. C'mere though.

SLIM *goes to her and curls up in her lap.*

Johnny Ace. Johnny Ace. Johnny Ace was cool. He was real cool, baby. Just like you. And he came East from Texas and no black guy had a hit record and no rock-and-roll boy had a hit record. And in rode Johnny Ace, from a moving train, pledging his love. That was his best song, man. What a great fucking song. And all the girls would cry when he sang. He sang all them pretty ballads. And one day when all the girls were waiting, when everybody paid their fare to see Johnny Ace on stage in person singing sad and dressed in black, Johnny Ace took out his revolver, rolled the barrel like his 45 record, played Russian Roulette like his last hit record, and lost. *Johnny Ace blew his brains out,* all the people jump and shout. All the people jump and shout *Johnny Ace blew his brains out.*

SLIM: You think that takes balls, I suppose. Do you?

CAVALE: Oh man. You're always saying that shit. Why don't you just play? Just play, it don't mean nothing, it's just a neat story. Fuck. You always wreck everything. Jus' like when I told ya about Villon. You never just listen, you always got to place stuff. And hey, fuck you, you asked me to tell you it. I ain't telling you no more stories. *(SHE gets teary and nervous)*

SLIM: Aw, come on, baby. Baby crow. Don't crow, baby crow. I'm sorry. I love ya. I love ya to tell me stories. It's like listenin' to the streets. Ya know? Like listenin' to summer sounds. Like it could be the dead of winter but some kind of sound like just a bunch of people laughing makes it sound like summer. That's why I love your stories. I'm sorry, baby.

CAVALE: Baby. Baby. Baby. Slim, I hurt my foot. *(SHE lifts up her foot. It's wrapped in a piece of ragged scarf)* Raymond bit it. Johnny Ace bit it, Villon bit it, a tarantula bit it. Summer bit it. Kiss it, will ya, Slim?

SLIM *bends down and licks her foot all over.* HE *growls like a coyote and howls.*

SLIM: It's them damn steel plates they put on yer foot when you was a punk. They called ya splayfoot, no 'count. I know. I know 'bout them jealous creeps. Lookin' at my crow like a freak. I'll kill 'em! I'll tear out their throats! I kiss your foot. I lick your toes. I suck your pinkie 'cause I love ya. How's that for openers?

CAVALE: Slim, don't tease me.

Pause.

SLIM: How's about a little lobster? Could ya go for a little lobster with drawn butter?

CAVALE: I guess.

SLIM: You don't dig lobster?

CAVALE: Sure.

SLIM: Who do we call for lobster?

CAVALE: Call the lobster man.

SLIM *goes to the phone and dials. Someone answers.*

SLIM: Listen, is this the lobster man? Good. Send us up some lobster with drawn butter and two scrambled eggs and four toasted bialys with cream cheese and some Pepsi-Cola and a bottle of Tequila with plenty of lemon. You got that? Good. *(HE hangs up)*

CAVALE: I'm not that hungry.

SLIM: Tell me about Nerval.

HE *holds her close and* THEY *dance while* SHE *talks; an old waltz or a fox trot.*

CAVALE: Nerval. Hey, Slim, really he's "de" Nerval, but we'll can that "de" stuff 'cause it's too fancy. Hey, Slim, tomorrow can we go into town and you buy me something fancy? I don't got nothing fancy. Oh, Slim, ya know what I want? Tap dance shoes. Red ones, red ones with pretty ribbons. Could we do that, huh, baby?

SLIM: We'll do that right now. Right now we'll do that!

HE *stands up and pulls her to her feet.* THEY *take an imaginary walk to the shoe store.* CAVALE *limps along,* SLIM *helps her.* THEY *walk through the room as though it were the city.*

Now ya gotta look sharp. Ya know what I mean. No limpin'. Try not to limp.

CAVALE: I can't help it, Slim.

SLIM: I know, I know. Just get it together. It won't be far now. Just a little ways. Up past Ridge Avenue, down through Ashland, we'll slide through Mulberry, and bingo! We'll be there.

CAVALE: It won't take long, will it, Slim?

SLIM: We'll be there before you can spit in a hornet's eye. In fact! In fact! In fact, you know what?

CAVALE: What?

SLIM: We're here.

CAVALE: Already?

SLIM: Yeah. Now just take yer pick. There's all them pretty dancin' shoes in the window there. Just take yer pick.

CAVALE: I want the red ones, Slim. The red ones with the ribbons.

SLIM: Okay, now I'm gonna break the window, so stand back.

CAVALE: But we got money.

SLIM: A good thief never hesitates.

HE *smashes the window and steals the shoes.* THEY *run away to another part of the room and sit down exhausted.* SLIM *puts a beat-to-shit pair of high-topped sneakers on* CAVALE.

Now, madam, if you'll just slip your foot into these, we'll see how they suit you.

SHE *tries them on.* SHE *takes a walk in them and looks them over.*

CAVALE: Oh, Slim, they're beautiful.

SLIM: Good. Now will you tell me about Nerval or "de" Nerval or whatever the fuck his name is?

CAVALE: Can the "de," baby. He's Nerval to me. He had a fucked-up foot too. Poor baby. Always banging into walls. Always dreaming when he's walking'. (SHE *spins around and tells the story singsong)* It hurts just to think about. Singing, I try to sing it out. Dead in winter. Two calico shirts. They cut the rope, that rope that cut him down. It hurts just to think about or how I'll do without him.

SLIM: Cut the shit, baby. You never knew that guy; he's a million years old. Just tell the story.

CAVALE: I do so, I do know him, Slim. He hung himself on my birthday. *My birthday.* And some lady tole my mom I was made from a hanged man. Poor bastard. And, Slim, he had a crow too. Just like Raýmond. I read this dream book Baudelaire writ, and he said Nerval came to him half-crow, half—half—half-ass. Nah. I'm just teasing. I'm sorry, Nerval. Slim, I don't wanna tell this story. It's stupid. I'm sick of telling about people killing themselves, it makes me jealous.

SLIM: Okay! Okay! Then don't tell me a story! Don't never tell me a story! Don't never tell me another fucking story! See if I care! Nobody gives a rat's ass anyway! I'm gonna play rock-and-roll! I'm gonna play some mean, shitkickin' rock-and-roll!

HE *goes to the electric guitar and starts playing loud rock with a lot of feedback.* HE *sings "Have No Fear."*

Have no fear
The worst is here
The worst has come
So don't run
Let it come
Let it go
Let it rock and roll
The worst has come.

Have no fear
The best is here
The best has come
So don't run
Let it come
Let it go
Let it rock and roll
The best has come

Every night I sit by my window
Watchin' all the dump trucks go by

Have no fear
The worst is here
The worst has come
So don't run
Let it come
Let it go
Let it rock and roll
The worst has come

CAVALE *plays dead on the floor with Raymond on her stomach. After a while* SLIM *stops.* CAVALE *stays "dead."*

Hey! Is that the lobster man? Hey! Cavale, did somebody knock? Cavale!

CAVALE *stays "dead" on the floor.*

Stupid broad.

SLIM *goes to the door and opens it. The* LOBSTER MAN *enters.* HE'*s dressed like a lobster and carries all the food* THEY *ordered.*

Oh, you must be the lobster man. Just drop everything in the middle of the floor.

The LOBSTER MAN *grunts, then goes center stage and drops all the food in a heap.*

Great. Thanks a lot. Just charge that to my office number. Gramercy 6-5489. Here's a little something for yourself.

HE *tips the* LOBSTER MAN. *The* LOBSTER MAN *grunts and exits.* CAVALE'*s still playing dead.*

The lobster man came. Cavale? You can stop playing dead now. We can eat. Cavale? Well, I'm going to eat, I don't know about you but I'm going to eat. (HE *sits on the floor and digs into the food)*

CAVALE: I'm dead, baby. Dead as dogshit. Dead and never baptized. Dead. Slaughtered. Without the Christian aid of water. Water makes me cringe.

SLIM: Cut the mystical horseshit and come eat.

CAVALE: *(runs to the food and starts overacting disgustingly)* Oh, man, look at all this neat shit. Have some cream pie, Raymond honey. Slosh up that shit, blackie baby. Shove a little sausage in that ole cracked beak. Here's tuna in yer eye.

SLIM: I'm gonna roast that fucking crow.

SHE *tells the story of Raymond as* THEY *slop around in the food.*

CAVALE: Hey, man. Watch that shit. Raymond's real sensitive. It's bad enough you don't let him in bed with us anymore.

SLIM: Gimme that sausage. Well, goddammit, it's sick. Fucking dead crow sucking me off in the morning. You went too far with that one, baby. There's nothing in my contract says I gotta have a rotting stuffed blackbird for a groupie.

CAVALE: Hey, shut up, will ya? Raymond's been a real chum. All them nights in that fuckin' hospital, all them electric shocks. All those hours they stole my dreams, all those people in white face masks saying I was crazy. Only ole Raymond stuck by me. Never gave me any shit. And the dirty fuckers broke his beak. Poor beak. (CAVALE *bandages Raymond's beak with an old piece of lace*)

SLIM: Poor beak, poor beak, poor beak. All I ever had was a dog. A dog. Like any good American boy. I had a dog. A live dog. A cattle dog. The reason I got him was 'cause he was a fuckup. He used to chase the cows out of the pasture instead a bringin' 'em for milking. He was a fuckup.

CAVALE: What was his name?

SLIM: Blaze. Blaze Storm. Named after the stripper.

CAVALE *sings something like "Put the Blame on Mame" in stripper style and picks up the Sears catalogue.*

CAVALE: Hey, Slim, I wanna electric dishwasher.

SLIM: We don't have any dishes.

CAVALE: But I want one. I don't have any housewife shit. I want some stuff ladies have.

SLIM: You don't want that shit, you're not the type. Look, tomorrow I'll take you into town and buy you a nice calico shirt. Just like your pal Nerval. How's that, my little rabbit?

CAVALE: Fuck Nerval. I wanna dishwasher. I wanna stovepipe and a scrambled egg maker. Here, Slim, we can get it all in the catalogue. All the stuff you always miss when you get like Mr. Yesterday. Then you'd be gladder, Slim. We could even get Raymond a little cradle. And a rattle. And booties. And a black baby lamb with a bell in its tail.

SLIM: I don't need no black baby lamb with a bell in its tail and I ain't gettin' no cradle for no dead crow. I have a baby! My own baby! With its own cradle! You've stolen me away from my baby's cradle! You've put a curse on me! I have a wife and a life of my own! Why don't you let me go! I ain't no rock-and-roll star. That's your fantasy. You've kept me cooped up here for how long has it been now? I've lost track of the time. A long time. A long fucking time.

And I'm still not a star! How do you account for that?

CAVALE: I don't know. I never promised nothin'.

SLIM: But you led me on. You tempted me into sin.

CAVALE: Oh, fuck off.

SLIM: Well, it's true. What am I doing here? I don't know who I am anymore. My wife's left me. She's gone to Brooklyn with the kid and left me. And here I am stuck with you.

CAVALE: You can go if you want.

SLIM: I don't want! I do want! I don't want! I want you!

CAVALE: Then stay.

SLIM: I want her too.

CAVALE: Then go.

SLIM: Good-bye!

SLIM *gets up and stomps over to the drums.* HE *starts bashing them violently.* CAVALE *goes through a million changes. Plays dead. Rebels. Puts on a bunch of feathers and shit to look alluring. Rebels. Motions like* SHE's *gonna bash the amps with a hammer. Hides in a corner. Then, shaping up,* SHE *grabs her .45.* SLIM *is still slamming.* SHE *yells over the drums.*

CAVALE: Look, you jive motherfucker, I'm still packing this pistol. I'm still the criminal. I'll fill you with—I'll—Hey, listen to me. I'm threatening your life. You're supposed to be scared. Look, baby, kidnapping is a federal affense. It means I'm a desperate . . .

SLIM: *(still slamming the drums)* It's "Offense," not "affense."

CAVALE: What? Hey, what do ya mean?

SLIM: *(stops drumming and sorta slumps over)* I mean your grammar stinks. I mean you talk funny. I mean—

CAVALE: Shit. Goddammit. How could you? How can you bust up my being a hard bitch with that shit? What a lousy thing. You know I'm sensitive about my talking. Shit. Just when I was really getting mean and violent. Murderous. Just like François Villon. You fuck it up. You wreck everything.

SLIM: Cavale?

CAVALE: Yeah?

SLIM: How come we're so unhappy?

CAVALE: Must be the time of year.

SLIM: Yeah. It's that time of year, all right. That must be it. Maybe we could change it.

CAVALE: What?

SLIM: The time of year. Let's change the time of year to Indian Summer. That's my favorite time of year. What's your favorite time of year?

CAVALE: Fall.

SLIM: Okay, we'll change the time of year to fall. Okay?

CAVALE: Okay.

SLIM: Okay, now it's fall. Are you happy?

CAVALE: Yeah.

SLIM: Good. Now tell me a story.

CAVALE: Stop asking me that. I can't tell no stories unless I'm inspired. Who wants to listen to something uninspired?

SLIM: Okay, then tell me what it means to be a rock-and-roll star. Tell me that. I'm supposed to be a rock-and-roll star. You're going to make me into a rock-and-roll star, right?

CAVALE: Right.

SLIM: So tell me what it means, so I'll have something to go by.

CAVALE: Well, it's hard, Slim. I'll try to tell you but you gotta stay quiet. You gotta let me fish around for the right way to tell ya. I always felt the rhythm of what it means but I never translated it to words. Here, hold Raymond. Come on. It's like, well, the highest form of anything is sainthood. A marvelous thief like Villon or Genêt . . . they were saints 'cause they raised thievery to its highest state of grace. Ole George Carter, black and beat to shit on some dock singing "Rising River Blues" . . . he was one. He sang like an ole broke-down music box. Some say Jesse James was one . . . and me . . . I dream of being one. But I can't. I mean I can't be the saint people dream of now. People want a street angel. They want a saint but with a cowboy mouth. Somebody to get off on when they can't get off on themselves. I think that's what Mick Jagger is trying to do . . . what Bob Dylan seemed to be for a while. A sort of god in our image . . . ya know? Mick Jagger came close but he got too conscious. For a while he gave me hope . . . but he misses. He's not whole. Hey Slim . . . am I losing ya? I mean, just tell me if I'm getting draggy. It's just hard and it's real important.

SLIM: No, baby, it's beautiful.

CAVALE: Well, I want it to be perfect, 'cause it's the only religion I got. It's like . . . well, in the old days people had Jesus and those guys to embrace . . . they created a god with all their belief energies . . . and when they didn't dig themselves they could lose themselves in the Lord. But it's too hard now. We're earthy people, and the old saints just don't make it, and the old God is just too far away. He don't represent our pain no more. His words don't shake through us no more. Any great motherfucker rock-n'-roll song can raise me higher than all of Revelations. We created rock-n'-roll from our own image, it's our child . . . a child that's gotta burst in the mouth of a savior. . . . Mick Jagger would love to be that savior but it ain't him. It's like . . . the rock-n'-roll star in his highest state of grace will be the new savior . . . rocking to Bethlehem to be born. Ya know what I mean, Slim?

SLIM: Well, fuck it, man. I ain't no savior.

CAVALE: But you've got it. You've got the magic. You could do it. You could be it.

SLIM: How?

CAVALE: You gotta collect it. You gotta reach out and grab all the little broken, busted-up pieces of people's frustration. That stuff in them that's lookin' for a way out or a way in. You know what I mean? The stuff in them that makes them wanna see God's face. And then you gotta take all that into yourself and pour it back out. Give it back to them bigger than life. You gotta be unselfish, Slim. Like God was selfish, He kept Himself hid. He wasn't a performer. You're a performer, man. You gotta be like a rock-and-roll Jesus with a cowboy mouth.

SLIM: You fucking cunt!

HE *jumps up and starts tearing the place apart, throwing things against the walls and screaming his head off.*

You stupid fucking cunt! Two years ago or one year ago! If it was then! If this was happening to me then, I could've done it! I could've done it! But now now! Not fucking now! I got another life! I can't do it now! It's too late! You can't bring somebody's dream up to the surface like that! It ain't fair! It ain't fucking fair! I know I could do it, but you're not supposed to tempt me! You're twisting me up! You're tearing me inside out! Get out of my house! Get the fuck out of my house!

CAVALE: This ain't your house. This is my house.

SLIM: It's nobody's house. Nobody's house.

HE *collapses, exhausted from his violence.* CAVALE *goes to him as if to soothe him, then realizes it's her dream being busted and not his.* SHE *starts yelling at him while* HE *just lies there wiped out.*

CAVALE: You're fucking right—nobody's house. A little nobody with a big fucking dream. Her only dream. My only dream. I spread my dreams at your feet, everything I believe in, and you tread all over them with your simpy horseshit. Fuck you. Fuck you. Poor, poor baby. I take your world and shake it. Well, you took my fantasy and shit on it. I was doing the streets looking for a man with nothing so I could give him everything. Everything it takes to make the world reel like a drunkard. But you have less than nothing, baby, you have part of a thing. And it's settled. And if it's settled I can't do nothing to alter it. I can't do shit. I can't give you nothing. I can't. I can't. You won't let me.

SLIM: Come here.

HE *pulls her to him.* THEY *hug each other. A pause.* THEY *lie on the bed.*

Listen to the traffic. It sounds like a river. I love rivers. I love the way they just go wherever they want. If they get too full they just overflow and flow wherever they want. They make up their own paths. New Paths. I tried to make a dam once in a river. It was just a little river. I put a whole bunch a rocks and sticks and shit in that river. I even put a tree in that river, but I couldn't get it to stop. I kept coming back day after day putting more and more rocks and mud and sticks in to try to stop it. Then one day I stopped it. I dammed it up. Just a little trickle coming out and a big pool started to form. I was really proud. I'd stopped a river. So I went back home and got in bed and thought about what a neat thing I'd done. Then it started to rain. It rained really hard. All night long it rained. The next morning I ran down to the river, and my dam was all busted to shit. That river was raging like a brush fire. Just gushing all over the place. Gushing up over the sides and raging right into the woods. I never built another dam again.

CAVALE: You're so neat. You're such a neat guy. I wish I woulda known you when I was little. Not real little. But at the age when you start finding out stuff. When I was cracking rocks apart and looking at their sparkles inside. Whe I first put my finger inside me and felt wonderment. I would've took you to this real neat hideout I had where I made a waterfall with tires and shit, and my own hut. We could've taken all our clothes off, and I'd look at your dinger, and you could show me how far you could piss. I bet you would've protected me. People were always giving me shit. Ya know what? Once I was in a play. I was real glad I was in a play 'cause I thought they were just for pretty people, and I had my dumb eyepatch and those metal plate shoes to correct my duck foot. It was *The Ugly Duckling,* and I really dug that 'cause of the happy ending and shit. And I got to be the ugly duckling and I had to wear some old tattered black cloth and get shit flung at me, but I didn't mind 'cause at the end I'd be that pretty swan and all. But you know what they did, Slim? At the end of the play I had to kneel on the stage and cover my head with a black shawl and this real pretty blonde-haired girl dressed in a white ballet dress rose up behind me as the swan. It was really shitty, man. I never got to be the fucking swan. I paid all the dues and up rose ballerina Cathy like the North Star. And afterwards all the parents could talk about was how pretty she looked. Boy, I ran to my hideout and cried and cried. The lousy fucks. I wish you were around then. I bet you would've protected me.

SLIM: Poor baby. *(pause)* Well, what're we gonna do now?

CAVALE: We could howl at the moon.

SLIM: Okay. Ready?

THEY *both let out howls, then laugh and fall on the floor.* THEY *play the coyote and the crow game on their hands and knees.* SLIM *talks in an old cracked, lecherous voice.*

Now, the coyote is mean. He's lean and low-down. He don't fool around with no scraggly crows. When he sees hisself somethin' he likes, he chomps it down.

HE *growls and goes after* CAVALE. SHE *scurries away.*

CAVALE: Little crow didn't do nothin'. Jes' out here peckin' in the desert. Checkin' out the sand for little corn grains. Jes' a little somepin' to nibble.

SLIM: Coyote gettin' hungry 'bout now. He ain't seen a chicken for he don't know how long. Crow look pretty good at this point. He don't care if it be fat and saucy. Just a little somepin' ta tear the wings off of.

CAVALE: Without no wings little crow bait have a hard time singin'. Starts to run all crazy through the night.

SLIM: Coyote he howl and chomp down on that crow now. Tear into that crow now!

HE *jumps on* CAVALE *and tears into her.* THEY *roll around on the floor for a while, then stop.*

Now coyote full. He ate up his tidbit. Now he roll on his back and make a big belch and fart and scratch his back against some cactus bush.

CAVALE: Little crow feel pretty good inside coyote belly. Not bad she says for a day on the range. Not bad at all. Though she may never see daylight again. Not bad at all.

A pause.

SLIM: Now what'll we do?

CAVALE: I don't know.

SLIM: We could call back the lobster man just for laughs.

CAVALE: Okay. Let me do it, Okay?

SLIM: Sure.

CAVALE: Goody. (SHE *runs to the telephone and picks it up*) Hello. Is this the lobster man? It is? Could you come back over here again? We need some cheering up. You would? Oh great! Thanks a lot. Bye. (SHE *hangs up*) He's coming right over.

SLIM: Good.

CAVALE: Let's play a trick on him when he comes, okay?

SLIM: Like what?

CAVALE: I don't know.

SLIM: What could we do?

CAVALE: Too bad he isn't a tuna fish. We could have a great big giant can and put him in it.

SLIM: Let's just talk to him when he comes.

CAVALE: What about?

SLIM: About what it's like to be a lobster man. It must be pretty weird, you know. Weirder than being us.

CAVALE: We're not weird, man. He's weird, but we're not weird.

SLIM: We could ask what the bottom of the ocean is like.

CAVALE: We could put him in a movie.

SLIM: What movie?

CAVALE: *Three Coins in the Fountain. The Prophet.*

SLIM: *The Swimmer.*

CAVALE: *You're just my Little Chicken of the Sea.*

SLIM: No, we gotta be nice to him. He's had a hard life.

CAVALE: How do you know?

SLIM: You can tell by his claws. He's got barnacles on his claws.

CAVALE: That means he's a wily old devil. He's outfoxed all the fishermen for years and years. He's never been caught.

SLIM: That's why he's so big. Lobsters never get that big.

CAVALE: He'll never be boiled, that one.

SLIM: We could boil him.

CAVALE: I thought you wanted to be nice to him.

SLIM: Did you ever hear a lobster scream when they hit the boiling water? It's awful. It's like a peacock fucking.

CAVALE: We can't boil him. We don't have any dishes.

SLIM: I could stab him with my switchblade. *(HE pulls out a giant switchblade and stabs it into the floor)*

CAVALE: Now, dear, don't get violent. Our company's arriving any minute now.

SLIM: I could cut through that hard shell and tear his heart out. I could eat his heart. You know that's what warriors used to do. Primitive warriors. They'd kill their opponent and then tear his heart out and eat it. Only if they fought bravely, though. Because then they believed they'd captured the opponent's strength.

CAVALE: What kind of strength does a lobster have?

SLIM: Ancient strength. Strength of the ages. Ancient sea-green strength. That's why I love lobster so much. They're very prehistoric.

CAVALE: But this one's a monster.

SLIM: You'd say the same thing about a Tyrannosaurus if he came in the door. I suppose you'd call him a monster too.

Loud banging on the door.

CAVALE: Jiggers, it's the lobster man! Quick, put away that knife. We don't want to scare him off.

SLIM *folds up his knife and puts it away.*

Okay. Ready?

SLIM: Ready.

More loud banging.

CAVALE: Coming!

SHE *goes to the door and opens it.* LOBSTER MAN *enters.*

Oh, Mr. Lobster Man. We're so happy to see you. We were just talking about you. Won't you come in?

LOBSTER MAN *saunters to center stage and grunts.* HE *looks ill at ease in the situation.*

SLIM: Have a seat.

LOBSTER MAN *sits on the bed and stares out at the audience.* SLIM *and* CAVALE *move around him.*

CAVALE: How long have you been a lobster?

LOBSTER MAN *grunts.*

SLIM: What'd he say?

CAVALE: He doesn't speak too clear. Could you try to speak up so we can understand you?

LOBSTER MAN *grunts.*

SLIM: Listen, the little lady here and I were discussing how we'd like to get to know you on a more intimate level. You know what I mean? I mean it's a drag to have servants just bringin' ya shit up the stairs and throwin' it down in the middle of the floor and then leavin' and you never get a chance to know them on a more intimate level. You know what I mean?

LOBSTER MAN *grunts.*

CAVALE: Yeah, you must be a very interesting person, and we don't even know you. That's not fair. We'd like to know your darkest nightmares, your most beautiful dreams, your wildest fantasies, your hopes, your aspirations. Stuff like that.

SLIM: What about it?

LOBSTER MAN *grunts.*

CAVALE: I think we oughta try a different tactic.

SLIM: Like what?

CAVALE: Like just ignoring him for a while. Pretend like he's not here. I mean, how would you feel if you walked into a situation like this?

SLIM: I never would.

CAVALE: I know, but just pretend you did. Let's just ignore him for a while.

SLIM: The whole point in bringing him over was so that we'd have something to do.

CAVALE: I know, but it ain't workin' out.

SLIM: So what're we gonna do then?

CAVALE: Let's go down to the deli and leave him here alone.

SLIM: He might rip us off.

CAVALE: So what? We don't need this shit.

SLIM: What about my drums? My guitar?

CAVALE: What about them? Man, you knock me out. You just gave it to me on the line. And like the Chinese say, sweetie, fuck the dream, you fuck the drum. Let the lobster man be the new Johnny Ace. It's the Aquarian Age. Ya know it was predicted that when Christ came back he'd come as a monster. And the lobster man ain't no James Dean. . . . Hey, honey, hit some hot licks on the fender. We're going out for a little shrimp cocktail.

SLIM: "Now what rough beast slouches toward Bethlehem to be born?" So now you want *him* to take *my* place. Is that it? You think this creep is gonna take me over! Is that it! You're gonna pour your magic gris-gris into this fool! Well, I'm gonna cut his ass wide open!

HE *pulls out his switchblade again and starts to threaten the* LOBS-
TER MAN.

CAVALE: Slim! Cut the shit! He's only a poor old lobster. Leave him
alone.

SLIM: *(to* LOBSTER MAN*)* Pretty sneaky. Pretty fuckin' sneaky. Squirmin'
yer way into our lives. Pretendin' dumb. We know you can talk.
We know you understand what's goin' on. You've got the silver.
You've got the gold. Out with it! Out with it, Lobster Man, or the
sun won't shine on your slimy shell.

CAVALE: No, don't, Slim. Leave him alone. He didn't do nothin'.
Leave my savior alone.

SLIM: Your savior? Your savior! He's supposed to be your savior?
Okay, we'll just see what kinda stuff he's made of then. We'll just
play him a little music and see what makes him tick. All right,
Lobster Man, this is your big chance.

SLIM *goes to the guitar and starts playing the old C-A minor—F-G
chords as* CAVALE *soothes the* LOBSTER MAN.

CAVALE: All right now, this won't hurt. Don't be afraid. I'll be right
back. Okay?

CAVALE *gets up and goes to the microphone.* SHE *begins to talk the
song "Loose Ends" as* SLIM *plays behind her.* HE *comes in on the
choruses, singing. During the song, the* LOBSTER MAN *gets up from
the bed and comes downstage. As the song unfolds* HE *begins to
break open and crack, revealing the rock-and-roll savior inside the
shell, dressed in black.*

I'm at loose ends
I don't know what to do
Always dreaming big dreams
Half dreams
Wanting him and loving you
To tell the truth I don't know which way to turn
Give me something to hold on to
Something I can learn
Oh come right here

*Come right here when you feel alone
And no one speaks for you
You can do it on your own*

Show me the way to it
You know I need a friend

A song to pull me from the hole I'm in
Give me something low-down
Give me something high
Pulling in the power of dark or light
To destroy to the left
Create on the right
Oh come right here

Come right here it's such a simple song
It'll cure all your misery
It won't move you wrong
So open up your mouth don't think about a thing
Feel the movement in you and sing

Sing sing sing sing

CAVALE *sings this part.*

Oh I was at loose ends
Now knowing what to do
I needed to open up
So I turned to you

SHE *talks.*

Help me to do it
I was always dreaming too high
Help me pull my star down from the sky
Down on the ground
Where I can feel it
Where I can touch it
Where I can be it

Oh I don't want to give up
I believe a light still shines
It shines for everyone
It's yours
It's mine
Oh come right here

CAVALE *talks the chorus,* SLIM *sings.* THEY *alternate lines.*

Come right here you know you're not alone
If you got no savior you can do it on your own

Open up your heart don't think about a thing
Feel the movement in you and sing

By the end of the song the LOBSTER MAN *is completely out of his shell and stands center stage as the rock-and-roll savior.* HE *stares out at the audience.* SLIM *sets down his guitar and goes to the gun.* HE *picks up the gun and goes to the* LOBSTER MAN. HE *holds out the gun for the* LOBSTER MAN *to take. The* LOBSTER MAN *takes the gun very slowly.* SLIM *smiles at the* LOBSTER MAN, *then crosses to the door.* HE *pauses a moment and turns to look at* CAVALE. THEY *stare at each other for a moment. Then* SLIM *exits through the door.* CAVALE *turns to the* LOBSTER MAN *and gives her speech very simply and softly, sitting on the edge of the stage. As* SHE *talks, the* LOBSTER MAN *spins the chamber of the gun, almost in rhythm with the speech. All through this* HE *stares at the audience.*

CAVALE: Nerval. He had visions. He cried like a coyote. He carried a crow. He walked through the Boulevard Noir inhuman like a triangle. He had a pet lobster on a pink ribbon. He told it his dreams, his visions, all the great secrets to the end of the world. And he hung himself on my birthday. Screaming like a coyote. The moon was cold and full and his visions and the crow and the lobster went on *cavale*. That's where I found my name. Cavale. On my birthday. It means escape.

As CAVALE *finishes, the* LOBSTER MAN *slowly raises the pistol to his head and squeezes the trigger. A loud click as the hammer strikes an empty chamber. The lights slowly fade to black.*

CURTAIN

The Rock Garden

The Rock Garden was first performed at Theatre Genesis, St. Mark's Church in the Bowery, New York, on October 10, 1964. It was directed by Ralph Cook, with the following cast:

> Boy: *Lee Kissman*
> Woman: *Stephanie Gordon*
> Man: *Kevin O'Connor*

The final scene of *The Rock Garden* was subsequently performed as part of the revue *Oh! Calcutta!*, which opened in New York on June 17, 1967. It was directed by Jacques Levy, with the following cast:

> Boy: *Leon Russom*
> Man: *Bill Macy*

SCENE 1

As lights come up we see a dinner table center stage. Seated at the head of the table facing the audience is a MAN *reading a magazine. Seated to the left of the table is a teen-age* GIRL. *A teen-age* BOY *sits opposite her. The* GIRL *and* BOY *are drinking milk.* THEY *take turns sipping the milk and exchanging glances. The* MAN *is completely involved in his magazine. For a long period of time nothing is said. The only action is that of the* BOY *and* GIRL *drinking milk. The* GIRL *drops her glass and spills the milk. Blackout.*

SCENE 2

A bedroom. There is a WOMAN *lying in a bed upstage with several blankets over her. To stage left is the teen-age* BOY *seated in a rocking chair. The lighting is a very pale blue. There is a large bay window behind the bed. The silhouettes of trees can be seen through the window. The* BOY *is dressed in underwear. As the lights come up there is no sound for a long while except the slow rocking of the* BOY.

WOMAN: Angels on horseback. That's what we called them. They're easy to make. Just salt crackers and marshmallows.

BOY: You have to toast them.

WOMAN: Yes. They're best when they're just barely toasted. Sort of a light brown so the marshmallow just barely starts to melt. *(a long pause)* It seems like they're for summer. We always had them in the summer.

BOY: It's summer now.

WOMAN: Yes. That's what I mean. In the summer. Angels on horseback. *(a long pause)* Pop liked them burned. You know? Burned to a crisp. Black and crispy. He'd sit there and chew all night on them. He'd sit in front of the fire and burn them all night. He loved them burned like that. It was funny.

BOY: Why?

WOMAN: I don't know. He just sat there a long time burning marshmallows and eating them. That's why his face was red. Everyone thought he just got out in the sun a lot but actually it was from sitting in front of the fire so long. He hardly ever went in the sun. It was funny. A whole beach and he stayed inside all the time. He'd look at the beach from the attic but he hardly ever went near it. The forest was what he liked. You know? He liked to go walking in the trees. He'd pick mushrooms. He could tell all the different kinds. He knew the poison ones from the edible ones. Once he made a mistake and got very sick. I remember. He picked up a lot of very small red ones that he'd never seen before. He made a big kind of stew out of them. He even mixed them with some of the other kind. He got very sick and threw up for a whole week. Poor Pop. He was a funny man.

BOY: Why?

WOMAN: He just was. I don't know. I mean he knew all about a lot of things but he still got sick. Like the mushrooms. And once he tried to make a tree house and fell down and broke his leg. Sometimes he just stayed in the attic. He'd stay up there for days and days and never come down. We thought he'd starved to death once because he'd been up there for ten days without food. But he was all right. He came out looking like he just had breakfast. He was never hungry.

BOY: Never?

WOMAN: Hardly ever. He would eat when we weren't around. He always ate alone.

BOY: Why?

WOMAN: He just liked to, I guess. He didn't like to eat around people. He ate with the cats in the attic. He had a lot of cats. He had one called Ty Cobb because it played ball so well. *(a long pause)* He was a funny man. He knew a lot of people. They'd stop by to see him but he was always in the attic. I always wondered why they kept coming back. He was always in the attic. He loved animals. He had a whole bunch of cats. He kept them in the attic though so nobody could bother them. Mother went up there once and she said the place stank so bad she never went back. I guess he never cleaned up after the cats. They just went all over the place and he never cleaned it up. Ty Cobb was his favorite one. I never saw Ty Cobb, but he told me that was his favorite.

BOY: He never let the cats out?

WOMAN: No, he kept them in the attic. He never let anyone up there. He'd stay up there for days.

BOY: What did he do?

WOMAN: I don't know. Mother told me he was a painter but I never saw him painting. He'd stay up there for days. I guess he was a painter. I don't know. Would you get me a glass of water?

The BOY gets up and goes offstage. HE comes back with a glass of water.

Thank you.

The BOY *sits.*

I'm really thirsty. *(a long pause)* Your legs are a lot like Pop's. Pop had the same kind of legs.

BOY: What do you mean?

WOMAN: Well I mean they were bony and—and kind of skinny.

BOY: They were?

WOMAN: Yes. And he had knobby knees.

BOY: He did?

WOMAN: And fuzzy brown hair all over them. He was a funny man. Would you get me another glass?

The BOY *goes off.* HE *comes back with the water and wearing a pair of pants.*

Thank you.

The BOY *sits.*

I really don't know how I caught this cold. It was probably from being out in the rain too much. I used to play in the rain all the time but now I catch colds. I used to listen to the rain when I was sleeping. I mean not when I was sleeping but when I was in bed. Just before I fell asleep I'd listen to the rain. It made me fall a-sleep. It was like music sort of. It always made me fall asleep. Your feet are almost identical to Pop's. I mean the way the middle toe is. You see the way your middle toe sticks way out further than the other toes? That's the way Pop's toes was. His middle one. The way it sticks out.

BOY: Oh.

WOMAN: Isn't that funny? Pop would have liked you. I can tell. Would you get me another blanket, please?

The BOY *goes off.* HE *comes back on with a blanket and wearing shoes.*

Oh, thank you. It's getting a little drafty. Can you feel it?

BOY: *(sitting)* No.

WOMAN: It feels a little drafty. It's probably coming from the windows. It probably is. But you know Bill. He says he'll put new putty in and he never does. He never gets around to it. All they need is some new putty and there wouldn't be any more drafts. It's very simple, you know? Even I could do it. I'll probably have to if I want it to get done. I don't think he's ever done that kind of work. I know he does physical labor but I don't think he's ever done any work with putty. Putty is a hard thing to work with. It's very—very tricky and it takes a lot of know-how. You can't just expect to pick it up and start working it right off the bat. You have to know what you're working with. It's a tricky kind of material. You have to know all about how to prepare it with the right kind of pastes and things like that. You can't just take it and start puttying. You have to really learn all you can about it before you can start working with it. He'll never learn. I don't think he wants to. Can I have another glass of water?

The BOY *goes off and comes back with a glass of water.*

Thank you.

The BOY *sits.*

He can't learn about putty by working in the orchard and things like that. He needs to practice with it a few times in order to get the feel of it. He could practice on the windows in the shed but I don't think he wants to. Just a little practice is all he'd need. He doesn't have to do all that physical labor that he does. He really doesn't. It doesn't do anything for him. He gets all sweaty and everything. It would be so much easier just to practice a little and putty the windows. I don't think he wants to do it though. *(a long pause)* It doesn't do anything for his physique. You know? He works and works all day and look at his physique. You've seen him without his shirt. You've seen his physique. He does all that labor for nothing. It's really too bad. You have the same kind of torso as he does. The same build. Only he works and you don't. That's the difference. He should just face up to it, that's all. It won't get any better. He's not going to develop any more by doing all that work. Could I have another glass?

The BOY *goes off.* HE *comes back with a glass of water and wearing a shirt.*

Thank you.

The BOY *sits.*

It doesn't really matter to me except that the draft isn't good for me when I have these colds. Otherwise the drafts are fine. It's just when I catch these colds that they bother me. I guess I should gradually become used to the draft but I can't help it. You're not supposed to have drafts on you when you have a cold. Aren't you cold?

BOY: No.

WOMAN: I'm freezing. Would you bring me another blanket?

The BOY *goes off.* HE *comes back on with a blanket and wearing an overcoat.*

Thank you.

The BOY *sits.*

It's really cold. I shouldn't have walked in the rain. That's the problem. If I hadn't walked in the rain I wouldn't be cold like this. It's just that I love the rain and whenever I get the chance I walk in it. I like it after the rain stops, too. I mean the way everything smells and looks. Right after a good hard rain. Those are two of my favorite times. When it's raining and right after it rains. I like it just before it rains too but that's different. It's not the same. I get a different feeling just before it rains. I mean it's a different feeling from the one I get when it's raining. It's not the same. It's like—

Footsteps are heard offstage. The footsteps get louder. A MAN *walks by the window from stage right to stage left dressed in a hat and overcoat. The* BOY *stands suddenly. The* MAN *can be heard scraping his feet offstage. The* BOY *runs off stage right. The* MAN *enters stage left.* HE *walks across the stage and exits stage right. After a while the* MAN *comes back on dressed in underwear.* HE *crosses to the rocking chair and sits. For a long while the* MAN *just sits rocking. The* WOMAN *stares at the ceiling.*

MAN: Kind of drafty.

WOMAN: Yes.

MAN: Must be the windows.

WOMAN: I guess so.

A long silence while the MAN *rocks. The lights dim down slowly.*

SCENE 3

The lights come up again on a bare stage except for a couch downstage left and a chair upstage right. The MAN *sits on the couch. The* BOY *sits in the chair facing upstage with his back to the* MAN. *The* BOY *never turns to address the* MAN *but delivers all his lines into the air.* THEY *are both dressed in underwear. At different moments the* BOY *nods out from boredom and falls off his chair.* HE *picks himself back up and sits again. The* MAN *goes on oblivious. There is a long pause as the* TWO *just sit in their places.*

Saturday afternoon—just after lunch, just before the ball game.

MAN: It's uh—the lawn doesn't seem too bad this time of year. *(a long pause)* Except around the sprinkler heads. It's always wet around the sprinkler heads so it grows all the time, I guess. *(a long pause)* It's harder to mow around them too, I guess. It's hard to get the lawn mower in there close, I guess. It's pretty hard to get it in there close so it cuts. I guess. *(a long pause)* The other house wasn't as bad as this one, was it? I mean the lawn wasn't. I mean the way the lawn was at the other place made it easier, I guess. I mean not the lawn itself but more the way it was. You know? The way it was just there. I mean it was just a square piece of lawn. You know? It wasn't the lawn so much as the way it was.

A long pause. The BOY *falls off his chair, then sits back down.*

The lawn here is different, you know. This one is different from the other one. It's the locality of it, I guess. You know? It's harder to get to. The other one didn't have as many sprinkler heads as this. The other one didn't have any, did it? No, the other one was easy. I remember the other one.

A long pause.

BOY: The other one was different from this.

MAN: Yes, the other was easier and didn't have so many sprinkler heads. *(a long pause)* If we can get the fence painted by next week it would be nice. You know? It's not a good fence but if we could get it painted by next week it would be nice, I guess. *(a long pause)* It needs to be saturated, you know? That way it will last. I remember the last one didn't last at all. You remember the last one, the way it fell down all the time? But if it had been saturated it wouldn't have fallen down at all. You know? *(a long pause)* There's a new kind of preservative you can buy that will be good for it. It only takes a couple of coats.

BOY: Two coats?

MAN: Yes, just a couple will do it.

BOY: Two?

MAN: Yes, two or three.

BOY: Three or two?

MAN: Just a couple.

BOY: Two?

MAN: Yes.

BOY: Good.

MAN: Yes. *(a long pause)* That ought to do it.

BOY: Good.

A long pause.

MAN: What color?

BOY: For the fence?

MAN: Yes.

BOY: What color is it now?

MAN: White.

BOY: White?

MAN: Yes.

BOY: How about white?

MAN: You mean paint it over white?

BOY: Yes.

MAN: Oh. Well, all right.

BOY: White would be good.

MAN: Sure. Maybe a kind of off-white. You know? What about a kind of off-white? You know what I mean? A kind of different white. You know? Just a little different. Not too much different from the way it is now. What do you think? A different kind of white. You know? So it won't be too much the same. I could be almost the same but still be a little different. You know?

A long pause. The BOY *falls off his chair.*

It would be fun, I think. Did you notice the rock garden? That's a new idea. It's by the driveway. You may have seen it when you pass by there in the mornings. It's not bad for my never having made one before. It's one of those new kind. You know? With rocks and stuff in it. It has a lot of rocks and stuff from the trip. We found afterwards that it was really worth carrying all those rocks around. You know? It's a nice rock garden. It gives me something to do. It keeps me pretty busy. You know? It feels good to get out in it and work and move the rocks around and stuff. You know? It's a good feeling. I change it every day. It keeps me busy.

A long pause. The BOY *falls off his chair.*

It's not the garden so much as the *work* it gives me. It's good to work in a garden. Remember when we found the rocks? I remember. That was a good trip, wasn't it? Maybe we can take another one and get some more.

BOY: Rocks?

MAN: Yes. We could start another garden. A bigger one.

BOY: Bigger than the one you have now?

MAN: Sure. We could start a whole lot of them. They're not hard to start, you know. All you need is some rocks. They have to be good rocks though. I mean they can't be any kind of rocks. You know what I mean? I mean they have to be the right size and shape and color and everything. They can't just be ordinary rocks, otherwise there wouldn't be any point in making a garden at all. You know?

That's why we'd have to go somewhere else to find them. Somewhere like Arizona or something. Like we did before. Do you remember? We went to Arizona before and we found a lot of rocks. We could really have some nice gardens like the one I have now. Only bigger and more fancy. I saw one with a fountain in it. We could put a fountain in ours. You know? And some of those Oriental statues and things like that. We could work on it together. You know? It wouldn't be hard. We could do it in our spare time.

BOY: Together?

MAN: Sure. And we could have bacon, lettuce, and tomato sandwiches afterwards.

BOY: After we work?

MAN: Sure.

BOY: With mayonnaise?

MAN: Yeah. And we both would have big appetites probably, from working so hard in the garden.

BOY: Hard?

MAN: I mean just working we would have appetites. Just from plain working.

BOY: We would?

MAN: Sure. *(a long pause)* It wouldn't be hard work at all. Just plain good steady work in the outdoors. It would be good for us. Don't you think? *(a long pause)* The orchard is the thing that really needs work. You know? It needs more work than the garden probably. It needs to be taken care of. It needs more water than it's been getting. You know what I mean. The new trees especially. They get brown pretty easily in this warm weather. I guess we should really take care of the orchard first. You know? Then maybe we can go to Arizona and pick up the rocks. We should disc the orchard first and then spray the new trees. It won't be hard once we get into it. It doesn't take a lot of work, really. You know? The irrigation needs to be worked on too. That will be the hardest. It's those damn pipes, you know? Whoever put them in when they were put in didn't put them in right. You know? They weren't put in right originally. That's the whole thing. They were put in wrong when they were first put in. You know what I mean? So I thought we'd take them all out and then put in some new ones. Some of those aluminum ones they have now. Have you seen the ones? They're lightweight. I thought we'd put some of those in.

BOY: We take all the ones that are in now out and then we put in some aluminum ones?

MAN: Yes.

BOY: And then we spray the new trees?

MAN: Yes, they need spraying. We could do all that and then go to Arizona. It wouldn't be bad at all once we got into it. This whole place will be looking like a new place. A new place. One of those new places with rock gardens all over and fountains. You know? You come up the street and there'd be a nice green lawn with a lot of rock gardens and the irrigation running and the new trees all—all sort of green. You know? And the fence all painted with a different kind of white paint and the grass cut around the sprinkler heads and all that. You know?

A long pause.

BOY: When I come it's like a river. It's all over the bed and the sheets and everything. You know? I mean a short vagina gives me security. I can't help it. I like to feel like I'm really turning a girl on. It's a much better screw is what it amounts to. I mean if a girl has a really small vagina it's really better to go in from behind. You know? I mean she can sit with her legs together and you can sit facing her. You know? But that's different. It's a different kind of thing. You can do it standing, you know? Just by backing her up, you know? You just stand and she goes down and down until she's almost sitting on your dick. You know what I mean? She'll come a hundred times and you just stand there holding onto it. That way you don't even have to undress. You know? I mean she may not want to undress is all. I like to undress myself but some girls just don't want to. I like going down on girls, too. You know what I mean? She gives me some head and then I give her some. Just sort of a give-and-take thing. You know? The thing with a big vagina is that there isn't as much contact. There isn't as much friction. I mean you can move around inside her. There's different ways of ejaculation. I mean the leading up to it can be different. You can rotate motions. Actually girls really like fingers almost as well as a penis. You know? If you move your fingers fast enough they'd rather have it that way almost. I learned to use my thumb, you know? You can get your thumb in much farther, actually. I mean the thumb can go almost eight inches whereas a finger goes only five or six. You know? I don't know. I really like to come almost out and then go all the way into the womb. You know, very slowly. Just come down to the end and all the way back in and hold it. You know what I mean?

The MAN falls off the couch. The lights black out.

CURTAIN

Cowboys #2

Cowboys #2 was first performed at the Mark Taper Forum in Los Angeles, in November, 1967, as part of an evening of plays entitled *The Scene*. It was directed by Edward Parone, with sets and lighting by Michael Devine, costumes by Mari Anna Elliott, and the following cast:

Stu: *Gary Hanes*
Chet: *Philip Austin*
Man Number One: *Lucian Baker*
Man Number Two: *John Rose*

The setting is a bare stage, very dimly lit. Upstage center is a sawhorse with a yellow caution light mounted on it. The light blinks on and off throughout the play. On each side of the sawhorse is a YOUNG MAN *seated against the upstage wall.* THEY *both wear black pants, black shirts and vests, and black hats.* THEY *seem to be sleeping. Offstage is the sound of a single cricket, which lasts throughout the play. As the curtain rises there is a long pause, then a saw is heard offstage, then a hammer, then the saw again.*

MAN NUMBER ONE: *(off left)* It's going to rain.

STU: Do you think so?

CHET: What?

STU: Uh, rain?

CHET: Oh . . . sure. Maybe.

STU: Could be.

CHET: Let's see.

MAN NUMBER ONE *whistles as if calling a dog off left. Pause.*

STU: It wouldn't be bad for my clothes.

CHET: Clothes?

STU: It'd be good for my clothes, I said. It'd be like taking a bath with my clothes on.

CHET: Sure. It'd be the same for me, I guess.

STU: Sure. Why don't you go over there and see if you can see any cloud formations?

HE *points downstage.* CHET *gets up and crosses downstage like an old man.* HE *stands center and looks up at the sky, then speaks like an old man.*

CHET: Well, well, well, well. I tell ya, boy. I tell ya. Them's some dark ones, Mel. Them's really some dark ones.

STU: *(talking like an old man)* Dark, eh? How long's it been since ya seen 'em dark as that?

CHET: How long's it been? Long? How long?

STU: Yeah. How long a time, Clem?

CHET: Long a time? Well, it's been a piece. A piece a time. Say maybe, off a year or so. Maybe that.

STU: A year, eh?

CHET: Yep. Could be longer.

STU: Longer?

CHET: Yep. Could be two or three year since I seen 'em all dark like that.

STU: That's a piece a time, Clem. That's for sure.

CHET: Yep! Yep! (HE *whistles loudly and starts doing a dance like an old man*)

STU: (*normal voice*) Hey! Come back!

CHET *stops short.* HE *walks back upstage like an old man and sits in his original position.* MAN NUMBER TWO *whistles from off right.* CHET *and* STU *look in the direction of whistling, then at each other.*

You know what?

CHET: What?

STU: I think I'll take a look.

CHET: Okay.

STU *stands and walks downstage like an old man.* HE *looks up at the sky and speaks like an old man.*

STU: By jingo! Them really is some dark ones.

CHET: Sure.

STU: Them's really dark like ya said, Mel!

CHET: Dark as they come.

STU: All dark and puckery like—like—

CHET: Like what?

STU: Well . . .

CHET: Like what?

STU: (*to* CHET, *in a normal voice*) Would you give me a chance?

CHET: Like what?

STU: Give me a chance to figure like what. I haven't even thought of it yet. So give me a chance.

CHET: Okay.

STU *turns back and looks at the sky;* HE *looks for a while.*

Have you decided?

STU *turns back to* CHET.

I'm sorry.

STU: Are you going to give me a chance or aren't you?

CHET: I said I'm sorry. So go ahead.

STU *turns back and looks at the sky again.*

STU: (*old man*) By jingo, them's really some dark ones, eh, Mel?

CHET: Fuck.

STU: (*turning suddenly to* CHET) Goddamn you!

CHET: Well, shit, why don't you say it? I'm not going to sit here all day.

STU: All right! (HE *turns back very fast to the audence and looks at the sky; HE says the lines rapidly*) By jingo, them's really some dark ones, eh, Mel? I haven't probably seen clouds as dark as them myself.

CHET: (*stands and yells at* STU) So!

STU: (*still facing the audience*) So it's important! Ya got to notice things like that! It's important!

CHET: *So!*

STU: So ya can stay alive or something. Ya got to notice things like that.

CHET: Why?

STU: So ya can tell when it's gonna rain! So ya can tell when it's gonna snow. So ya can tell when—when—so ya can tell!

CHET: I seen 'em already!

STU: Good!

CHET: I seen 'em lots a times in Utah and in other places.

STU: (*turns to* CHET) So?

CHET: So I already seen 'em. If I already seen 'em, there ain't no point in me lookin' agin.

> CHET *sits abruptly. There is a pause, then* STU *starts doing jumping calisthenics, clapping his hands over his head.* HE *faces* CHET *as* HE *does this.*

STU: Clap, clap, clap. Clapping, clapping. Clap.

CHET: What are you doing?

STU: This?

CHET: That.

STU: Oh. Well, you remember yesterday?

CHET: Yesterday what?

STU: Remember yesterday when I was sitting and my feet fell asleep?

CHET: Yeah.

STU: Well, this is for that.

CHET: Oh. To get the blood going and circulating?

STU: Yes. To get the blood going the way it should.

CHET: So it runs.

STU: So it runs.

CHET: So it doesn't stop and get clogged up?

STU: Right.

CHET: You know, you may have something like, uh, diabetes.

STU: (*stops and looks at* CHET) Diabetes?

CHET: Yes. It may be a low sugar content.

STU: No. That's diabetes.

CHET: Yes.

STU: Well, that's what I don't have. *(HE starts jumping again)*

CHET: You don't know. You can't really tell.

CHET gets up and crosses to STU. HE walks around STU in a circle, talking to him as STU continues jumping.

Diabetes is a strange thing. Very strange. It's been known to lie dormant for years, then one day it just pops up. And there you are.

STU stops as CHET continues to walk around him.

STU: Where?

CHET: There you are, lying in bed or sitting on a subway or walking down the street or eating a hamburger or drinking a Coke or smoking a cigarette.

STU: There I am.

CHET: There you are and you fall over.

CHET falls on the ground. STU stands looking down at him.

You fall out. You breathe harder and you get weaker and weaker. There was this kid I remember in junior high school. He had it. He collapsed one day right in math class. Just fell out of his chair and collapsed on the floor. Well, we had to bring him sugar. That's what it takes. Sugar. Each one of us had to go to the cafeteria and bring him back a bowl full of sugar. Each one of us.

STU: How did he do?

CHET: What?

STU: How did he pull through?

CHET: Oh. Shh!

STU: What?

CHET: Shh! Listen.

CHET stands slowly. THEY both stand facing the audience and listening. The sound of rain is heard faintly offstage; it builds as THEY continue the scene.

STU: Is it?

CHET: Sounds like it.

Smiling, THEY look up at the sky.

STU: I think it is.

THEY start doing a dance and laughing, slowly building and getting more hysterical.

CHET: It's them clouds!

STU: Rain! Rain, mother!

THEY *take off their hats and wave them over their heads.*

CHET: It's comin' down.

THEY *become the old men again.*

STU: Here we go!

CHET: Look at it!

STU: Rain, bitch! Rain!

THEY *laugh hysterically.*

CHET: My clothes!

STU: You could tell by them fuckin' clouds!

CHET: Rain on me!

STU: Come on, baby!

CHET: It's like the great flood of 1683!

STU: Everything's wet!

CHET: Wet all over!

STU: Look at the mud!

CHET: Mud!

THEY *fall on the floor and roll around in the imaginary mud.*

STU: Mud! You're beautiful!

CHET: All this mud!

STU: Mud all over!

CHET: Kiss me, mud!

STU: Dirty mud!

CHET: *Aaah!*

STU: Muddy, muddy!

CHET: Dirty gook!

THEY *kiss the floor and throw mud on each other.*

STU: Muck and slime!

CHET: *Aaah,* mud!

STU: Fucky, fuck!

CHET: Mud and guck!

The rain sound stops suddenly.

STU: Oh, mud.

CHET: Mud.

STU: Mud.

THEY *slowly stop laughing and roll over on their backs.* THEY *stare at the ceiling.*

CHET: You know, some girl asked me about the Big Dipper and I couldn't tell her.

STU: You couldn't tell her what?

CHET: I couldn't tell her anything about it. The big one.

STU: Is that the big one? *(HE points to the ceiling)*

CHET: That's what she asked me and I couldn't tell her, so how can I tell you?

STU: Is that the big one or the little one? *(a pause)* Is that the big one or the little one?

CHET: It looks like the little one to me.

STU: Can't you tell? *(a pause)* Can't you tell?

CHET *stands suddenly and walks upstage looking at the ceiling.*
You don't know?

CHET: I said before that it looks like the little one. I said that. Now what?

STU: Then it is the little one, isn't it?

CHET: I guess! Yes! Why not?

STU *stands and walks up to* CHET. CHET *walks around the stage looking up at the ceiling as* STU *follows close behind him.*

STU: It should be the little one, if you say it's the little one.

CHET: I guess.

STU: I guess it is, Chet.

CHET: I guess it is, Stu.

STU: You're probably right. I've never seen either one really, so I can't tell.

CHET: I've never seen them together.

STU: They don't come out together, do they?

CHET: I don't know.

STU: That's the only way to compare them. To see them together.

CHET: I guess.

STU: That looks like the little one though.

CHET *turns suddenly to* STU; THEY *stare at each other.* MAN NUMBER ONE *and* MAN NUMBER TWO *whistle back and forth across the stage, then stop.*

CHET: *(old man's voice)* Clem, I though we was in the Red Valley.

STU: *(old man's voice)* Red Valley? That's right, Mel. This here's the Red Valley area.

CHET: Is that right?

STU: That's right, boy. Come on down here.

STU leads CHET downstage center. THEY look out over the audience.

CHET: What?

STU: Come on. Now see that? *(HE points off in the distance)*

CHET: What?

STU: See all that out there? That area all out in there?

CHET: Yep.

STU: That's it, Clem.

CHET: This whole area's the Red Valley?

The sound of horses running can be heard faintly offstage.

STU: That's right, Mel.

CHET: This here's the same Red Valley you was referrin' to back in Des Moines?

STU: This here's the very same area.

The horses get louder.

CHET: The very same place? Clem, I think you was either lyin' to me or you was misinformed somehow.

STU: How's that, Mel?

CHET: Listen.

The horses get louder.

STU: What's that?

CHET: Well, that's what I mean.

STU: What?

CHET: That.

HE points in the distance. The sound of Indians screaming joins in with the horses and becomes very loud.

STU: Damn.

CHET: We got to do somethin', boy.

STU: Get down behind them barrels and get out yer rifle.

THEY kneel down and hold imaginery rifles.

CHET: Sure is a lot of 'em, Clem.

STU: Well, we can hold 'em for a while.

CHET: Don't have much ammo . . .

STU: We'll fight 'em with our rifle butts after that.

The sound offstage gets very loud and is joined by gunfire.

CHET: Wait till they get up close.

STU: Okay.

CHET: Okay. Fire!

THEY *make gun noises and fire at imaginary Indians.*

STU: Fire!

CHET: Fire!

STU: Damn! Look like Apaches!

CHET: Some of 'em's Comanches, Clem!

STU: Fire!

CHET: Good boy, ya got him!

STU: Fire!

CHET: Got him again. One shot apiece, Clem.

STU: Get em, Mel.

CHET: Fire! Got me a brave! Got me a brave!

STU: Good boy!

CHET: Thought he was fancy, ridin' a pinto.

STU: Your left, Clem. Got him! Tore him up!

CHET: Good boy. Got him in the head that time. Right in the head. Watch it!

STU: Fire!

CHET: Atta baby!

STU *grabs his shoulder, screams and falls back.* CHET *stands and yells out at the audience, firing his rifle.*

You lousy red-skinned punks! Think you can injure my buddy? Lousy red assholes! Come back and fight!

The sound fades out. CHET *pulls* STU *upstage and props him up against the wall.*

STU: My arm . . .

CHET: Ya okay, boy?

STU: Got me in the arm.

CHET: Take it easy. Easy. I'll take care a ya, boy. Take it easy.

STU: Redskins all over.

CHET: Red Valley area. (CHET *rolls* STU's *sleeve up and breaks off an imaginary arrow*) Easy, boy.

STU: My arm . . .

CHET: I'll get it. Gonna be okay.

STU: Bad arm.

CHET: Bloody, blood.

STU: Mud.

CHET *crosses downstage center.* HE *kneels down on the edge of the stage and takes his hat off.* HE *dips his hat in an imaginary stream as though the edge of the stage were the bank.*

CHET: Water. Gonna get ya some a this. (HE *pours water on his head from the hat.* HE *dips his hat again and pours more water on his head)* Good water. *Aaah.* All sweet and everything.

HE *dips his hat again and carries the hat carefully upstage.* HE *throws the water in* STU's *face.* STU *jumps up.* THEY *talk in normal voices.*

STU: What the fuck are you doing!

CHET: I was—I was trying to cool you off.

STU: Thanks.

CHET: Okay.

STU: I don't need it.

CHET: Oh.

STU: I'm cool already.

CHET: Oh.

STU: So thanks anyway.

CHET: That's all right.

STU *crosses downstage center and sits.* HE *takes off his shoes and socks and puts his feet in the stream.* HE *sits on the edge of the stage. A pause.* CHET *remains upstage looking at* STU.

STU: Nice.

CHET: What?

STU: Air.

CHET: Air?

STU: Yep. Used to be lots of orange orchards around here, you know.

CHET: Really?

STU: Yep. Lots. All over. You could smell them.

CHET: I guess. I'm sorry about the water.

STU: They were all over. Then they cut them all down, one at a time Every one. Built schools for kids and homes for old flabby ladies and halls for heroes and streets for cars and houses for people.

CHET: I was trying to cool you off, Stu.

STU: Then buses for kids to go to the schools and buses to take them back. Peacocks. Peacocks for mansions. For gardens. Peacocks screaming like mothers and daughters. Peacocks screwing on top of people's houses. Peacocks shitting in people's driveways. On people's cars. They can hardly fly. Fat, ugly birds with no wings and overlong tails. Tail feathers that people put in vases and set on

top of fireplaces and dust collects on them. They dust them off.
Green feathers with eyes in the middle. Blue eyes in the middle of
green feathers. You can't eat peacocks. They're too tough.

CHET: I'm sorry, Stu.

STU: Pheasant is the thing they eat.

CHET: Stu?

Car horns are heard offstage. STU *stands and looks out over the
audience.*

STU: Bird of paradise. That's a flower. They grow like that. Acres full
of bird of paradise. Truck comes by in the morning and picks them
up. They take them to another town and sell them. They go in
vases, too. Peacock feathers and bird of paradise. They just leave
them in vases and let the stems rot and the water get all smelly and
green.

HE *picks up his shoes and socks and crosses slowly upstage.* HE
walks backward looking at the audience; as HE *does this* CHET
slowly crosses downstage, also looking out at the audience.

They have turtles, too. Turtles, with painted shells from the county
fair. A dozen turtles in bowls and pans, with water and rocks and
turtle food floating around. Then the turtles die and the water gets
all green and slimy and smells. The whole house starts smelling
from dead turtles and rotten stems and slimy water. Pens full of
sheep and lambs. Chicken coops with chicken-do hanging in the
wire. The chickens walk all over it and through it. Their feet rot
after a while from walking in their own crap so much.

Car horns are heard offstage.

They start eating it after a while, and it gets inside them and infects
their throat and their liver. Their livers rot and their feathers fall
out. Their skin gets all blue and pus starts coming out their noses.
They bleed from the mouth and can't control their bowels. It just
runs out of them like water. They lie there in a pool of shit and pus
and feathers and cluck. It's a little cluck in the back of their throat.
Their wings throb and they make this clucking sound and they just
lie there.

CHET *sits on the edge of the stage.* STU *lies down on his back upstage. The car horns continue. There is a long pause.*

CHET: It's a nice morning though. (HE *takes off his shoes and socks and
puts his feet in the stream)*

STU: Hm.

CHET: I like mornings. Any kind of a morning. You know what I like
best about mornings? Hey, Stu!

STU: Hm?

CHET: Do you know what I like about mornings more than anything?

STU: What?

CHET: Food. All the different kinds of food.

STU: Food's food.

CHET: Not in the morning. Food is more than food in the morning.

STU: It's breakfast food.

CHET: I wasn't talking about any kind of food. I was talking about food being different in the morning because you're most hungry in the morning.

STU: Why?

CHET: Because you haven't eaten all night. So when you get up, you're really hungry.

STU: I see.

CHET: You know, I could go for some breakfast.

STU: Already?

CHET: Yep. Some scrambled eggs and hot chocolate and toast. Rye toast.

STU: This early?

CHET: Sure. Some farina. Hot farina with cold milk and prune juice. Maybe some pancakes, with butter and maple syrup and powdered sugar. About ten pancakes on top of each other. You know, they have all different kinds of cereals here. Cold and hot. Cornflakes, Rice Krispies, oatmeal, Sugar Corn Pops, farina, Malto-Meal, Nutrina, Purina, and many others.

Car horns sound offstage. While CHET *continues speaking,* MAN NUMBER ONE *and* MAN NUMBER TWO *carry on their conversation.* THEY *are unseen.*

CHET: And eggs. Poached eggs on toast, with hot milk and butter, and when you break the yolks the yellow part drips down into the hot milk and mixes with the toast. Salt and pepper and coffee and hot chocolate. Then just something plain on the side. A little sour cream maybe, on the eggs. Then some sausage. Bacon. Or eggs sunny side up and turned over lightly. Some

MAN NUMBER ONE: The rent's down to a dollar a month now.

MAN NUMBER TWO: Oh yeah? How did you manage that?

MAN NUMBER ONE: Something about the City Health Department or Rent Commission.

MAN NUMBER TWO: Well, that's good.

MAN NUMBER ONE: I guess so.

hashbrown potatoes fried in deep butter. A tall glass of milk with water on the outside of the glass. Then two glasses of water and another cup of coffee and some cigarettes.

More car horns. CHET *sits looking out over the audience.* HE *smells his armpits, then his feet.*

You know, Stu, we really stink. We really do. My feet smell like cheese. Blue cheese. It's really strong.

HE *picks his toes.*

MAN NUMBER TWO: We got enough food to last for a while.

MAN NUMBER ONE: Sure.

MAN NUMBER TWO: Don't take much to live on.

MAN NUMBER ONE: A buck a month.

MAN NUMBER TWO: That's as cheap as you can get.

MAN NUMBER TWO: I guess so.

MAN NUMBER TWO: I guess for free would be cheaper.

It's toe-jam. That's what they call it. That's what stinks. It's not our feet. It's the toe-jam. Whew! (HE *lies back*) It's in our clothes, too. My clothes smell just like my body smells, only worse. Sweat. (HE *sits up and looks at the sky*) We're going to go on sweating, too. In this sun we're going to go on sweating and smelling more and more. (HE *squints his eyes and looks at the sun*) It's just morning and look at the sun. It's really early. (HE *stands suddenly still, looking out*) Hey, Stu! It's morning and look at the sun already. What time is it, Stu? (HE *turns upstage*) Stu!

HE *turns back very slowly toward the audience and becomes an old man again, shielding his eyes from the sun.* MAN NUMBER ONE *and* MAN NUMBER TWO *whistle back and forth, then stop.*

Well, well, well. The sun's up already and it ain't even time. It's early yet. It's comin' down, boy. That heat. It's gettin' hot, Mel. I seen it like this before. (HE *turns and runs upstage to* STU) Mel, ya got to get up, boy. Ya got to get up now. (HE *shakes* STU *by the shoulder*) Enough sleep! We got to look for some water, boy! (HE *turns to the audience*) You don't seem to realize the situation, Mel. We're in fer some heat. We're in fer some hot days now, and we got to find water. All right! All right! I'll look fer the water and you sleep. Don't move, boy. Just sleep and I'll get the water. (HE *pulls his vest up over his head and wanders around the stage searching*) Where shall we look? Can't exert. Got to save our strength. (HE *paces back and forth*) Good thing we got a lot a clothes, otherwise we'd be sunburned to death. Oh, it's really hot. It's really hot. I wonder how hot it is right now. Must be ninety at least. What if it's ninety, Mel? If it's ninety that means it could get up to a hundred or a hundred and ten or a hundred and twenty. We'll be scorched and boiled. We got to find some shade. Mel! (HE *switches to his normal voice*) Okay, Stu, this isn't funny. I don't think it's funny. You're going to sleep all day while I bust my ass looking for shade? Come on. I'll get you into some shade.

HE *drags* STU *slowly downstage as the lights come up very slowly; the lights should reach their full brightness at the end of the play. Car horns are heard softly offstage.*

Come on down here. There's better shade down here. Come on, boy. That's it. Let me get ya some water. (HE *dips his hat in the stream and pours it over* STU's *face;* HE *does the same to himself.* HE *looks up at the sky, then stands slowly.* HE *talks like an old man*) By jingo, looky there. We're really in trouble, Mel. Them birds. See them birds, Mel? See what they're doing? I seen them things in Utah. Vultures. Condors or somethin'. Mean, nasty birds. They eat cows, Mel. I seen 'em eat a whole goddamn cow like it weren't nothin'. Come on, come on. (HE *drags* STU *back upstage*) Got to get ya back. Get ya in the other shade.

The horses and Indians join with car horns offstage and build in volume to the end of the play.

Better shade back here. Gettin' worse, Mel. Can't feel my tongue no more. Worse. Need some shelter, boy. (HE *stands and yells at the birds*) Get away from here, you mothers! This ain't funny! (HE *runs downstage, waving his hat at the birds*) This ain't no joke, you shitty birds! What do ya think this is? TV or somethin'? I ain't gettin' et by no vultures. Get out!

HE *runs upstage and drags* STU *back downstage again. As* HE *does this* MAN NUMBER ONE *and* MAN NUMBER TWO *come on from opposite sides of the stage with scripts in their hands.* THEY *are both dressed in suits and are the same age as* CHET *and* STU. THEY *read from the scripts in monotone, starting from the beginning of the play. The sound builds to its full loudness; the lights come up all the way as* CHET *continues.*

Better shade, boy. Shade down here. Take it easy. Easy. Come on, boy. (HE *takes off his shirt and vest and covers* STU's *head with them.* HE *kneels, looking out at the audience*) Keep the sun off. Got to keep it off. Sunburn. Tongue's cracked down the middle. All around the edges, Stu. Get away, birds! Get out a here! This ain't the place! Go look fer some cows! Get out! Get out!

The sound offstage stops suddenly. CHET *stares at the sky.* MAN NUMBER ONE *and* MAN NUMBER TWO *continue reading in monotone as the lights dim down.*

CURTAIN

Sam Shepard
9 Random Years [7 + 2]

By Patti Smith

. . . when he was grown
had hubcaps of his own
on a Hudson Hornet car
and rolled the pretty ladies
and often went too far
he rode to Chicago
he flew to Kalamazoo
slid into Nashville
raced in Tolkume
he slipstreamed Salinas
he plunged off a cliff
the people all gathered
and pointed to him
they said there goes a bad boy . . .

1956

In full moonlight Sam Shepard totaled his red Renault
Dauphine while stoned on Benzedrine.

1958

In white winter he drove down to Fire Place Road in an
ole '40 Ford. The road where Jackson Pollock took his great
last ride; white and stretching out like canvas. Sam
scratched the icebanks in search of blue housepaint clues,

Jacksons footprint or an old Texas license plate.
He slapped blue paint on his nose . . . howled like fire . . .
leaped and shouted for Jackson to come out and
fishback . . .
All night he celebrated the drunken painters dance and split
and stamped and bled and vomited till the grounds
resembled Pollacks own pain, his own Blue Poles, his own
jazzy dripping.

Sun came up.

1961

Sam was still dancing. Often he was found all spent in a field
or stretched out on a mountaintop

Nights
Sky was clawed and bitten by a mad attempt
to exorcise his racing spirit from the limiting
shell of his body.
Skin on fire.
All the inner forces were a whirlpool.
Release.
The thrashing tiger
the wolverine wants to thrash and claw
the snowy egret longing to soar above him.
Harboring his own private zoo he sped to South Dakota.
Searching for the immense he scored the great statue of
Crazy Horse, the rise of Mount Rushmore, the towering
plaster dinosaurs with huge headlight eyes.
He was bad
la-lu-lid
a drunken kid
He yodelled like a cowboy, rolling and sliding
all over them big dinosaurs.
People stared up at him, he didn't care
he was a renegade with nasty habits
he was a screech owl
he was a man playing cowboys.

1964

Sam was still playing with monsters

He swore to the great waters:
   engulf my spirit
   give me room
   a new rhythum
He lost himself in rivers:
   the Snake River
   the Colorado River
   the North Platte River
   the Mississippi River
He drank up the ocean—any ocean.
Ocean . . . he was lost for days.
He fed on sand and seaweed, squid and the sting
of jelly fish
flying fish
silver fish
There were sun spots in his eyes, his tongue was
thick like fur.
Not a woman in sight   he masturbated
and came for hours
like a river.

. . . .

December 30. Sam Shepard wrote his first play *Cowboys* in
true pioneer style . . . on the back of used Tootsie Roll
wrappers.
There were ice caps on the waters. He laid waiting for the
year to end and the white buffalo to come raging from the
ocean.

. . . .

1965

Sick of sea and pleased with his Cowboy aria etched in
sticky chocolate, he headed East.
Theatre in his pocket and a salamander in his shoe he
thumbed it toward the great white way.

Broadway.
People shouted at him.
Theres something fishy about you boy.
He didn't care.

The moon was in first quarter.
It was getting mighty cold so he ran the roads
to warm up.
He shouted . . . he challenged that moon:
Open up you fool . . . make a circle . . . get hot.

Speeding his way was a badass and shining
Eldorado pimp car.
with pinstriping
with a continental kit
shaved. chopped. channelled.

Nick was a gambler. Sam had nothing to lose.
they were true brothers.
they left the moon behind and fell to crime.
Not only the worldly crimes of passion
the poetry of Speed:
  the fast moving car
  the engine
  the black mustang pony
  the electric guitar.

1967

Cut with a new demon . . . rock n' roll. With an amplifier
for a heart he slid into Detroit.
The motor city: cars and radios.
His father was a Dixieland drummer
The roots of his theatre was music too.
  The Five Spot
  Charles Mingus
  The Fables of Faubus
  The Black Saint & Sinner Lady
  Danny Richmond: "The greatest drummer on 2 feet"
His theatre encompassed all those rhythum trade-offs all
those special dialogues of the heart.

Neon New York kept flashing through him. he had one last
banquet of Rock and Pontiacs and sped back East . . .
leaving Nick in a pool hall with a fist full of juke box
quarters.

1969

He hit it big in Hollywood, bought five cars . . . one of
which was a green Packard Clipper . . . had a special garage
built around them . . . and left them . . . heading East in
an old Chevy milk truck

1970

Sam and his best friend Fritz drove a 1936 black Plymouth
4-door sedan suitable for Doug Schultz himself . . . into the
fields of Massachusetts. They smashed it to shit . . . under
full starlight . . .
with crowbars
sledge hammers
rocks and screw drivers.
Fritz packed up his tool box and moved on.
Sam had a half moon branded on his left hand.
Sam danced one more time in some used car lot
in New Jersey.
Sam watched six straight hours of silent cowboy
reruns.
Sam moved on.

1971

Sam Shepard can usually be found parked down at the docks
. . . stretched out in the back of his Hudson Hornet car . . .
with a six-pack of Carta Blanca and a daily Racing Form.
But he seldom bets the horses
not unless there's a spot-back Appaloosa
or a sheen-black mustang pony in the running
which is almost never.
So Sam just looks out on the river.
the badlands keep pulsing through his anatomy
the kind of bad that's open and innocent:
    the passion of a forest fire
    the beauty of a poisonous flower, scorpion, snake.
Flames: the shot of silver:
James Dean's death car . . . the silver Porsche
the stiletto . . . the pushbutton blade
the sliver of moon carved on his fist
mad dog dawn foaming at the mouth
heart like a garage
car . . . speeding like a demon.

LITERATURE

Bataille, Georges
Story of the Eye,
120 p. / Cloth $5.

Bresson, Robert
Notes on Cinematography,
132 p. / $6.95 / paper $3.50

Brodsky, Michael
Detour, novel,
350 p. / Cloth $8.95

Cohen, Marvin
The Inconvenience of Living, fiction,
200 p. / Cloth $8.95 / paper $4.95

Ehrenburg, Ilya
The Life of the Automobile, novel,
192 p. / Cloth $8.95 / paper $4.95

Enzensberger, Hans Magnus
Mausoleum, poetry,
132 p. / Cloth $10.00 / paper $4.95

Hamburger, Michael
German Poetry 1910-1975,
576 p. / Cloth $17.50 / paper $7.95

Handke, Peter
Nonsense & Happiness, poetry,
80 p. / Cloth $7.95 / paper $3.95

Innerhofer, Franz
Beautiful Days, novel,
228 p. / Cloth $8.95 / paper $4.95

Kroetz, Franz Xavier
Farmyard & Other Plays,
192 p. / Cloth $12.95 / paper $4.95

Shepard, Sam
*Angel City, Curse of the Starving
Class & Other Plays,*
300 p. / Cloth $15.00 / paper $4.95

MOLE EDITIONS

Clastres, Pierre
Society Against the State,
188 p. / Cloth $12.95

Elias, Norbert
The Civilizing Process, Vol. 1 & 2,
400 p. / Cloth $15.00 each Vol.

Gibson, Ian
The English Vice,
364 p. / Cloth $12.95

Preface by Erich Heller
Panorama of the 19th Century
212 p. / Cloth $15.00

ECONOMICS

DeBrunhoff, Suzanne
Marx on Money,
192 p. / Cloth $10.00 / paper $4.95

Howard, Dick
The Marxian Legacy,
340 p. / Cloth $15.00 / paper $5.95

Linder, Marc
Anti-Samuelson, Vol. I,
400 p. / Cloth $15.00 / paper $5.95
Anti-Samuelson, Vol. II,
440 p. / Cloth $15.00 / paper $5.95

CONTEMPORARY AFFAIRS

Andrew Arato / Eike Gebhardt (Eds.)
*The Essential Frankfurt School
Reader,*
554 p. / Cloth $17.50 / paper $6.95

Augstein, Rudolf
Preface by Gore Vidal
Jesus, Son of Man,
420 p. / Cloth $12.95 / paper $4.95

Burchett, Wilfred
Southern Africa Stands Up,
Cloth 12.95 / paper $4.95

Kristeva, Julia
About Chinese Women,
250 p. / Cloth $8.95

Ledda, Galvino
Padre, Padrone,
Cloth $9.95

Sartre, Jean-Paul
Sartre by Himself,
136 p. / photos / Cloth $10.95 / paper $3.95

Steele, Jonathan
Inside East Germany,
300 p. / Cloth $12.95

Stern, August
The USSR vs. Dr. Mikhail Stern,
420 p. / Cloth $12.95

Write for a complete catalog and send orders to:
Urizen Books, Inc., 66 West Broadway, New York, N.Y. 10007
212 · 962-3413